SANCTUARY AND ASYLUM

SANCTUARY AND ASYLUM

A Social and Political History

LINDA RABBEN

[signature: Linda Rabben]

A Capell Family Book
University of Washington Press
Seattle & London

The Capell Family Endowed Book Fund supports the publication
of books that deepen the understanding of social justice
through historical, cultural, and environmental studies.

Manufactured in the United States of America

Frontispiece: South China Sea: Crewmen of the amphibious
cargo ship USS *Durham* (LKA-114) take Vietnamese refugees
aboard a small craft, April 1975. Photographer unknown.
Courtesy of the National Archives and Records Administration
and Wikimedia Commons.

UNIVERSITY OF WASHINGTON PRESS
www.washington.edu/uwpress

Library of Congress Cataloging-in-Publication Data
Names: Rabben, Linda, 1947– author.
Title: Sanctuary and asylum : a social and political history /
    Linda Rabben.
Description: Seattle : University of Washington Press, 2016. |
    Includes bibliographical references and index.
Identifiers: LCCN 2016012898| ISBN 9780295999128 (hardcover :
    alk. paper) | ISBN 9780295999135 (pbk. : alk. paper)
Subjects: LCSH: Asylum, Right of–History. | Asylum, Right of.
    | Refugees.
Classification: LCC K3268.3 .R335 2016 | DDC 342.08/3–dc23
LC record available at https://lccn.loc.gov/2016012898

The paper used in this publication is acid-free and meets the
minimum requirements of American National Standard for
Information Sciences–Permanence of Paper for Printed Library
Materials, ANSI Z39.48–1984.∞

In memory of Miep Gies (1909–2010),
Howard Zinn (1922–2010),
Nicholas Winton (1909–2015),
and thousands of other sanctuarians;
and with thanks to JE, for giving me shelter

Not like the brazen giant of Greek fame,
With conquering limbs astride from land to land;
Here at our sea-washed, sunset gates shall stand
A mighty woman with a torch, whose flame
Is the imprisoned lightning, and her name
Mother of Exiles. From her beacon-hand
Glows world-wide welcome; her mild eyes command
The air-bridged harbor that twin cities frame.
"Keep, ancient lands, your storied pomp!" cries she
With silent lips. "Give me your tired, your poor,
Your huddled masses yearning to breathe free,
The wretched refuse of your teeming shore.
Send these, the homeless, tempest-tost to me,
I lift my lamp beside the golden door!"

— Emma Lazarus, 1883

Contents

Acknowledgments

Many people in several countries gave me help – and refuge – from 2006 to 2015, as I researched and wrote *Sanctuary and Asylum* and its predecessor, *Give Refuge to the Stranger*.

At home in the sanctuary city of Takoma Park, Maryland, Rev. Phil Wheaton and Michael McConnell gave me informative interviews about their work for the 1980s Sanctuary Movement. Zelda Bell provided practical assistance that made it possible for me to do research in the United Kingdom and France, and Alice Haddix helped arrange my 2008 visit to Tucson.

In Tucson, sanctuarians Reverend Ricardo Elford, Reverend John Fife, John Heid, Paul Barby, the Community of Christ in the Desert, Lois Martin, Sarah Roberts, Frederick Neidhardt, Rev. Jim Wiltbank, Rev. Alison Harrington, the Samaritans, Rosemary and Bill Hallinan, Rev. Robin Hoover, Mike Humphrey, John Miles, Sebastian Quinac, Rachel Wilson, Geoff Boyce, and others kindly gave me interviews in 2008 and 2014. Abby Root and Lauren Raine offered hospitality and a listening ear. Linda Green, Kathryn Rodriguez, Sarah Launius, Kent Walker, and Jean Boucher helped in other ways. Rosa Robles Loreto, in sanctuary at Southside Presbyterian Church, and Francisco Perez Cordova, in sanctuary at Saint Francis in the Foothills United Methodist Church, graciously consented to be interviewed in November 2014.

Nicole Kligerman introduced me to the New Sanctuary Movement of Philadelphia. In El Paso, Joe Heyman was tremendously helpful during my visit in 2010; afterward he read chapter 2, made useful suggestions for changes, and became a friend. Also in El Paso and environs, sanctuarians Kathleen Erickson, Delia Gomez, Fernando

Garcia, Ruben Garcia, and Rev. Peter Hinde gave inspiring interviews that increased my understanding of old and new sanctuary movements. In Juarez, Mexico, Sr. Betty Campbell and Sr. Mary Alice shared their experiences with me.

In Saint Paul, Minnesota, the matchless Nelly Trocmé Hewett shared her encyclopedic knowledge of her parents André and Magda Trocmé, Le Chambon-sur-Lignon, France, and the surrounding region; she also read chapter 6 and corrected many errors, small and large.

In Le Chambon-sur-Lignon, Annik Flaud and Gérard Bollon graciously provided a great deal of information in a very short time. Thanks also to John Graney, MD, who drove me to Le Chambon with dizzying proficiency along the winding back roads of the Haute Loire.

I am grateful to interviewees "Mary" and "Pierre," who requested anonymity. They and other asylum seekers whose stories are told in chapter 1 are heroes whose courage and persistence continue to inspire me.

In Britain, Mahamad Al-Shagra, Rev. John Arnold, Sally Daghlian, Bob Deffee, Emma Ginn, Jim Gomersall, Eveline Louden, Roger Norris, Dele Olawanle, Kate Roberts, Jan Shaw, Debora Singer, Ahlam Souidi, Chris Williams, and Jean Wilson gave me interviews and inspiration. Conor Gearty was a gracious and encouraging host at London School of Economics' Center for the Study of Human Rights, where I was a visiting fellow in 2007–2008. My colleague at CSHR, Michael Welch, was helpful to me in London and after. The Scottish Refugee Council in Glasgow gave me shelter for a week in 2008 and taught me much about integration. Thanks also to Gary Christie, Celia Clarke, Jonathan Cox, Rev. Moyna McGlynn, Rev. Nicholas Sagovsky, and Jeremy Seabrook, who were especially encouraging. Zoe Stevens and Rev. Patrick Wright kindly facilitated visits to detention centers. Moyra Ashford, Sue Branford, Sue and Patrick Cunningham, John and Elizabeth Nurser, Jan Rocha, Patti Whaley, and Rob Wheeler provided indispensable hospitality and friendship over the years.

In the Netherlands a volunteer social worker, several asylum seekers, Patricia Brunklaus, and Esther van den Broek of the Dutch Refugee Council in Tilburg, Tycho van Lummel of the Netherlands Justice Ministry Migration Directorate, and residents of Noelhuis (Catholic

Worker house) of Amsterdam were kind enough to meet with me in 2014. I am especially grateful to Veerle Slegers and her family for their generous hospitality. *Bedankt!*

Librarians and archivists, such as Wendy Chmielewski, curator of the Swarthmore College Peace Collection, and Patricia Chapin O'Donnell of Swarthmore College Friends Historical Library; Josef Keith and Lisa McQuillen of Friends House Library, London; Clement Ho, international studies librarian at American University; and Steve Lafalce, reference librarian at Washington College of Law's Pence Library, gave me valuable assistance. Thanks also to employers and colleagues who gave practical help as I was writing *Give Refuge to the Stranger*: Juan Mendez, the late Robert Goodland, Marie Marr Jackson, and Virginia Bouvier, who made me aware of Colombian peace communities.

Several experts were kind enough to steer me through the shoals of asylum policies and practices: Celia Clarke of BID, Steve Symonds of Amnesty International UK, Prof. Wendy Chan of Simon Fraser University, Grant Mitchell, director of the International Detention Coalition, Lucy Bowring, MENA coordinator of the International Detention Coalition, and Prof. Claudia Tazreiter of University of New South Wales, Australia, reviewed parts of chapters 8 and 11 and made helpful comments. Prof. Jayesh Rathod of Washington College of Law commented on chapter 10. Michael Matza of the *Philadelphia Inquirer* gave me indispensable help with the story of Tiombe Carlos, told in chapter 1. Imam Daoud Nassimi and Prof. Steven Caton graciously provided information about sanctuary in Islam.

My relationship with the University of Washington Press goes back to 1998, when they published the first US edition of my book on Brazilian indigenous movements, *Unnatural Selection*. Over the years my editors there have consistently provided moral support and helpful advice. My heartfelt thanks go to them and to anonymous readers who made constructive suggestions for changes.

I am grateful to copyright holders who gave me permission to reproduce their work: Australian Human Rights Commission, Lydia Besong, Angie Morton, Rutgers University Press, United Nations Archives, and UNICEF.

Chai was my faithful research assistant. John Eckenrode's generosity, encouragement, and example have made all the difference to
my life and work.

If I have forgotten anyone who helped, I beg pardon. The mistakes in this book are my own, and I ask forgiveness for them, too.

SANCTUARY AND ASYLUM

Introduction

Fleeing the threat of genital mutilation, seventeen-year-old Fauziya Kassindja left her home in the West African country of Togo in late 1994. Unlike many girls in her ethnic group, she had avoided "cutting" because her father did not approve of the practice. But after he died his kin decided to marry her off to a forty-five-year-old local leader who insisted that she undergo the procedure (Kassindja and Bashir 1998).

With the help of her mother and sister, Fauziya fled Togo on the first plane she could board, to Germany. After a short stay there, she acquired a false passport and came to the United States, where she had relatives. She requested asylum on arrival. Although she was a minor who should not have been detained, the Immigration and Naturalization Service kept her in various jails and prisons for seventeen months. During her incarceration she was housed with convicted felons, although she had not committed any crime. She fell ill, suffered from suicidal depression, and was prevented from practicing her religion. Fauziya was lucky, however. Unlike most detained asylum seekers in the United States, she received pro bono legal representation and moral support from human rights organizations and activists.

I read about Fauziya's plight in a *Washington Post* op-ed early in 1996. As a human rights activist working for Amnesty International, I found the story of her ordeal difficult to believe. Could the United States' asylum system really be so unjust, so cruel? I started writing to Fauziya in prison and sent her care packages of toiletries and (at her request) Islamic literature. By this time the *New York Times* was covering her case in the Metro section of the paper, because she had been detained in northern New Jersey. I contacted her pro bono law-yers and asked for the case records, in which I found many details not mentioned in the *Times* articles. Amnesty International USA (AIUSA) suggested that I write a letter to the editor of the *Times*, urging her release. The newspaper published my letter across from an editorial calling for her to be released while her case was adjudicated. About a week later she was released, and six weeks later she was granted asylum. The decision in her case set an important precedent, mak-ing it possible for young women threatened with genital mutilation to gain asylum in the United States.

That was how my involvement in asylum began. I started attend-ing meetings of a group of Washington organizations that work on migration issues, represent asylum seekers, do public outreach and advocacy, and educate Congress and policy makers. Trained as an anthropologist and not as a lawyer, I found the intricacies of US immigration law daunting. Focusing on Brazil and writing books on human rights had taken most of my time and energy in the 1990s and early 2000s. But I could not let go of the asylum issue. As an Amnesty International researcher and volunteer, I had several opportunities to enjoy the pleasures of rescue, when I helped survivors of human rights abuses get out of jail or gain asylum. I visited detention cen-ters, wrote expert affidavits on behalf of Brazilian asylum seekers, and assisted other asylum seekers who struggled against great obstacles to gain refuge in the United States.

After 9/11 the situation for asylum seekers became even more difficult. Draconian laws against them were implemented in many countries. After finishing a book about Brazil in 2005 – almost ten years after I had first heard about Fauziya Kassindja – I was looking for a new subject. I found an article I had published back in 1997 about detention conditions for asylum seekers. Almost a decade later, those conditions had changed little. Despite the concerted pressure of human rights organizations over the years, the immigration ser-vice (now known as Immigration and Customs Enforcement, or ICE) was still mistreating thousands of asylum seekers and other immi-gration detainees.

As immigration issues acquired greater political visibility in 2006,

I started doing research on sanctuary and soon found that its roots go deep into human history. As a result, my research ranged widely over thousands of years of refuge given to strangers around the world. It took me to archives, libraries, detention centers, courtrooms, offices, and communities in the United States, the United Kingdom, France, and the Netherlands. I interviewed asylum seekers and refugees and acquired more knowledge along the way by working for a refugee resettlement agency and volunteering for a center for torture survivors.

As an anthropologist, I wondered where the idea of asylum came from, how it evolved, and whether it was a human universal – a feature of language, belief, or behavior that exists in all or almost all societies. First I wanted to find out if my own discipline could provide a framework for analyzing and interpreting asylum and sanctuary in many cultures. It was not difficult to find numerous works on the human hostility toward and avoidance of "the other," but studies of cooperation and sociability among humans of different groups were much less common.

My hypothesis was that sanctuary might have begun both to help females avoid incest and to diversify the gene pool of receiving communities. But subjects I had thought important to look into, such as endogamy and exogamy (marriage inside and outside a group or community), were no longer in fashion among anthropologists, and I could find few modern publications on those topics. Late nineteenth- and early twentieth-century anthropologists such as Edward Westermarck may have been the last people to be interested in them. The most useful studies of sanctuary I found were written in 1887 (by Thomas de Mazzinghi, a classical scholar) and 1911 (by John Cox, a church historian). One of the academic readers who reviewed an early version of my manuscript doubted that such antique sources could be acceptable in this day and age. (Because they were very carefully documented, I thought they were still relevant, and so I cited them.) Even the Human Relations Area Files, which include ethnographic studies on hundreds of subjects, contained nothing on sanctuary more recent than the 1980s.[1]

Studies of chimpanzees and bonobos, our primate cousins, were more promising. Primatologists such as Frans de Waal have done important research on altruistic behavior within and among communities of those species. Their sophisticated studies have found that "aiding others at a cost or risk to oneself is widespread in the animal world," and "helpful acts that are costly in the short run may produce long-term benefits if recipients return the favor" (de Waal 1996: 12).

Frans de Waal has not shied away from pointing out similarities between primate and human behavior. He and other primatologists have gone beyond the debate over rigidly deterministic (and, to my mind, reductionist) theories of the "selfish gene," which could not explain altruism, by studying primates' behavior over time in captivity and in the wild.[2] Their observations have shown that primates give refuge to strangers, especially females fleeing to other communities after incestuous approaches or violent attacks by male kin. These findings reinforced my interpretation of sanctuary as rooted in primordial rules of exogamy and the incest taboo (which Westermarck correctly analyzed a century ago). My approach takes into account sanctuary's apparent universality in our species, as well as its altruistic character. I could not find any other account of sanctuary among humans that took such an approach.

Discussing sanctuary and asylum comparatively, across thousands of years and many societies, is a bold exercise. Several reviewers wanted me to give more attention to the "social and cultural factors that shape people's actions and national policy and practice," the "social, economic or other conditions [that] promote positive responses to the asylum seeker" and the "factors [that] turn people against refugees." But I found I could not take a conventional approach to social causation by pointing to abstract "factors" or "forces" in the face of a richly contradictory reality. Risking their lives and livelihoods to help despised strangers, the sanctuarians whose stories I tell often defied powerful social, cultural, and political rules and norms. Those who abided by the rules thought they were misguided, selfish, crazy, or criminal to act as they did.

For example, it is difficult to explain, by invoking social or economic factors, why Oskar Schindler – who profited from Jewish slave labor and fraternized with Nazi officials while allowing his workers to sabotage production – risked his life to rescue Jews. Schindler seemed to act quixotically, against his own best interests; his motives remain mysterious. I even wondered if he might have taken sociopathic pleasure in fooling the Nazis from whom he was stealing. But such an analysis would be invidious, considering the life-saving success of Schindler's altruistic behavior in the eyes of anyone but a Nazi. At any rate, I do not believe that altruistic actions can be satisfactorily explained by social science that assumes that human behavior is rational, orderly, and consciously self-interested, in accordance with functional social norms. Life is messier and more confounding than that. As Charlie Chan once said, "Theory like mist on eyeglasses, obscures facts" (R. Bernstein 2010: 16). In the interests of scholarship, however, those who are theoretically inclined are welcome to use this book as a launching pad.

Still, I have tried to put sanctuarians' behavior in its social, political, and economic context, precisely because it may be inexplicable without such background. For example, it would be difficult to understand why Catholic churches in late medieval Britain insisted on giving permanent sanctuary to thieves and other criminals without knowing something about the Church's losing struggle with the state for political dominance. That kind of contextual information is woven throughout the stories I tell.

Because this subject ranges so widely, I had to place limits on what I covered. For example, I have limited my discussion of the social construction of the other or the history of refugees in the twentieth century; these have been the subjects of many other books. Instead I focus, especially in the later chapters, on asylum seekers and their experiences with the state apparatus. To do this, I had to explain how asylum systems work. Accordingly, I describe in detail modern asylum policies and practices, about which most people know little. It is important for citizens to be aware of how their government treats people seeking refuge and what kinds of policies their taxes pay for. I also wanted to educate the public about the many grassroots, community, and nonprofit organizations that seek to help asylum seekers and refugees.

I write as an activist as well as an anthropologist, because I want to encourage those who work on asylum and immigration issues to continue their important work. As a defender of asylum and an admirer of sanctuary, I do not pretend to be neutral, but I am committed to being accurate and coherent and backing up my claims. I have cited and quoted journalistic sources and "gray literature" (by nonacademics), as well as academic sources and primary research, crossing disciplinary boundaries in the process. This book is intended to be useful to diverse readers, from students and scholars to activists and resettlement workers.

Today asylum is under threat in many countries that once welcomed asylum seekers. Before the 2015 Syrian refugee crisis, the number of asylum seekers arriving in the United States, the United Kingdom, and other countries had decreased markedly because governments had instituted policies to prevent their entry.[3] Those who managed to request asylum on or after arrival in another country often failed in the attempt. Host societies are still increasingly hostile to asylum seekers. Many endure destitution, illness, and the isolation of exile, sometimes for years, only to be deported back to the place where they were persecuted. Some die as a result.

Asylum gained greater international attention in recent years through the notorious cases of Julian Assange and Edward Snowden, who sought refuge from prosecution for publishing government secrets. These cases are not at all typical. Most asylum seekers are unknown, even in their own countries. They may be ordinary people who fall victim to arbitrary government repression; community activists who call attention to government corruption; women or children who flee abuse from which the state cannot or will not protect them. When they cry out for help or justice, few hear them.

Yet thousands of groups and individuals in countries around the world offer help to these threatened, vulnerable strangers. Throughout history, people have organized or made special efforts to welcome the stranger, sometimes at great risk to their own lives. The compelling question this book raises is: Why? *Sanctuary and Asylum: A Social and Political History* traces the evolution of sanctuary from its ancient beginnings up to the present day. I focus not only on the asylum seekers and the authorities who give or refuse asylum, but also on the social groups and individuals who mobilize to provide sanctuary, often outside the law and at great risk. Finally I speculate about the future of asylum in a world overwhelmed by strife and persecution. What does the persistent human proclivity to give refuge say about our species and its prospects? Will the history of asylum have a happy or a tragic ending? Fortunately, it is too soon to give a final answer to these questions; we are still in the midst of the struggle for the right to refuge.

Since *Give Refuge to the Stranger* was published in 2011, I have traveled across the United States and Europe to talk about sanctuary and asylum with a great variety of people. One of the most striking things I have noticed in my travels is how little citizens know about asylum seekers and the inhumane and ineffective system of detention, adjudication, and deportation their tax dollars support. When I tell people that in the "land of the free and home of the brave," people guilty of no crime, survivors of systematic abuse, are incarcerated for months or even years without legal representation and then deported without mercy by our government, they are incredulous. The stubborn reluctance of the US government to improve detention conditions and of lawmakers to reform the immigration system could lead any caring person to despair.

And yet thousands of organizations and people of goodwill are trying to change this depressing state of affairs. Having already published *Fierce Legion of Friends: A History of Human Rights Campaigns and Campaigners*, about the generations of activists who have mobilized to advance human rights, I felt it would be worthwhile to focus on the people who are working against the odds, with courage and determination, to help asylum seekers, refugees, and migrants in the United States and other countries.

I decided to write this new book as I watched asylum policies and movements change, sometimes radically, after the publication of *Give Refuge to the Stranger* in early 2011. Governments that had acknowledged the futility of punitive, inhumane policies during the first decade of the twenty-first century reverted to the old failed policies as political pressure escalated. In response, sanctuary movements, which had been quiescent for years, suddenly revived. These developments made parts of the previous book outdated, but they also confirmed my conviction that although asylum is under threat, sanctuary will always be with us. I felt compelled to bring the story up to date in *Sanctuary and Asylum* and to keep encouraging people to work on this issue.

Over more than a decade, my research has given me many opportunities to meet and learn from sanctuary givers and seekers. I hope their stories are as inspiring and heartening to readers as they have been to me. And I hope they move you to take action, however modest, to protect and advance the ancient, noble institution of sanctuary, a vital part of our human heritage.

1   Asylum and Sanctuary Seekers' Stories

A well-founded fear of being persecuted

– Convention Relating to the Status of Refugees, 1951

Every day, thousands of individuals seek asylum in scores of countries.[1] In so doing they are exercising a basic human right as defined in article 14 of the Universal Declaration of Human Rights (1948): "Everyone has the right to seek and to enjoy in other countries asylum from persecution" (Center for the Study of Human Rights 1992: 7). The vast majority do not immediately obtain refuge through the elaborate systems established by international and national laws and policies. Many wait years for a definitive decision. In the meantime they may go underground, living precariously or in destitution, denied social welfare benefits, the right to work legally, and the right to participate freely in their adopted society. Others, including torture survivors, children, pregnant women, the elderly, and the seriously ill, may be detained for indefinite periods in jails, prisons, or detention centers. Only a few have the opportunity to tell their story to the public. Often these stories remain unread, except by government officials and lawyers. For the most part, asylum seekers are voiceless, invisible, forgotten. As a result, many citizens of the countries in which asylum seekers exist have only the vaguest notion – or none at all – of what or who they are.

An asylum seeker could be said to be a person who is trying to become a refugee. According to the UN Refugee Convention of 1951, a refugee is a person who "owing to a well founded fear of being persecuted for reasons of race, religion, nationality, membership of a particular social group or political opinion, is outside the country of his nationality and is unable or, owing to such fear, is unwilling to avail himself of the protection of that country; or who, not having a nationality and being outside the country of his former habitual residence as a result of such events, is unable or, owing to such fear, is unwilling to return to it" (chapter 1, article 1[2]).[2]

Governments use this rather narrow definition to exclude or accept asylum seekers.[3] In many countries, they are confused or conflated with illegal immigrants or even criminals and treated as scapegoats, falsely accused of causing economic and social problems. They may be subjected to xenophobic reactions and even lethal violence that deepen their isolation and suffering.

A relatively small proportion – usually no more than 30–40 percent in major receiving countries such as the United States and Britain – do gain asylum and the benefits that go along with this legal status.[4] They may succeed because they arrive with copious documentation of the persecution they have suffered and with the financial resources to hire a good lawyer or the luck to find skillful pro bono representation. But most do not.

Then there are the sanctuary seekers, who arrive under varying circumstances, usually outside the law. These days they are called by different names: illegal aliens, illegal immigrants, undocumented, unauthorized, migrants, overstayers. They remain in the shadows, hoping to escape notice, until some mischance – a broken tail light, missing identification, an injury while crossing the desert – brings them to the attention of the authorities. Some of them end up in detention and are served, after a perfunctory or prolonged legal process, with a deportation order. Some look for refuge "underground." Others are sent back to the place they came from, only to return again and again.

The following are a few of the stories of asylum and sanctuary seekers that have come to light in recent years. They give an idea of what thousands of people experience when they search for refuge. Some of their stories remain unfinished, the protagonists lost in a Kafkaesque maze of red tape and systematic cruelty. Other seekers eventually find their promised land.

Mary in Limbo

The most dangerous moment of Mary's year in prison came in the solitary confinement cell, when a guard demanded that she kneel before him.[5] She refused, saying, "That is an act of worship, and I worship only God; I will not kneel before any man." Mary is not sure what he did to her after that; the next thing she remembers is waking up in the intensive care unit of the local hospital, shackled to the bed.

After much pleading and bargaining, she was unshackled and the guards were allowed to watch television in her room (against regulations). She stayed in the hospital for a week. Eventually she was released and allowed to work, but she was instructed to keep immigration authorities informed of her whereabouts until her case was decided – if it ever was decided.

Mary was no criminal; she was an asylum seeker. In the early 1990s, after the assassination of a relative who was a high-ranking government official, she fled her home country in Africa. Most members of her family also fled and now live in various European and Asian countries. She sought refuge in the United States.

In her search for asylum, Mary was unfortunate to encounter a series of incompetent, overcommitted, or crooked lawyers who took her money but did nothing. Her case got lost in a backlog of hundreds of thousands of cases. After several years, having heard nothing from her lawyer or the immigration authorities, she presented herself at the district office of the Immigration and Naturalization Service (INS, now known as Immigration and Customs Enforcement, whose grimly apposite acronym is ICE). There she learned that an immigration judge had signed an order to deport her after she failed to appear at a hearing she had known nothing about. She was taken into custody at the immigration office and sent first to a local jail, then to a maximum security prison two hundred miles from the town where she had been living.

The next year was a trial by ordeal, marked by physical and psychological abuse that violated federal detention guidelines, not to mention international law. Transferred to a prison in another state in the middle of the night without warning or explanation, malnourished because she was lactose intolerant, kept in a cell with a murderer, denied vegetarian food required by her religious beliefs, unable to contact her lawyer because she had no money to pay for a long-distance call, Mary kept her sanity by documenting the mistreatment she and other detainees endured. After she and two others threatened to expose conditions at the prison to federal authorities, they saw some improvements. The detainees were taken out of cells housing convicted felons and placed in a warehouse with no windows.

It took months of dedicated efforts by a pro bono attorney and Amnesty International to secure Mary's release on parole. Years later, she was unwilling to discuss her experience publicly for fear of retaliation by ICE or corrections officials. She had to pay the government a hefty annual fee for permission to work. In 2006, asked how it felt to have her case still unsettled, she replied, "Dreadful – I cannot make plans. I cannot visit my family. I cannot leave the country." Asked when she began seeking asylum, Mary said sadly, "1992." How long could the process go on? "Forever," she thought. Mary finally gained asylum in 2013, after more than twenty years in limbo.

Lydia Besong Tells Her Story

"I would not have left my own country if I had not been in danger for my life.[6] I was a member of the political group South Cameroon National Council, and members of the group are always persecuted by the government. They came for me one day in 2006. They took me into prison, and the conditions in prison are very filthy. When I was in prison I suffered a lot. I was tortured. If you look at my legs you will see the scars. Women suffer many things that it is hard to stand in public and speak about. It is very hard for a woman to say that she has been raped. I myself felt very shy to speak about this. I suffered a lot of beatings. I was released not because they wanted to release me but because my health was so bad. As soon as I was released I went into the hospital. When I knew they were going to come for me again, I had to run away for my life.

"When I arrived in the UK with my husband, I thought that I would be safe. I went to the Medical Foundation [for the Care of Victims of Torture], and they saw the scars. They supported my claim for asylum. But then I realized it wasn't going to be as I thought. I was refused asylum. The Home Office just said that they didn't believe me. I was not allowed to work, but I kept myself busy by volunteering with a women's group and I wrote a play with Women Asylum Seekers Together Manchester. This play, *How I Became an Asylum Seeker*, tells the story of what we go through in the asylum process. The first time it was performed was in Manchester on 3 December 2009.

"But just six days later I was arrested by the Home Office. I spent Christmas in Yarl's Wood Detention Centre. I thought I was going to be deported, and then I knew my government would put me back into prison. The thing that kept me going was that I received many, many Christmas cards from my supporters. Every time I opened a card, I felt very emotional, to know that many people were thinking of me and I could not be with them.

"But in Yarl's Wood there were many women who did not even receive one card. I met one girl who was only eighteen, who had come here seeking asylum from Nigeria because of the harm she had suffered in her traditional community. Nobody knew she was in detention. She was totally alone. She was crying all the time.

"Although I was released after Christmas and appealed against my refusal, I was refused asylum again and put in detention again on 10 January 2012. For me, being locked up reminded me so much of being put in prison back home, it brought back all the memory of torture. They put me on suicide watch because I was so depressed; they were watching me 24/7. I don't know how I would have kept going except that I had so much support from people outside.

"The second time I was detained, Women for Refugee Women made sure that people like Michael Morpurgo and Joan Bakewell were writing to the newspapers.[7] And the grassroots groups I work with in Manchester were my support. They made calls, they faxed the airline, so no matter what the immigration was doing to me, I still felt strong. Sometimes you think, should you give up – but then you think, no, you are not fighting the fight alone. Other people act like your pillar: if you feel you are going to fall, they keep you standing. And in the end I was given refugee status. It was agreed that I had been tortured and I would be in danger if I was returned to my home country. I should be free of all the dark times now.

"But when I left detention, Yarl's Wood followed me to Manchester. Sometimes I feel like I'm in a trance, I feel I hear the footsteps of the officers, I hear the banging of the doors and the sound of their keys. Even though I'm out of detention, I'm not really out – I still have those dreams. I wish the politicians could understand what they are doing to women by detaining us like this when we have already been through so much. Asylum seekers are not criminals. That's why I wanted to speak out . . . because I believe that if people speak out, then change will come one day. If we do not speak out, then we are dying in silence."

Detained to Death: Two Stories

HIU LUI (JASON) NG

At age seventeen in 1992, Hiu Lui (Jason) Ng entered the United States from China on a tourist visa. According to a *New York Times* article of August 13, 2008, he "stayed on after [the visa] expired and applied for political asylum. He was granted a work permit while his application was pending, and though asylum was eventually denied, immigration authorities did not seek his deportation for many years" (Bernstein 2008).[8]

Jason worked his way through community college and became a computer engineer, working in the Empire State Building. In 2001 he married, and his wife petitioned for him to be granted a green card (permanent residence) as the spouse of a US citizen. The couple waited more than five years for this request to be processed.

Meanwhile the immigration bureaucracy was looking for him as a rejected asylum seeker. A notice ordering him to appear in court went to a nonexistent address, and as a result Jason did not show up for a hearing in 2001. At that time the judge automatically issued a deportation order for him.

Unaware of this turn of events, Jason and his wife appeared for a green card interview in July 2007. ICE agents arrested him under the old deportation order and sent him to two jails and then a federal detention center in New England. "Over the next year," the *Times* reported, "his family struggled to pay for new lawyers to wage a complicated and expensive legal battle."

In April 2008, still in detention, Jason began complaining to his family about severe back pain and skin irritation. At the time, he was in a county jail in Vermont that had no medical personnel. He asked to be transferred to Wyatt Detention Facility in Rhode Island because it had medical staff who he hoped could provide treatment for his extreme pain. For the first three days at Wyatt, he was kept in a dark isolation cell. "Later," the *Times* reported, "he was assigned an upper bunk and required to climb up and down at least three times a day for head counts, causing terrible pain." He told his sister he had informed the nursing department he was in pain, "but they don't believe me. . . . They tell me, stop faking." The *Times* described him as "once a robust man who stood nearly six feet and weighed 200 pounds. . . . Mr. Ng looked like a shrunken and jaundiced 80-year-old."

Other detainees helped Jason go to the toilet, brought him food, and called his family. "He no longer received painkillers, because he could not stand in line to collect them," the *Times* reported. When his lawyer tried to visit him on July 26, 2008, he was too weak to walk to the visiting area, and he was denied use of a wheelchair. Detention center officials refused to arrange for an independent medical evaluation of his condition.

Jason's final ordeal began on July 30. According to affidavits obtained by the *Times*, "Guards . . . dragged him from his bed . . . , carried him in shackles to a car, bruising his arms and legs, and drove him two hours to a federal lockup in Hartford, where an immigration officer pressured him to withdraw all pending appeals of his case and accept deportation." Then they drove him back to the detention center.

Calling this treatment "torture," one of his lawyers filed a habeas corpus petition on his behalf. A US District Court judge ordered that Jason be taken immediately to a hospital for testing. "The results were grim: cancer in his liver, lungs, and bones, and a fractured spine," the *Times* reported. After waiting three days for the detention center director to give permission, his family visited him in the hospital, "hours away from death and still under guard." Jason died on August 6, 2008. He was thirty-four years old and left a wife and two children, all US citizens.

TIOMBE CARLOS

Born on the Caribbean island of Antigua, Tiombe Carlos came legally with her family to the United States as a four-year-old in the early 1980s. At age fourteen, she was diagnosed with paranoid schizophrenia. According to the *Philadelphia Inquirer*, "She was often in and out of hospitals and had convictions for trespass, shoplifting and assaults, mostly fighting with police when they arrested her" (Matza 2013). Eventually she spent several years in prison for various crimes. Her status as a legal permanent resident was revoked, and ICE moved to deport her because of her criminal convictions when her sentence ended in 2010. Carlos then spent almost three years in immigration detention, in an ICE facility in Boston and at York County Prison in Pennsylvania, which contracts with the federal government to hold immigration detainees.

Tiombe was not easy to detain. According to a review of her case by ICE's Office of Professional Responsibility, she spent much of her time at York "in segregation due to her assaultive nature, and misconduct and mental health issues. . . . [She] had a history of violent criminal activity to include arrests for assault, robbery and resisting arrest" (Division Director 2014: 1, 3). She was physically and verbally abusive at times, suffered from extreme mood swings, and was considered a danger to herself and others.

In 2011, at her lawyer's request, a clinical psychologist affiliated with Physicians for Human Rights interviewed Tiombe at York. He determined that she was severely mentally ill. Her lawyer wrote to ICE asking that they suspend her deportation because of her condition. He cited "Carlos' arrival in the United States as a young child; long-term permanent residency; lack of immigration-specific violations; lack of ties to Antigua; close family bonds in America; and a U.S. citizen daughter, born in 1999 during one of Carlos' hospitalizations. The child, now 14, lives with her grandparents" (Matza 2013). He asked that she be kept in a group home with regular medication.

A supervisor at the Philadelphia Department of Behavioral Health said she could be considered for residential treatment, but an immigration judge upheld the deportation order.

Carlos could not be sent back to her home country unless the Antiguan government issued travel documents for her. Antigua's deputy consul general in New York said in an interview, "What am I sending her to? If she has a diagnosis of schizophrenia and her family is here, who am I sending her home to? It's like sending her home to die" (Matza 2013). The Antiguan government did not provide the travel documents, and Carlos remained in detention at York County Prison. She was placed in disciplinary segregation eight times and in the Intensive Custody Unit twice.

In August 2013, after an altercation with an inmate, Carlos tried to hang herself; the prison's emergency response team cut her down. An official reported that she "was crying and said, 'It's not fair, I don't wanna live'" (Division Director 2014: 15). The prison did not inform her family of this suicide attempt, which the medical staff regarded as a "cry for help" rather than a serious attempt. It was a great shock to her family when on October 23, 2013, at age thirty-four, she killed herself.

ICE promised to review her case and its policies and procedures for detention and removal of mentally ill migrants. A review was completed in the summer of 2014 but not released until January 2015, after *Inquirer* reporter Michael Matza asked ICE to comment on his follow-up story about her case.

The review found many deficiencies in the treatment of Carlos by the prison and ICE. Although she was placed on suicide watch five times between 2011 and 2013, the prison's medical staff gave no clearance for her to be transferred to a suicide prevention cell, nor did they prepare a psychiatric treatment plan for her. Days before her death and two months after her first suicide attempt, a deputy warden asked ICE to consider placing her in a psychiatric facility. "The local ICE office said an appropriate alternative to incarceration was unavailable," Matza wrote (2015b).

The review revealed that corrections officers took "disciplinary" actions that were improper. "When Carlos acted out, guards soaked her with pepper spray" but did not take measures to decontaminate her (Matza 2015b). In 2011 a guard wounded her with a stun gun, which ICE forbids in its contract with the prison. Apparently the guard did not know she was an immigration detainee.

Carlos's lawyer, who was unaware of the review until Matza showed it to him, said it showed that officials knew how severe his client's mental illness was but did not address it properly. (Reading the ICE review, one gets the impression that the authorities did not know what to do. It seems obvious that she belonged in a psychiatric facility, not a prison.) Her family's lawyer filed a Freedom of Information Act request for the review in June 2014 but received no reply. Families for Freedom, an advocacy group for migrants, concluded, "Ms. Carlos' case is emblematic of all that is wrong with mandatory detention."

The Survivor

Layla was teaching international law at a university in Libya when she was arrested for saying the wrong things about the country's dictator, Muammar Gaddafi. Layla's family was associated with the former king of Libya, whom Gaddafi had overthrown, and her father had died after being arrested and tortured. A student had denounced her. For six months she was imprisoned, tortured, raped, and told she would be executed. "My survival is a miracle," she told Jeremy Seabrook, who interviewed her for his book *The Refuge and the Fortress* (2009: 161–63).

Alone in a secret prison in Benghazi, she heard the cries of the tortured but saw nobody. "They sentenced me to death with no trial, no court." She asked to see her mother, who raised a huge amount of money to bribe a guard to help her escape. "I walked out unchallenged. I just got in the car and sat down beside someone I had never seen before. He took me to a small farm near the airport." There her mother and sisters joined her. A people smuggler arranged for her to board a plane bound for London. "You can buy anything in Libya. Even freedom. I came from a wealthy family. If we had been poor, I'd have been executed."

When Layla arrived in London, she couldn't speak a word of English. Immigration officials stamped her false French passport without looking at it. The people smuggler took her to a fast-food restaurant for a meal, then gave her enough money to get to Lunar House, the government office where immigrants and asylum seekers must report, the following morning. She spent the night in a phone booth.

Layla arrived at Lunar House at 4:20 a.m. "There was a long queue. It was December, I was cold and hungry. I was seen at 4 p.m. I told the truth. . . . I was met with discrimination, contempt, disbelief. I was sick, but the interpreter said I was acting. . . . I needed a doctor and asked her to translate. I had had no sleep for two days. It was a nightmare."

At one in the morning a bus took her and other asylum seekers to a detention center on the coast. She was twice denied asylum and sent to the Refugee Council, a nongovernmental organization, where "there was an endless queue." She spent most of the next three days in the queue. "The security man hit me as I tried to enter the building. Someone said, 'She's been here three days.' He said, 'I don't care if she's been here a year.'"

Layla entered what is known as the destitution underground: "I was homeless for eight months. I slept rough, spent nights in churches and mosques. I was so tired I couldn't walk." People at a mosque looked after her. "I was bleeding because I had a miscarriage. When I was raped in the jail in Libya I was a virgin, and didn't know I was pregnant." Finally she was referred to the Medical Foundation because she was suffering from severe depression, and a doctor treated her. Medical Foundation staff found a place for her to live after she had been in Britain for nine months. She studied English and did volunteer work for mental health consultants. She was not allowed to work for pay during this period.

After a private lawyer failed to help her, she went to the Refugee Legal Centre (which later fell victim to government funding cuts). She gained refugee status in May 2005, more than two years after she had arrived in Britain. Two weeks after she gained asylum, Layla found a job, first working for a private company, then for a local health agency. When Seabrook interviewed her, she was planning to study to be a mental health professional. "I want to use my experience constructively, to help others," she told him. In 2014 Layla reported that she had gotten married and completed her master's degree in mental health. Seabrook reflects, "In many ways, although she is still fragile, she considers her life in Britain to have been a success" (personal communication, December 2014).

Pierre Finds Safety

When I first met Pierre in 2008, I felt sure he would succeed in the United States.[9] He was personable, highly intelligent, resourceful, and above all, self-confident. He had fled West Africa in 2007, at age forty. At home he was a tenured professor, owned his own house, had servants and a comfortable life. But he made the mistake of refusing to join the ruling political party. When he started receiving death threats, he left the country, and his wife and children moved to his family's village. She lived there in danger, fear, and uncertainty for three years.

Pierre spent his first year in the United States seeking asylum and living in a shelter managed by a local church. He searched the Internet for resources; there he found pro bono immigration lawyers from a nonprofit organization who helped him. As soon as he gained asylum, he looked for work. His first job in the United States was earning minimum wage as a baggage handler at an airport. He was eligible for food stamps, but he refused to sign up for them because that would mean he was poor. Soon he was promoted to customer service agent.

His priority was to save enough money – $8,000 – to bring his wife and children to America. After two years of "working like crazy," he met them at the airport where he worked. The long separation had had traumatic effects. His seven-year-old son did not recognize him at first; he took one year to embrace Pierre, two years to stop fearing that Daddy would leave. His wife also had difficulty adjusting to life in the United States. When I first met her, she was very shy and unable to speak English. Eventually she went back to school and found friends and part-time work as a caregiver.

After two years of working at the airport, Pierre found a job related to his professional training. He improved his English by watching PBS programs and the National Geographic Channel, listening to National Public Radio, and reading *Ferdinand the Bull* to his son.

Pierre told me, "Overall I'm very happy to be in America, because I'm free of fear." But he avoids his compatriots. After living under an authoritarian regime, where people were constantly spying on one another, even in the United States he does not talk about what happened to him, for fear of hurting his family at home. Still, he has hope, not only for himself but for his family. "America has accepted me. That's something I really cherish. . . . That's priceless." He became a US citizen in early 2015.

Pierre was far luckier than Stephen, another political dissident from the same West African country who also arrived in the United States in 2007.

> He left behind his wife and infant son when he fled to the United States after his life was threatened by his government. After waiting three years for his individual court hearing, the immigration court continued Stephen's hearing to 2012 because the judge presiding over his case retired and his case was assigned to a different judge. . . . A month before that hearing was to occur, the court again continued Stephen's case, this time until August 2013. . . . [Stephen's case was subsequently moved up to June 2012.] On that date, the judge heard testimony, but was unable to complete the case and rescheduled it for September 2014. Stephen's attorneys filed another motion to advance and had a hearing in August 2013. On that date, he was granted asylum. Stephen's case was so protracted that by the end, it had been handled by five different pro bono attorneys and was before three different judges. It took six years for him to be granted asylum, during which time he was separated from his wife and child. (McCarthy 2015: 13)

A Case of Stolen Identity

Neda Soltani was teaching English at Karadj Azad University in Iran in June 2009, when postelection demonstrations erupted in Tehran and other cities. She did not participate in the uprising, but media outlets confused her with Neda Agha Soltan, shot to death by a sniper during a protest. Neda Soltani's Facebook photo was used to illustrate the story of the sniper victim, and it took some time for the dead woman's family to correct the mix-up. Meanwhile the secret police arrested Neda Soltani, threw her into prison, accused her of participating in subversive activities, and psychologically tortured her. After police left her on a street corner in a state of shock, friends convinced her to leave the country. Soltani was able to escape from Iran because she had a visa to attend an academic conference in Greece. Her friends bribed a Tehran Airport official to stamp her passport. She arrived safely in Athens via Istanbul in June 2009.

Aiming for Britain, she ran afoul of Schengen Convention rules, which guaranteed that she would be sent back to Greece if she sought asylum in any other EU country.[10] A US official told her that if she sought asylum in the United States, she would be detained and then would have to find a way to support herself. With no money or friends in the United States, she decided to go to Germany, where she knew people who would help her. She spoke no German, however.

In Germany she was sent to a refugee camp. When she asked an official how long she would have to stay there, he replied, "Well, from six months to several years. When you choose to be a refugee, you give up your autonomy." Soltani thought to herself that she had not chosen to be a refugee but said nothing. After three months, she had a Kafkaesque asylum interview, during which an elderly Afghan man who spoke Dari, not Farsi, did his best to translate words such as *Facebook* into German for the immigration judge. Then she was transferred to a different camp to await the judge's decision.

In her gripping memoir, *My Stolen Face*, Soltani recounts the story, including her time in the two camps, where she stayed for about nine months. She became severely depressed and suffered from survivor guilt as conditions worsened in Iran, but she managed to learn enough German to interpret for other detainees and do volunteer work with refugees. She kept hearing that international media were still reproducing her photo as Neda Agha Soltan's. Her pro bono lawyer repeat-

edly contacted them, to no avail. Newspaper accounts of her plight led
to hate mail from people who refused to believe her story, feeling it
damaged Neda Agha Soltan's image as a martyr. Eventually a German
court upheld her complaint against the publications, although some
newspapers continued to reproduce her photo as Soltan's.

Neda Soltani received asylum in February 2010, about eight months
after her arrival in Germany.

> I had told everyone that the minute I would be granted asylum, I would
> leave the camp. By the time I had found an apartment, nevertheless, I
> was crippled with fear and helplessness. Now that the new life I had
> craved was real, I realized how abominably frightening it was. . . . Now
> my real life had started, and . . . it looked even emptier than the life
> in the camp. . . . It took me several more weeks to orientate myself
> step by step and focus on the three things that I reckoned were vital
> for my new life: learning German, fighting for justice, and looking for
> opportunities to get back into the world of books, research and aca-
> demia. . . . No day went by without missing my old life and missing
> my loved ones back in Iran. (Soltani 2012: n.p.)

Soltani built a new life in Germany, published her memoir, and
went on to teach at a university in the United States. In her book's
acknowledgments, she writes:

> I am enormously indebted to the individuals who helped me survive the
> whirlpool of events back in June 2009. Without the help of my friends,
> who risked many things to rescue me, I would not have had a chance
> to survive. I owe thanks to all the people who reached out to help me
> from across the borders. . . . Living the life of a refugee is a trauma-
> tizing experience, and I owe boundless thanks to my German friends
> who devotedly supported me in every single move I made to stabilize
> my new situation. I owe them thanks for their unstinting support and
> endless compassion and understanding. [They] did everything in their
> power to make me feel at home under their roof.

Them and Us

These cases are not unique or even unusual. Neda Soltani did not have to spend years in a refugee camp as she had feared, but without the sanctuary her friends provided she might not have found refuge anywhere. The theft of her identity was a primordial loss that many refugees experience but few have written about so eloquently.

Pierre is one of the few asylum applicants who find refuge in the United States in a timely manner, with legal representation and relatively few complications. In contrast, Mary and Jason both presented themselves voluntarily to immigration authorities and were immediately detained because of outstanding deportation orders. Neither had received notice of an asylum hearing held years before. At such hearings, the judge automatically issues deportation orders to anyone who does not appear, no matter what the reason, and then the cumbersome, arbitrary system moves clumsily and haltingly into action. Immigration authorities took years to find Mary and Jason, by which time they had established themselves as taxpaying US residents. Jason had started a family, whose other members were US citizens. All the people described in this chapter suffered family break-ups, as a result of either exile, detention, or expulsion.

Both Jason Ng and Tiombe Carlos were thrown into jails and prisons and detained there for many months under inadequate and inhumane conditions. In those facilities, the staff callously, even viciously, violated the basic human rights of the detainees in their care. Their apparent negligence may have caused Jason's agonizing and premature death and contributed to Tiombe's suicide.

ICE reported more than seventy deaths of immigrant detainees between 2003 and 2008, and families attempted to sue the government in some of those cases. In response to public outcry, US Rep. Zoe Lofgren and Sen. Robert Menendez introduced the Detainee Basic Medical Care Act (HR5950). It did not pass, but ICE made some improvements in immigration detention health care. Nevertheless, by the end of 2013, 141 immigration detainees, including asylum seekers, had died in custody in US facilities (United States Department of Homeland Security 2014).

Layla and Lydia were subjected to cruelty or discrimination in the British immigration system. Lydia is one of many African women asylum seekers who have been sexually assaulted, either in their home country or in Britain.[11] In general it is extremely difficult for Africans, especially women, to gain asylum in Britain, even from countries with a high level of internal conflict and government repression. Furthermore, the British government reportedly shipped planeloads of refused asylum seekers back to Uganda, Congo, Zimbabwe, Iraq, Sri Lanka, and other dangerous countries between 2009 and 2013. Often these countries either refused to accept the deportees or immediately threw them into prison.

Mary suffered the dire consequences of bad lawyering: years of delay, prolonged detention, and apparently endless uncertainty. Pierre was more fortunate, obtaining asylum with the help of a pro bono attorney, reuniting with his family, and finding work in his professional field. He lives at peace in America, but even so the exile's shadow sometimes falls over him. The suffering of asylum seekers such as Neda Soltani, Layla, Mary, and Lydia Besong lingered long after they were released from detention.

The Nature of the System

At one time or another, asylum or sanctuary seekers are subjected to what scholars and advocates call "a culture of disbelief," which permeates immigration bureaucracies. Officials tend to assume that asylum claimants are all liars who present fraudulent documents and deliberately misrepresent their reasons for seeking refuge.

These and many other stories give the impression that asylum systems are designed *not* to work – or at least designed to deny asylum in most cases, to deserving and undeserving applicants alike.[12] Despite a well-developed body of international and national laws that are supposed to protect their human rights, asylum seekers are often treated more harshly than criminals. Although guilty of no crime, they are detained without any indication of when they will be released or why they are incarcerated. At every opportunity, legislatures and governments pass laws and implement policies that make it increasingly

difficult for victims and survivors of harassment, discrimination, torture, genocide, and other crimes to find a safe haven where they can
remake their lives and contribute to their new societies.

Meanwhile the arbitrary and convoluted workings of the immigration system deny undocumented migrants the opportunity to make
a decent living and support their families. Instead they live for years
in constant fear of separation from their loved ones and banishment
to a place they might not even know. Although immigration officials
call deportation or removal an administrative measure, banishment
is traditionally one of the most severe punishments, short of death,
that anyone can suffer.

In the face of systematic abuse, what can be done to ensure that
asylum seekers can exercise their human rights? Can undocumented
migrants overcome the obstacles that keep them from living in peace
and security? Despite unfavorable public opinion and official obstruction, myriad groups and individuals try to help them by lobbying,
advocating, protesting, and providing sanctuary inside or outside
the bounds of the law. They follow an ancient tradition, at least five
thousand years old and perhaps much older than that. Along with
rejecting and expelling outsiders, giving refuge to strangers is one of
the fundamental acts of humanness.

2 Sanctuary's Beginnings

I was a stranger, and ye took me in.

— Matthew 25:35

Homo sapiens is a migrating species. Scientists have traced our wanderings across continents and oceans through a history that stretches back more than two million years. During this long process, we have adapted to our varied surroundings by developing diverse practices and beliefs, as well as forms of behavior that distinguish us from our primate relatives. And in the hundreds of thousands of years during which we have had language, we have evolved further, from discrete, isolated communities into a worldwide community. According to anthropologist Adam Kuper, "Five hundred years ago, the history of the human population began to come together again into a single process, for the first time since the origin of modern humans. After a history of dispersal and differentiation that lasted perhaps a quarter of a million years, there is once more something approaching a single world economy, culture and political system" (1994: 95).

A highly sociable species characterized by sharing, exchange, cooperation, and hospitality, we are also quarrelsome and violent, excluding and rejecting those we define as different from ourselves. Many social commentators have argued that conflict and competition for scarce resources, such as food, status, and mates, characterize human societies. Yet anthropologists have studied societies in which food, status, and mates are not particularly scarce; the only generalization one can make with assurance about human beings is that our circumstances and actions vary considerably – within certain broad limits determined by biology, environment, and culture.

As both anthropologists and biologists acknowledge, we have in common with other species a tendency to act altruistically. The great primatologist Frans de Waal observes, "Aiding others at a cost or risk to oneself is widespread in the animal world." Like other primates, humans extend help not only to their biological kin but also to unrelated individuals or groups. "Helpful acts that are costly in the short run may produce long-term benefits if recipients return the favor," de Waal notes (1996: 12). Such reciprocal altruism follows rules laid out by biologist Robert Trivers in 1972:

1. The exchanged acts, while beneficial to the recipient, are costly to the performer.
2. There is a time lag between giving and receiving.
3. Giving is contingent on receiving. (de Waal 1996: 24)

De Waal links reciprocal altruism among primates to the evolution of morality, "a tendency to develop social norms and enforce them, the capacity for empathy and sympathy, mutual aid and a sense of fairness, the mechanisms of conflict resolution, and so on" (2001: 34). Morality among humans extends beyond single communities, as disparate groups meet to socialize, trade, court, and perform. Anthropologists have documented how the social relationships that develop at such gatherings endure over long periods and great distances. De Waal points out that human societies differ from those of chimpanzees in that kin bonds extend well beyond the group's boundaries, partly through exchange of females in marriage (34).

De Waal goes much further when he writes: "Early human societies must have been optimal breeding grounds for survival-of-the-kindest aimed at families and potential reciprocators. Once this sensibility had come into existence, its range expanded. At some point, sympathy for others became a goal in and of itself: the centerpiece of human morality and an essential aspect of religion. It is good to realize, though, that in stressing kindness, our moral systems are enforcing what is already part of our heritage" (2006: 181).

Thus giving asylum or sanctuary may be seen as one of the basic manifestations of altruistic behavior and human morality. In the face of conflict, humans wander or even flee, sometimes thousands of miles from home, seeking safety among strangers who may have little apparent reason to welcome us. We seek sanctuary from pursuers and offer asylum to strangers in this richly contradictory context. Sanctuary and asylum are ancient, perhaps primordial, institutions, part of the foundation of our species. Why should that be so? Aside from saving the lives of those fleeing persecution, what larger purposes does sanctuary serve?

Other primates' social lives may be suggestive. *Homo sapiens* is not the only species whose members offer or seek sanctuary. Among our closest primate relatives, the chimpanzees and bonobos, females often move from one group to another, fleeing sexual overtures or attacks by local males they do not want to mate with, perhaps because they are related to them.[1] According to primatologists, female primates are more averse to incest than males and therefore more likely to leave home to avoid it. About chimpanzees, primatologist Lynne Isbell writes: "Because inbreeding is more costly to females than to males, selection should favor females that minimize incestuous matings. Males disperse because limited mating opportunities in their natal groups or home ranges create greater mating opportunities in other groups or home ranges, all else being equal" (2004: 96). Chimpanzees manage to find shelter in groups where they have no relatives, even though their social life is characterized by chronic conflicts, including raids and killings, between communities. Perhaps sanctuary or asylum could even be considered an integral part of intergroup hostility within a species, since it can be defined as the reception and protection of a fleeing member of a strange or "enemy" group.

However one chooses to interpret primate migration, it is a delicate business to extrapolate from other primates' behavior to our own. Humans differ from chimpanzees and other primates in important ways. Most strikingly, we form enduring nuclear and extended families; we keep in touch with distant relatives; unrelated humans become friends and maintain those friendships for long periods; we maintain elaborate kinship groups, based on social as well as biological ties; we socialize and trade with hundreds or even thousands of other humans, creating huge communities that span continents; we make war, but

we also make peace; we codify and change social rules; and we give
refuge to unrelated individuals and groups on a scale unknown to
other primates. As a result, our sociability is far more complex than
theirs, and to a far greater extent we are an unfinished species. We
have tried to take our evolution into our own hands through wholesale alterations of the natural environment, with unforeseen and as
yet unknown results. Our evolution is still going on.

Kuper warns us "not to expect to learn very much about our present nature from a study of remote ancestors scratching a living some
40,000 years ago" (1994: 101). Nonetheless, it is instructive to look
at the long history of human groups to find the commonalities that
define us as members of one species. Nineteenth-century theorists
disagreed about the mechanisms of human evolution on the basis of
their observations of other species, ancient Greek and Roman sources,
and reports on recently contacted human groups. In his 1865 book
Primitive Marriage, John McLennan speculated that early human males
had avoided incest by seizing women from outside their local group.
Darwin played down ideas about generalized promiscuity among early
humans by pointing out that mating is never random, but Freud
apparently believed that such promiscuity had existed. In contrast,
early twentieth-century anthropologists, including Westermarck and
Malinowski, theorized that incest was the first human taboo.

Westermarck went further, proposing that association with close
relatives during childhood inhibits later sexual attraction in humans
and other primates; this has come to be known as the Westermarck
effect. Evolutionary biologists' research over the past hundred years
has proven him right. They have also found that in some primate
species, such as chimps and bonobos, males tend to be philopatric
(remaining in their birth communities), while females migrate to
other communities to mate. Thus primates, including humans, practice exogamy (mating outside their family or community) to avoid
incest, which has damaging effects on reproductive fitness over time.

In the process, humans create and maintain trade and other relationships outside their home community. Relations with other communities may be friendly, antagonistic, or both: strangers may be seen
as important sources of information or potential exchange partners

rather than dangerous interlopers or deadly assailants, but which of these cannot be known in advance (Chapais and Berman 2004: 401). For this system of communication and exchange to work, communities must take in strangers at least some of the time.

Furthermore, "social inclusion is absolutely central to human morality, commonly cast in terms of how we should or should not behave in order to be valued as members of society. . . . Universally, human communities are moral communities; a morally neutral existence is as impossible for us as a completely solitary existence," de Waal maintains (1996: 10). However, he insists, our sympathy for others is not boundless. We give it most readily to our own family and clan, less to other members of the community, and least of all to outsiders (88). Accepting strangers makes them part of the moral community. That is the basis of sanctuary. But the ever-present tension between incorporating and rejecting strangers limits humans' willingness to bestow it.

In many societies, sanctuary is only temporary or is hedged with restrictions. Inspiring stories of Christian Holocaust rescuers sheltering Jewish children at the risk of their own lives must be juxtaposed against today's punitive and exclusionary asylum policies, which break up families or return refugees to die in the country that persecuted them. Decisions about whom to accept and whom to reject may seem arbitrary, but they are not; they are based on our willingness to incorporate members of certain groups but not others into our moral community. The criteria we use to make such decisions change over time, depending on a complex combination of economic, social, and political factors and circumstances. And sometimes sanctuary is given *despite* these factors, as individuals and groups defy custom and law, risking their lives and livelihoods to give refuge to strangers.

Ancient Sanctuary Traditions

Often these decisions come out of deeply held beliefs that form the foundation of our moral community. Almost every major religious tradition includes concepts and rules governing sanctuary. Religious texts codify customs that probably existed long before the texts were

written. For example, rules establishing "cities of refuge" for manslayers are laid out in the Old Testament, in the Book of Numbers and
Deuteronomy, compiled more than 2,500 years ago. Siebold explains:
"Exodus XII:14 ruled that whosoever transgressed against his neighbor, killing him by cunning, should be removed from the altar and
slain. Deuteronomy marked a new epoch in the administration of
criminal justice: blood vengeance was divested of its private character and replaced by public punishment; the purchase of freedom
from punishment by the murderer was no longer permitted; and a
clear distinction was made between premeditated and unpremeditated
crimes. All shrines were abolished except for the temple at Jerusalem,
where the entire cult was centralized, and the institution of sanctuary was completely transformed" (1937: 534).

The ancient Hebrews created six cities of refuge, linked to former
religious sanctuaries and intended only for those who had committed unpremeditated murder. Over time, protection of the innocent
and punishment of the guilty became the public features of secular
law (Siebold 1937: 534). Bau (1985) points out that the city of refuge
lessened the harshness of the blood feud by giving refuge to such
unintentional killers, who were in a different category from murderers. Once they had arrived in the city of refuge, manslayers had to
undergo a trial to prove that they had killed accidentally. Then they
could stay in the city until the reigning high priest died. After that,
they could return home safely.

Traditions of sanctuary in the Mediterranean world are even older.
Among the ancient Egyptians, Siebold notes, "in the earliest times
every shrine, including places dedicated to the gods, royal altars, pic-
tures and statues of the ruler, or sites used for the taking of oaths,
was a protected region sought out by all the persecuted, by mistreated
slaves, oppressed debtors and political offenders" (1937: 534).

The word *asylum* comes from the ancient Greek *asylos*, "inviolable." Three thousand years ago, the goddess Diana's sanctuary at
Ephesos was famous throughout Greece as a place of asylum, and
people also sought refuge in groves, temples, and other places associated with the gods. Boundary markers, including rocks and trees,
marked sacred and inviolable space. Nothing could be damaged and

no one harmed there with impunity. Fugitives could sit at the foot
of a statue or an altar or tie themselves by a rope to a statue, and no
one was supposed to touch them, John Pedley, a historian of ancient
Greece, wrote. Sometimes the area around a sanctuary, such as all the
space within bow-shot range of the corner of the roof of the temple
of Ephesos, was sacred (Pedley 2005: 57–58).

Outlaws and refugees, guilty and innocent alike, fled to sanctuaries. It was believed that severe punishment such as a plague would
befall anyone who broke the rules protecting them. These sanctions
could also affect the community of someone who violated sanctuary.
Defeated soldiers, slaves, exiled politicians, or social outcasts could
cross the boundary into the sacred space and be safe. No one could
remove them by force (Pedley 2005: 97).

The Greek city-states were constantly at war with one another,
producing a stream of refugees and exiles seeking sanctuary with
their enemies. Sanctuaries on the frontiers of city-states were well
known. Promontories, considered sacred to the god Poseidon, often
served as places of asylum because they were accessible by both land
and sea. According to Siebold, "Temples enjoyed the character of
sanctuaries and under all circumstances could protect the oppressed
and the persecuted, slaves, debtors, malefactors and criminals. Even
deliberate murderers and those under sentence of death had a claim
to protection and could dwell in the sanctuary grounds surrounding
a temple, secure under the sheltering wing of the divinity, until death
overtook them" (534).

Under Roman rule during the third and second centuries CE,
Greek sanctuaries were still giving shelter to fugitives, often escaped
slaves. A Roman emperor, hearing that sanctuaries were being violated, referred the matter to the senate. Its decisions usually favored
the sanctuary seeker on the basis of ancient practice. Romans thought
the Greeks knew best about maintaining sanctuaries (Pedley 2005: 98).

Although the ancient Romans were not known to be merciful, they
also considered certain places as sanctuaries. Westermarck writes that
an old Roman tradition held that "Romulus [the mythical cofounder
of Rome] established a sanctuary, dedicated to some unknown god or
spirit, on the slope of the Capitoline Hill, proclaiming that all who

resorted to it, whether bond or free, should be safe" (1909: 162). He also
notes that a temple built to honor Julius Caesar in 42 BCE, two years
after his assassination, gave sanctuary to fugitives. Statues of Roman
emperors were considered places of sanctuary as well. According to
Siebold, during the imperial period their protective power extended
to persons and objects connected with the cult of the divine emperor.
Statues, portraits, and temples of the caesars, as well as military flags
and eagles, were imbued with the properties of asylum (535).

Sanctuary in Other Societies

Cultures and societies remote from Western civilization also have
long traditions of sanctuary and asylum. Ethnographers, historians,
explorers, invaders, and travelers since the fifteenth century have
observed and reported on such traditions, which may date from
ancient times. Margaret Mead observed in her study of the island of
Manus, in Papua New Guinea: "In a primitive community, sanctuary and hospitality are so intermixed that it is difficult to distinguish
between them" (1956: 315).[2]

　　In cultures where honor is a central virtue, it usually includes the
obligation to wreak vengeance, provide safeguard and sanctuary, protect the integrity of women, and guarantee hospitality (Masters 1953:
180). These ideals predate major religious traditions in the Middle
East and Mediterranean, and some continue up to the present. For
example, in the 1960s the Bedouins of western Egypt preserved an
ancient practice, the *nazaala*, "the act of taking refuge": "If a killing
is committed, the killer immediately seeks protection by going to the
residence of a neutral third party. . . . During the period of sanctuary,
it is hoped that two things will happen: that the killed man's group
will be placated and agree to compensation rather than retaliation as
a means of conflict regulation; and that over this period of one year
the killer's family will pay the [compensation]" (Obermeyer 1969: 201).
Seeking or giving sanctuary or asylum to forestall blood vengeance is
a frequent theme in the anthropological literature.

　　Sanctuary also serves other purposes in "honor" cultures. Boehm
wrote that when Montenegro was a Balkan tribal society, malefactors

might be exiled temporarily or permanently. In Montenegro and the Turkish territory that surrounded it, refugees from trouble of one sort or another kept showing up and asking for permission to stay. The local moral code made sanctuary an imperative (1984: 75).

In many African societies, sanctuary was based on animist religious beliefs and thus was a sacred institution. Among the Igbo, a major ethnic group in Nigeria, "the shrine of the goddess became a sanctuary for such social offenders as thieves, adulterers, debtors and those sent there as gifts to the goddess. . . . As the stream was considered sacred, all creatures in it were considered sacred and taboo by the community" (Amadiume 1987: 53).

Among many examples of sanctuary throughout the world, Westermarck cites one from India: "Among the Kafirs of the Hindu-Kush there are several 'cities of refuge,' the largest being the village of Mergron, which is almost entirely peopled by . . . descendants of persons who have slain some fellow-tribesman" (1909: 161).

Half a world away, Native American groups that had tense relationships with one another still offered and received sanctuary. After their rebellion against the Spanish in the 1680s, for example, the Tewa fled west and sought refuge with the Hopi. Anthropologist Harold Courlander notes: "The Hopi mesas were a sanctuary for Lagunas, Acomas and others seeking escape from Spanish authority virtually throughout the seventeenth century. At one time or another there were Eastern Pueblo settlements close to every one of the extant Hopi villages" (1987: 12).

In what later became New York state, Seneca of the eighteenth century gave sanctuary to indigenous people of diverse origins. Many of them were assimilated into Iroquoian society (Deardoff 1951: 82). A *History of American Indians*, published in 1775, describes "peaceable towns" among the tribes of the Southeast: "They seem to have been formerly 'towns of refuge,' for it is not in the memory of their oldest people that human blood was ever shed in them, although they often force persons from them, and put them to death elsewhere" (Westermarck 1909: 161).

Hawaiians were more forgiving, although their system of *kapu* (taboos) was rigid and all-encompassing: "The authority of the high chief and the priests to regulate the patterns of ancient Hawaiian society, especially as they related to social and religious customs, was unquestioned. Those who disregarded the traditional restrictions were susceptible to the most extreme punishment. One avenue of succor was available to them, however, consisting of escape to a place of refuge. These were the only checks to the king's absolute power of life and death over his subjects" (Rhodes and Greene 2001: 219). These places, called *pu'uhonua,*

> were sacred areas, not necessarily enclosed, to which murderers, kapu-breakers, and other transgressors who had incurred the wrath of the ruler could hastily retreat to gain sanctuary from reprisal. . . . Theoretically, no one pursuing this person, including a high chief, the king, or enemy warriors, could enter the enclosure without risking death at the hands of the resident priest or his attendants. The one seeking asylum usually remained several days and then returned home, absolved of his misdeeds by the gods. Fugitives from battle also fled to these places; during times of war white flags waved from tall spears placed outside the walls at each end of the enclosure. . . . Ten *pu'uhonua* existed on the island of Hawai'i, the one at Honaunau being the largest in the Hawaiian Islands. (219)

Pu'uhonua O Honaunau (City of Refuge) is now a US national park, and its sanctuary has been carefully restored.

Sanctuary Transformed

Over the past five hundred years, as societies changed under the pressure of Western colonialism and imperialism, they transformed ancient traditions to respond to modern conditions. For example, Catholic Church historian John Noonan points to the reuse of ancient concepts of sanctuary in nineteenth-century America, "when churches were to be used as safe places for slaves who had fled their masters in slave states. . . . Here sanctuary was not incorporated into the law to limit the law but operated in bold defiance of the law. Nonetheless the ancient idea of the special character of a holy place was at work. Somewhere on earth, it was believed by religious people, the hunted should be beyond their pursuers" (quoted by Bau 1985: 2–3).

Members of the Sanctuary Movement in the United States often cited Canon 1179 of the Catholic Church's 1917 Code of Canon Law to justify giving refuge to Salvadorans, Hondurans, and Guatemalans during the Central American wars of the 1980s. Ignatius Bau quotes the canon: "A church enjoys the right of asylum, so that guilty persons who take refuge in it must not be taken from it, except in the case of necessity, without the consent of the ordinary, or at least of the rector of the church" (1985: 91; and quoted by Lippert and Rehaag 2013: 26). Despite its omission from the Code of Canon Law of 1983, this provision continued to have moral force for some Catholics. Bau, the first writer to put the Sanctuary Movement in historical, religious, and political context while it was most active, called the provision "shocking to the secular mind. How can there be any place within the confines of a nation that the law does not operate? How can religion claim a privilege to say it is beyond the law? How can the law stultify itself by acknowledging that in certain places the law ceases to hold sway? Religious history teaches otherwise" (2). Thus modern sanctuary givers have sought legitimacy in ancient traditions.

* * *

Human cultures are characterized by diversity and variety, and contradictory tendencies to exclude and to integrate strangers are both widespread in our species. As a result, it is incorrect to assume that human nature leads inevitably to rejection of the other. We are as likely to accept strangers as to drive them away, depending on complex factors that cannot be reduced to the immediate self-interest of a particular group. Sanctuary and asylum may be informally or spontaneously given, but they are rule-bound institutions based on shared values and well-established cultural codes. Nevertheless, individuals and groups may defy powerful social, political, and economic forces and norms to give sanctuary.

Giving refuge to strangers is an act of reciprocal altruism, an adaptation we share with our primate relatives and other species. It may have its roots in the avoidance of incest and the practice of exogamy in various species. Sanctuary is often associated with sacred or otherwise special places where extraordinary exceptions may be made to normal rules, punishments, and restrictions. Asylum may be given to complete strangers from distant societies or to known individuals from neighboring communities or nearby kin groups. Whoever gains sanctuary is protected from violence, usually temporarily but sometimes permanently. The religious nature of sanctuary is a constant across cultures and millennia.

3 A Thousand Years of Medieval Sanctuary

God in heaven forbid
We should infringe the holy privilege
Of blessed sanctuary! Not for all this land
Would I be guilty of so deep a sin.

—Shakespeare, *Richard III*, Act 3, Scene 1

In the fourth century CE, the Roman Empire made a transition from one state religion to another by transforming pagan practices and institutions into Christian ones. Sanctuary was already an ancient custom among many peoples of the empire, from Germans to Hebrews. The first Christian emperor, Constantine, embraced the institution of sanctuary.

The Theodosian Law Code of 392 formally codified church sanctuary, limiting it according to the type of crime and the character of the accused. Debtors, embezzlers of state funds, Jews, heretics, and apostates were to be excluded from its benefits. Around 450 CE, Theodosius the Younger extended sanctuary from the church interior to the churchyard walls or precincts, including the bishop's house, cloisters, and cemeteries. About fifty years later, Justinian's Law Code excluded public debtors, tax officials, murderers, rapists, and adulterers from sanctuary. But such people often did obtain refuge on church premises over the next 1,100 years.

Catholic Church councils laid down rules for church sanctuary throughout the Christian world. As early as 344 CE, the Council of Sardia officially recognized sanctuary in churches, but it did not proclaim any *right* to asylum in churches. (It would be anachronistic to talk of any individual right in this context.)

Fourth-century church fathers such as Augustine, John Chrysostom, and Ambrose personally protected fugitives and preached on the inviolability of churches. The Council of Orange, 511 CE, declared, "No one was permitted of his own authority to remove by force from churches those who had fled to them, but they had to apply to the bishops, who took cognizance of the complaints of the slaves, and the wrongful acts of their masters, and interposed to obtain pardon for the former, guaranteed by an oath of the master to observe it or pay two slaves to the church" (Mazzinghi 1887: 90).

In the late seventh century, the Council of Toledo declared excommunication as the penalty for violating sanctuary. It should be kept in mind, however, that transportation and communication were so poor and the rule of law so precarious that legal codes and conciliar proclamations often had little effect, unless officials, clerics, and secular rulers saw the advantages of upholding and enforcing them on the local level. On the one hand, rulers understood that the peace of the church was also the king's peace (Sartain 2002: 34). On the other hand, the Catholic Church struggled to exert exclusive control over sacred spaces and objects, such as relics housed in churches. To maintain the sanctity of church premises (and the power of the church as an institution), it was necessary to protect everything and everyone, even fugitives, within them.

Above and beyond secular law codes, the church exercised its authority by regulating sanctuary. Pope Leo I (440–61 CE) decreed that church officials were to examine all sanctuary seekers. As sanctified personages, bishops could then grant sanctuary. They could act as intercessors and advocates on behalf of fugitives, becoming intermediaries between accused wrongdoers and those seeking private vengeance or legal redress. They also assumed the authority to subject sanctuary seekers to "penitential discipline" and "spiritual punishment" (Siebold 1937: 535). The Council of Reims, 630 CE, decreed that "a person delivered by the church from pain of death had to promise before he left to make penance for his crime and to fulfill whatever canonical punishment might be imposed" (quoted by Sartain 2002: 42). The church undertook to exercise mercy and dispense justice in a world that had little time for either.

As far as the church was concerned, its power to grant sanctuary came from God and thus superseded that of the state. As a result, secular officials were not allowed to pursue sanctuary seekers into the church. Such pursuit would amount to sacrilege. Public authorities' legal right to seize a sanctuary seeker was thereby suspended (Siebold 1937: 535). Meanwhile conflicts between church and state over the extent and exercise of each institution's authority led to a gradual erosion of church power, a process that took many centuries.

During early medieval times in European countries and Britain, the secular legal system was thoroughly corrupt and ineffective when it existed at all. The king was the lawgiver, and if he was absent from the kingdom or in conflict with the nobility, lawlessness reigned. Gangs composed of nobles or their vassals controlled parts of kingdoms. Men of lower rank carried knives and gentlemen wore swords, so any quarrel could end in bloodshed, especially since society viewed the willingness to engage in violence as a valuable male quality (Bellamy 1973: 25). Armed men could bribe, intimidate, or even kill judges, juries, and witnesses and get away with it. Crime was not the monopoly of the lower orders. Violent feuds were common among the nobility and gentry, and private individuals avenged killings with impunity. Nobles and gentry were as likely to commit crimes as the poor, although most crimes were thefts caused by poverty. Penalties were severe. In England the penalty for stealing goods worth more than 1 shilling was death. It was in this context that people (usually men) accused of serious crimes fled to church sanctuary.

To the clergy, crime was the consequence of man's fall from grace, and the church stood for mercy to sinners (Bellamy 1973: 32). Thus violence within the church's sacred precincts was forbidden. Sanctuary seekers had to sign an oath upon entry that they would not commit violent acts in the church. Innocent people also sought sanctuary. During the limited time they were allowed to stay in the church (three to forty days, depending on the period and the place), negotiations could be conducted with the secular authorities to forestall private vengeance killing.

The German tribes that came into contact with the declining Roman Empire did not provide sanctuary in their temples to crimi-

nals (Cunningham 1995: 221). But under the Merovingian kings, who
ruled in the former Roman province of Gaul from the mid-fifth to the
eighth centuries, Roman and German concepts of sanctuary merged:
Criminals could find refuge from private vengeance and severe punishments but remained subject to the public legal system. The sanctuary seeker who was delivered to the secular court was protected
from capital punishment and brutal treatment. The German kings
also borrowed exile and banishment, accompanied by confiscation
of personal property, from Roman law.

Charlemagne, who united most of Western Europe between 800
and 814 CE, allowed sanctuary but intervened to prevent feuding and
assert the royal right of pardon and punishment. His Saxon Capitulary
of 785 declared, "If anyone seeks refuge in a church, no one should
attempt to expel him by force, but he should be permitted to have
his peace until he presents himself to judgment; and his life should
be spared in honor of God and Holy Church" (quoted by Jones 1994:
27). However, Charlemagne reserved the power to send the fugitive
wherever he pleased. He was one of many kings who tried to bend
the ecclesiastical system to their own political purposes, proclaiming
themselves monarchs by divine right and challenging the authority of
the pope and his bishops.

Meanwhile, in Arabia

In the seventh century CE, the Prophet Muhammad was creating what
would become the world religion of Islam. Encountering resistance
and violent persecution, the Prophet "sought a more receptive environment for his message, which he eventually found in Medina, a
mainly agricultural community in western Arabia. In 622 AD, Muhammad and his first followers, who became known as *al-muhajirin* (the
migrants) left Mecca and settled in Medina" (An-Na'im 1990: 12). This
flight to sanctuary is known as *hijra*, and that year marks the beginning of the Muslim calendar.

Hijra had ancient roots in Arab traditions of hospitality. According to Westermarck (1909: 162), "At certain Arabian shrines the [pre-

Islamic] god gave shelter to all fugitives without distinction." Among the desert Arabs, any tent could be a sanctuary for a short period (Bau 1985: 127–28). In many tribal cultures that adopted Islam, sanctuary was (and is) connected to the practice and prevention of vengeance. In Afghanistan, for example, the traditional Code of Pashtunwali includes not only vengeance and feuding but hospitality and sanctuary. The traditional Bedouin practice of *nazaala* is an example of the link between sanctuary and conflict resolution (Obermeyer 1969: 201; see chapter 2).

Muslim religious practices have preserved and continued these venerable traditions. In late nineteenth-century Morocco, "the tombs of saints and mosques offer shelter to refugees, especially in those parts of the country where the Sultan's government has no power" (Westermarck 1909: 161). Muslims have taken the idea of sanctuary with them as they spread their religion around the world, from Arabia to Indonesia to Detroit, Michigan. A recent study of Iraqi refugees in the Detroit metropolitan area found that many considered themselves *muhajirin* on a migration from "the Domain of Disbelief to the Domain of Faith," as they struggled to maintain their Islamic beliefs in a secular society. A Sunni man told an interviewer, "The Prophet said that he who escapes with his faith from one land to another, even if it is only the distance of an inch, will be worthy of Paradise" (Shoeb et al. 2007: 449).

The Relationship between Church and State

In the medieval West, sanctuary was consolidated through royal edicts, laws, and clerical customs. The first Christian king in England, Ethelbert of Kent (c. 560–616), set up a penalty for violation of the peace of the church, or *fryth*, in a law code of 597. One of the foundations of sanctuary, fryth was immanent in the power of the church and any sacred place. The Germanic root of the word refers to sacred woods (Bau 1985: 135).

In Anglo-Saxon England, sanctuary was again related to blood feuds and vengeance. The offender was subject to punishment by the group or individual that had been injured, and his offense was considered a crime against the entire community, clan, or tribe. The victim or relatives had the right to carry out vengeance. In some societies, however, compensation substituted for violent punishment.

The church served as an intermediary between the fugitive and the offended group, helping to determine what punishment or compensation would be levied. Later the crown or the state intervened, turning compensation into a fine and vengeance into capital punishment or imprisonment. Thus a public legal system gradually emerged over many centuries from rougher, private forms of justice. But over a thousand years, by stepping between the accused perpetrator and the injured parties, church sanctuary played an important role in the progression from private vengeance to public law.

In 680 King Ine of Wessex provided for sanctuary as an alternative to punishment or death in his law code, and in 887 King Alfred gave his protection to all churches and some monasteries, which could give temporary refuge to fugitives with the expectation that they would soon leave sanctuary and be reconciled with their enemies (Jones 1994: 21). Alfred offered "immunity from peremptory retribution" if the sanctuary seeker confessed and surrendered to local authorities. Under his law code, sanctuary seekers could gain refuge for seven to thirty days. Anyone harming the fugitive during that time had to pay compensation to the fugitive's kin for breaching fryth.

Another of Alfred's laws extended the number of days the fugitive could stay in sanctuary but did not allow the church to provide food, thus guaranteeing his eventual departure. Even so, church officials were supposed to ensure that sanctuary seekers did not suffer capital punishment or torture after leaving sanctuary, in line with the church's duty to ensure mercy for sinners.

Toward the end of the first millennium CE, kings granted sanctuary privileges to almost two dozen abbeys, monasteries, minsters, and other religious houses throughout England. These included Beverley Abbey, Durham Cathedral, Wells Cathedral, York Minster, and Westminster Abbey. Royal laws imposed fines to protect the inviolability of sanctuaries, depending on the distance from the altar where violations took place. A violation of the altar itself was irredeemable.

This rule had momentous consequences in the twelfth century, when King Henry II's vassals assassinated Thomas Becket, the archbishop of Canterbury, inside the cathedral near the altar. One chronicler recounts that Becket had resisted Henry's repeated denials of sanctuary, and for this and other reasons Henry ordered his assassination (Cox 1911: 35). In addition to being archbishop of Canterbury, Becket was also the provost of Beverley, one of the most important sanctuary abbeys in England.

Becket's murder on December 29, 1170, had tremendous repercussions, including the development of a cult in his honor that brought numerous visitors and considerable revenues to Canterbury Cathedral. (Chaucer portrays the pilgrims in the *Canterbury Tales* as they wend their way to the cathedral to worship at Becket's shrine.) Henry had made progress in consolidating the justice system and the state's power over the feudal lords. But his involvement in Becket's murder made it impossible for him to exercise effective control over the church. Becket's killing had the unintended effect of strengthening the church's control of sanctuary.

As sanctuary law developed, it began to reflect conflict and competition between church and state. In 1014 King Ethelred's law conferred sanctity on churches themselves rather than the clerics who officiated there. The church collected fines for violations of sanctuary under this royal law. As time went on, "the churches and the clergy would claim that the sanctuary privilege was rooted in the sanctity of the place, irrevocable by the monarch. On the other hand, the king would claim that the privilege was merely a personal privilege granted to the clergy, revocable at the king's will" (Bau 1985: 141).

In the second half of the eleventh century, William the Conqueror's laws affirmed church sanctuary and established stiff fines for its violation. Such fines were to be paid not only to the church but also to the king. The secular law was supposed to approximate or be modeled on divine justice. As it developed, it protected the guilty and the innocent through due process. Secular procedures such as habeas corpus (which appeared in England in the twelfth century) and the concept that one is innocent until proven guilty may have evolved from royal laws protecting sanctuary seekers. In the twelfth and thirteenth centuries, English and French kings created a criminal justice system in which royal courts claimed a monopoly over criminal prosecution, making formerly private justice public.

The crown had strong reasons to support sanctuary, however. If private parties summarily executed a criminal, the crown would lose the revenue (fines, seized property) it could hope to gain if it successfully prosecuted him. Sanctuary gave the crown time to prepare a prosecution and made it more likely the criminal would be brought to justice. The monarch also used sanctuary to protect a particularly stigmatized group, the Jews, on whom he often depended for funds to fight both civil and foreign wars. In the twelfth and thirteenth centuries, threatened by great public hostility and pogroms, Jews survived in Britain only because their loan contracts stipulated that they could take refuge in royal castles (Winder 2004: 47).

Abjuring the Realm

Sanctuary could be and was abused by criminals who used the church as a safe house. Some abbeys, such as Westminster, could even provide permanent sanctuary from private vengeance or the king's justice. In reaction, kings placed restrictions on sanctuary: felons could remain in a church for only forty days, during which time they were expected to confess their crimes and abjure the realm (Siebold 1937: 536).

Abjuration of the realm was a form of voluntary exile. It apparently arrived in England from Normandy and was first mentioned in a royal document around 1130. Bracton's *On the Laws and Customs of England*, compiled in the mid-thirteenth century, described the procedure in detail. After gaining sanctuary, the fugitive publicly confessed the crime before a royal official, called a coroner, who came to the church for that purpose. Coroners kept legal records of sanctuary cases, some of which still exist today. These and other documents indicate that around a thousand people a year may have gained church sanctuary in England over several centuries. Fugitives could either surrender to the secular authorities for trial or abjure the realm. In the latter case, they were required to swear before the coroner: "Hear this, justices or ye coroners, that I shall go forth from the realm of England, and shall not return thither again, except with the license of the lord the king or of his heirs, so God me help" (quoted by Cox 1911: 14).

Bracton's law treatise, *De Corona*, describes what happened next:

> If having acknowledged his misdeed he has elected to abjure the realm, he ought to choose some port by which he may pass to another land beyond the realm of England. . . . And there ought to be computed for him his reasonable traveling expenses as far as that port, and he ought to be interdicted from going out of the king's highway, and from delaying anywhere for two nights, and from entertaining himself anywhere, and from turning aside from the high road except under great necessity or for the sake of lodging for the night, but let him always continue along the straight road to the port, so that he shall always be there on the appointed day, and that he shall cross the sea as soon as he shall find a ship, unless he shall be impeded by the weather; but if he does otherwise, he shall be in peril. (Cox 1911: 13–14)

Other sources say the abjurer was to wear white sackcloth, carry a cross in his hand, and go bareheaded and barefoot. The usual port of departure was Dover, but some northern abjurers would walk to Berwick and thence to Scotland. Sometimes the coroner gave the abjurer little time to reach the port, and he or she might have to walk as many as thirty-three miles a day. Once at the port, he was supposed to wade into the water up to the knees (some sources say up to the neck) and hail a boat. However, most abjurers probably did not leave the kingdom. Medieval courts were so weak that the best they could hope for was for abjurers' identities to become widely known (Jones 1994: 25). From exile, abjurers could petition the king to be allowed to return to England, and a few records indicate that some were allowed to return after paying a large indemnity. Abjurers could be pardoned only once, however.

The Boundaries of the Law

With its elaborate rules, privileges, and restrictions, sanctuary was
one of the most powerful and important medieval institutions. Three
types of sanctuary existed: first, a general privilege inhering in every
parish church and churchyard; second, sanctuary chartered by the
king, where permanent refuge was possible; third, secular sanctuary controlled by the local lord in churches under his jurisdiction,
beyond the king's authority. In all cases, sanctuary could be used
to settle or resolve conflict, not only as a way for criminals to avoid
punishment and retribution (Musson 2005: 5). It also served broader
purposes, defining the boundaries of the law and the sacred meaning of justice.

Musson points out that sanctuary demonstrated the redemptive
quality of punishment that permeated early medieval culture (2005:
39). That is, doing wrong injured not only the victim of crime but the
soul of the wrongdoer. Redemption lay in the perpetrator's making
an offering to God in search of forgiveness. Retribution for wrongdo-
ing was supposed to be "an offertory act of conciliation and repair,"
mediated or supervised by the church without violence (42). Punishment would lead to justice only if it included mercy and charity. The
wrongdoer could return to the community of believers by making a
sacrifice, an act of penance, which "reflected an acknowledgment
that by strict justice, all were lost. One could only achieve reunion
through grace, be it the Deity's, lord's or victim's" (46).

The Catholic basis of sanctuary survived until the Reformation in
Europe and Britain, but the rules governing it changed as the state
increased its control over the justice system. With adoption of the
Magna Carta in 1215, trial by jury became part of secular law. Sanctuary seekers who wanted to avoid trial in the royal courts had to abjure
the realm. Thus sanctuary continued to be a recourse for fugitives,
but increasingly kings sought to limit its use. They tried to prevent
traitors, debtors, and other categories of criminals from gaining refuge in churches and even went to the pope to gain support for their
policies. For example, in 1486 Henry VII obtained a bull (decree) from

Pope Innocent VIII regulating sanctuary in England. It proclaimed that sanctuary men (as they were called, although women also sought refuge) could not return to sanctuary if they committed crimes after leaving the premises. Sanctuary men's goods were not protected from creditors, and the king might send guards to the church to watch any sanctuary seeker accused of treason (Mazzinghi 1887: 112).

Religious and secular sanctuaries marked the limits of royal authority. The courtyards of feudal lords were out of bounds to state authorities and private seekers of vengeance. Entire cities, including Durham, were classified as "liberties," where royal authorities could not pursue fugitives. During periods of civil war, armed vassals and soldiers could flee to a liberty and stay there permanently, leaving them effectively beyond the reach of the law.

Numerous disputes among the king, the city, and the church ensued over liberties and sanctuary during the late Middle Ages. By the fifteenth century, kings were trying to undermine the institution at every opportunity. Legal authorities also disliked it. In 1399, English judges issued a manifesto against the erection of new sanctuaries, declaring that the king could not give away his prerogative of pardoning felons. Alleged abuses of sanctuary gave the monarch an excuse to limit or abolish it. But medieval laws limiting sanctuary were often ineffective: "Medieval legislation was always in the nature of a manifesto of policy, or the enunciation of a wholesome principle, to which practice should but frequently did not conform" (Thornley 1924: 187).

Despite royal restrictions, churches continued to take in fugitives during the fourteenth, fifteenth, and sixteenth centuries. They had strict rules. For example, at Durham Cathedral two men were stationed in chambers inside the north door to receive fugitives at all hours. The sanctuary seeker would ring the bell or bang the knocker and, before witnesses, declare why he was there. Once inside, he donned a black gown with a yellow cross on the left shoulder and was allowed to remain in designated areas of the cathedral for a maximum of thirty-seven days. From 1464 to 1524, Durham's records indicate that 332 fugitives involved in 243 crimes stayed in the church. Almost

200 of the crimes were homicides. At Beverley, 469 sanctuary seekers included 173 murderers and 200 debtors between 1478 and 1539 (Kesselring 1999: 348).

In 1456–57, the regulations of Saint Martin le Grand in London declared that the sanctuary seeker could bring no weapons into the church. Sanctuary men who went out at night or during the day to commit crimes would be forced to stay inside the church (Cox 1911: 90). Counterfeiters, strumpets, and bawds were not allowed entry, and betting was prohibited. Barbers were not to work on Sundays or feast days, though many tradespeople did live and carry on business within protected church precincts.

Sometimes sanctuary seekers waited many years, even decades, before fleeing to the church. Kesselring reported one man who abjured the realm in 1519 for a murder he had committed forty years earlier. Some sought sanctuary far from the scene of the crime. Others confessed to a felony committed nearby on the same day they fled to the church. Christopher Brown sought sanctuary in July 1477 after "he insulted one Thomas Carter who was riding and holding in front of him his little boy of three years of age; whereupon the said Thomas hastily dismounting on account of the insult, suffered his son to fall on the ground, and the horse, by an unfortunate accident, set its feet upon the child who died within two days from the wounds. Christopher, recognizing that he was the indirect cause of the child's death, hastened to Durham" (Cox 1911: 110).

The Decline of Sanctuary

By the late Middle Ages, sanctuary was a tarnished institution in Britain. The Elizabethan poet Michael Drayton expressed a common sentiment when he wrote,

> Some few themselves in sanctuaries hide
>   In mercy of that privileged place,
> Yet are their bodies so unsanctified,
>   As scarce their souls can ever hope for grace,
> Whereas they still in want and fear abide,

> A poor dead life this draweth out a space,
> Hate stands without and horror sits within,
> Prolonging shame, but pardoning not their sin!
> (quoted by Mazzinghi 1887: 112)

Criticisms of sanctuary focused on the abuses it led to, not on the institution itself (Kesselring 1999: 354). Thieves and debtors who used sanctuary as a base or to escape punishment were particularly despised. People knew and disapproved of the fact that fugitives could lead comfortable lives in permanent sanctuary in the liberties. Those with trades and skills a monastery could use to maintain itself might become lay brothers. During periods of civil conflict, liberties welcomed sanctuary seekers who were able fighters. In 1487, on receiving the false news that rebels had defeated Henry VII, Westminster sanctuary men joined together to rob the houses of the king's supporters, who were with him in the field (Thornley 1924: 186).

Westminster Abbey's precincts, which extended quite some distance beyond the church, were part of a sanctuary chartered by the king. In a famous incident in 1378, Sir Robert Hawley, an escapee from the Tower of London, was killed in the choir of the Abbey Church during the reading of the Gospel at High Mass (MacMichael 1970: 12). Cox notes: "This murder in such a place, apart even from the peculiar sanctuary privilege, aroused the deepest feeling of dismay. For four months the abbey remained closed to all religious rites, and even the sittings of Parliament were suspended lest they should be contaminated by assembling near the scene of the outrage" (1911: 52). As a result, Parliament gave Westminster permanent sanctuary status.

Art historian Gervase Rosser describes the abbey's residents as "a large assembly of marginal types, destitute or criminal, or both, who were glad of this protection from the law. At the same time, the sanctuary population also included a substantial minority of wealthy merchants. . . . To a trader desiring both complete immunity and convenient proximity to the city, nowhere offered greater safety than the sanctuary of Westminster Abbey" (1989: 156). Merchants accused of theft and fraud sometimes lived within the abbey gates for many years. Political dissidents also found a home in the abbey. The most famous was the poet laureate John Skelton, who wrote broadsides in verse against Cardinal Wolsey during the reign of Henry VIII. He died in sanctuary in 1529.

Westminster Abbey had special status as a sanctuary because the land around the abbey was an independent liberty. The king's writ and royal officers had no authority there (MacMichael 1970: 11). The fifteenth century, dominated by the Wars of the Roses, was the heyday of sanctuary at the abbey. Among the prominent sanctuary seekers there were Eleanor, Duchess of Gloucester, in 1441; Henry Holland, Duke of Exeter, in 1454; and Queen Elizabeth Woodville (wife of Edward IV) in 1470 and 1483.

As the Tudor kings consolidated state power by force and through the law, the church lost its dominance; sanctuary declined as a result. Determined to prevent traitors from gaining sanctuary, Henry VII and Henry VIII severely limited its operation. A series of parliamentary acts between 1529 and 1540 decisively damaged the institution. Abjuration of the realm was abolished in 1530, and anyone claiming sanctuary had to remain there permanently under pain of death. This law may have been passed because people with expert knowledge, such as mariners, were abjuring the realm and taking state secrets and technical expertise abroad. A law of 1534 declared that traitors could not gain refuge, and in 1540 serious felons were excluded from sanctuary.

All sanctuaries except for churches and churchyards were abolished after Henry VIII dissolved the monasteries and ended the chartered privileges of the country's major abbeys. The Reformation effectively destroyed not only the primacy of the Catholic Church but also sanctuary as a refuge from and alternative to secular law. Henry VIII established eight cities of refuge based on the Old Testament model. Apparently the inhabitants of the eight cities objected, and few if any fugitives went there.

Queen Mary Tudor, a Catholic, allowed sanctuary at Westminster Abbey but did not try to restore it in all places. Near the end of her reign, in 1558, the abbot of Westminster successfully defended the abbey's privileges in Parliament, noting that "all princes, throughout the history of Christendom, had preserved 'places of succour and safeguard for such as have transgressed laws and deserve corporal pains'" (quoted by Kesselring 1999: 355). He argued that places of refuge could legitimately temper the law.

Mary's successor, Queen Elizabeth I, weakened sanctuary by restricting it to debtors. During her reign, voluntary abjuration of the realm was transformed into "transportation," the secular judicial penalty of exile in the colonies. In 1624, during the reign of James I, Parliament finally ended sanctuary. It continued to exist until the early eighteenth century in a few churches, but it was finished as a recognized legal institution in Britain. Even so, in Scotland debtors could – and did – gain sanctuary at the royal palace of Holyroodhouse in Edinburgh until 1880. Debtors' prisons, which allowed them and their families to live unmolested in relative comfort until they could find the money to repay their outstanding debts, could also be seen as a continuation of sanctuary.

The Afterlife of Sanctuary

Even as the religious institution of sanctuary was declining, however, the underlying principles of sanctuary survived in the new secular invention of asylum. Under the Treaty of Westphalia (1648), asylum became an important part of international law as a right of nation states and an attribute of national sovereignty.

During the Counter-Reformation, the Catholic Church tried to preserve sanctuary in predominantly Catholic countries such as France, where King François I had abolished it in 1539. The Council of Trent (1545–63) declared sanctuary a divinely instituted right of the church. A papal bull of 1591 pronounced church buildings inviolable, and fugitives were not to be removed without the rector's permission. Violation of this rule would result in excommunication. As late as 1727, Pope Benedict XIII threatened secular officials with excommunication if they violated sanctuary but barred street robbers, assassins, political offenders, and counterfeiters from refuge in churches. Although severely restricted, sanctuary was tolerated in some parts of southern and eastern Europe as recently as the nineteenth century (Jones 1994: 35). The 1917 Code of Canon Law upheld sanctuary but dropped excommunication as a penalty for its violation.

Ironically, in his 1937 article on asylum in the *Encyclopaedia of the Social Sciences*, Siebold remarked, "In an orderly state with a systematized legal procedure sanctuary is superfluous" (537). At that moment, thousands of refugees from the Spanish Civil War were receiving sanctuary in France, Mexico, and other countries, and late in the following year charitable organizations began sending almost ten thousand Jewish children from Germany, Austria, and Czechoslovakia to sanctuary in Britain. During World War II, Catholic clergy, including the future Pope John XXIII, revivified sanctuary by hiding Jewish and other refugees from the Nazis in churches, monasteries, convents, and other religious houses. The 1983 Code of Canon Law did not include sanctuary at all, but at about that time Catholic, Protestant, and Jewish clergy and laypersons in the United States were risking federal prosecution by giving sanctuary to refugees from the Central American wars.

The elaborate belief structure of medieval sanctuary, mandating forgiveness and mercy, existed in a brutal world of blood feud, summary killing, torture, and trial by ordeal. Since then, the world has changed in some ways but not in others. Church sanctuary's success as an institution can be measured chiefly by its enduring influence, in Western societies and beyond, up to the present day.

4   From Religious Sanctuary to Secular Asylum

A permanent residence ought not to be denied
to foreigners who, expelled from their homes,
are seeking a refuge, provided that they submit
themselves to the established government and
observe any regulations which are necessary to avoid
strifes.

– Hugo Grotius, *De jure belli ac pacis*, 1625

On August 3, 1492, Isabella and Ferdinand expelled the Jews from Spain. A few left with Columbus that day for the New World. Some others fled to England, where they lived very quietly indeed, since the Jews had been expelled from that country two centuries before, in 1290. James I expelled their descendants in 1609, but from the mid-1620s on, small numbers of Jews again sought to enter England. During the Protectorate of Oliver Cromwell, in 1656, twenty Jews arrived in London, declaring themselves refugees from the Spanish Inquisition. In essence, they were asylum seekers. Because they identified themselves as anti-Catholic, the government allowed them to stay and practice their religion (Winder 2004: 76). More followed, establishing a small community in the East End of London. By the end of the seventeenth century, they numbered about a thousand.

The Jews were not the only, and certainly not the largest, group to seek refuge in Britain from religious persecution. Protestants from other nations, such as the Huguenots who left France after the Saint Bartholomew's Day Massacre of 1572, fled to Protestant England during the Reformation. Many other foreigners arrived in the country for economic and political reasons. In the fourteenth century, Flemish weavers fled unrest on the Continent and settled in England, where protectionist trade policies helped them prosper. These economic immigrants were much disliked, however. Riots in London drove Italian merchants out of the city in 1456–57, and unemployed people aimed their rage at foreigners during the May Day riots of 1517. Parliament repeatedly passed laws against "aliens" and restricted their economic activities. The British crown also had extradition treaties with other states; it used these agreements to get rid of "traitors" (people we would now consider political refugees) as well as criminals. Yet despite a generally negative attitude toward outsiders, the British became known for their willingness to take in strangers, especially when doing so served their economic interests.

English law divided aliens into two categories, friends and enemies. The Jews were defined as eternal enemies until the courts overruled that designation in 1697. As far back as the sixteenth century, the government had feared that foreigners were arriving under false pretenses, claiming to be religious refugees but actually coming to take jobs from native-born subjects. Throughout that century, rabble-rousing pamphlets aimed hostility at foreigners, who were commonly called "fugitives," as if they were criminals. Queen Elizabeth set an example for monarchs by allowing in certain kinds of people, such as Protestant Walloons from Flanders, while mercilessly expelling others, such as German Anabaptists, who did not believe in the Trinity. Her government also kept strict records of the numbers of foreigners in the kingdom. Nevertheless, European Protestants referred to Britain as "asylum Christi."

Even so, British Puritans could not find the religious toleration they craved in their native land and sought refuge first in Holland, then in the New World, which they considered a sanctuary from persecution. The Massachusetts Bay Colony and other early European settlements in America did not have sanctuary laws, but some did give refuge to religious and political dissidents who fled other colonies.

The first recorded sanctuary case in the American colonies took place in the 1660s, when Edward Whalley and William Goffe, officers in Cromwell's army and members of the court that had condemned King Charles I to death fifteen years earlier, arrived in the New Haven Colony (Bau 1985). They were fleeing indictments handed down under Charles II, who sent officers to the colony to arrest the two and return them to England for trial. A pastor in New Haven preached a sermon to the officers in support of sanctuary, and the Puritans hid the fugitives in a cave. The two stayed in the colony for ten years before dying of natural causes. Nobody invoked sanctuary, but it was given.

The first people to be called "refugees" in English were the Huguenots, who fled to England for a second time after the revocation of the Edict of Nantes in 1685. As many as 250,000 Huguenots left France in the following years for England, Germany, Switzerland, Holland, Denmark, Sweden, Russia, and America. The origin of asylum as a legal concept in international law predates this event, however.

The Peace of Westphalia, which ended the Thirty Years' War in 1648, established in Europe a community of nation-states that had certain rights, including sovereignty. The idea of state sovereignty based on physical territory was an invention of this peace treaty. It followed that the native inhabitants of a state had a natural right to live there, as opposed to outsiders or strangers, who had to obtain special permission to enter or reside in the territory. The Peace of Westphalia brought new order, based on international laws and agreements, to the relations among European nations. Part of sovereignty was the state's right to give asylum to anyone it wished and for other states to respect that right (Gibney and Hansen 2005: 1:23). An important aspect of asylum was the limitation it established on a state's right to ask for extradition of enemies who had fled to another state. It should be kept in mind that modern asylum came into formal existence as a universal right of *states* to grant, not of *individuals* to receive. In contrast to sanctuary, a religious institution in Europe, asylum was and is a secular and political institution, a part of the modern international system of sovereign states.

The acceptance of the Huguenots as refugees was an important early test of the new system. They were granted permanent asylum in their new countries, and their descendants live and prosper there to this day. Each generation in Europe received a group of refugees who came seeking refuge outside their native land. For example, some forty thousand émigrés arrived in England during the French Revolution. Although the British government supported the French monarchists, it feared that revolutionary spies might be sent to England to overthrow the British king. As a result, Parliament passed the first law regulating asylum in Britain, the Aliens Act of 1793, which dictated that refugees must register upon arrival in the country. This requirement has been included in successive British immigration laws for more than two hundred years.

Often governments admitted refugees only to expel them later. Charles Talleyrand, prime minister and foreign minister of France, was granted asylum in England in 1792, during the Reign of Terror, but expelled two years later; he spent two more years in exile in the United States before returning to France. In 1803 King George III issued a proclamation ordering 1,700 French refugees to leave the country. After being refused entry in France, they returned to England and were allowed to stay. In these instances, the enemy of England's enemy was England's friend – for a while.

During this very repressive period in Britain, when public meetings and even private correspondence on political matters could lead to treason charges, paranoia became official policy. In 1798, the Act for Establishing Regulations Respecting Aliens distinguished "between persons who either really seek refuge and asylum from oppression and tyranny . . . and persons who, pretending to claim the benefit of such refuge and asylum . . . have or shall come to . . . this kingdom with hostile purposes" (quoted by Stevens 2004: 21). This suspicion of strangers can be found in almost all asylum legislation and policy up to the present, where it survives in the bureaucratic "culture of disbelief" – the assumption that all asylum seekers are liars.

The Alien Acts passed during the Napoleonic Wars allowed the government to deport enemy aliens, and 218 were removed between 1801 and 1815. Even so, the government made exceptions to its draconian rules on a case-by-case basis. In 1802 the British secretary of state allowed the Bourbon princes to find refuge in Britain, saying, "His Majesty . . . feels it to be inconsistent with his honor, and his sense of justice, to withdraw from them the rights of hospitality, as long as they conduct themselves peaceably and quietly" (quoted by Stevens 2004: 22). This is an example of the state granting or withholding asylum for political purposes, as an instrument of state power in foreign affairs.

In the United States, the Alien Act of 1798 gave the president the authority to deport anyone he found dangerous to national security. This law and the accompanying Sedition Act were highly unpopular. In general, US borders were open, and regulation of immigrants was the responsibility of local authorities until the late nineteenth century.

Nineteenth-Century Asylum in Britain and the Continent

The British Parliament continued to pass Alien Acts from time to time during the nineteenth century, but between 1836 and 1905 the government did not deport a single refugee, including hundreds of revolutionaries who had been expelled previously from various European countries. The most illustrious political exiles included Giuseppe Mazzini and Karl Marx, who lived in Britain for decades. Thus Britain consolidated its reputation as a free country. A conspiracy bill targeting refugees who plotted attacks on European rulers did not pass Parliament and brought down the government in 1858, so great was the public opposition (Stevens 2004: 24).

Fifty thousand refugees were registered with the British police in 1851, one hundred thousand in 1871. Public attitudes toward them were contradictory. On the one hand, in 1849 the *Times* called England "the favoured receptacle of all the scum and refuse which the continental revolutions have thrown up" (quoted by Stevens 2004: 22). On the other hand, the same newspaper proclaimed in 1853, "Every civilized people on the face of the earth must be fully aware that this country is the asylum of nations, and that it will defend the asylum to the last ounce of its treasure and the last drop of its blood. There is no point on which we are prouder or more resolute. . . . We are a nation of refugees" (quoted by Stevens 2004: 27). In line with this sentiment, an 1870 law specifically protected political exiles from extradition.

Thousands of European political dissidents began to move to England and France in the early 1830s, after revolution swept from France and Belgium to Holland, Switzerland, Germany, Italy, and Poland. Around twelve thousand Poles departed to Western Europe and England in 1830–31. Thousands more fled from Portugal, Spain, Italy, and Germany. The French government reacted by placing restrictions on refugees. They were dispersed to parts of France where they would not threaten national security, and they had to carry identity cards after 1837. Sometimes they were forced to join the Foreign Legion and fight in colonial campaigns. They could be imprisoned. Or they might be expelled or extradited if they left the place to which they had been sent or if their home country wanted to prosecute them. Refugees could stay in France only if they lived quietly and avoided political activity (Bade 2003: 136).

The revolutions of 1848 brought another wave of refugees to France and Belgium. For political and economic reasons, both governments tried to discourage them from staying, although Belgium had achieved independence with the help of refugee soldiers and officers in 1830. Even before 1848, Karl Marx was expelled from France and went to Belgium. Then he was expelled from Belgium and eventually went to England in 1849. Other revolutionaries left Europe for the United States. But many European exiles wanted to stay as close to their home country as possible, so they could continue to influence political developments there. Political refugees were relatively few, but they represented the opposition in exile. Their writings and group activities abroad made them visible at home, and their influence was disproportionately large compared to their small numbers (Bade 2003: 138).

Pressured by the French government, the Belgians made it more difficult for political refugees to stay in the country. In 1849, for example, they prevented scores of Italians and Hungarians from crossing their border because another country (France) had previously taken them in. About 150 years later, European Union member states promulgated similar regulations under the Schengen and Dublin agreements to restrict the entry of asylum seekers.

Similarly, Switzerland pushed asylum seekers on to England and the United States in 1848–49. Only those who could not return to their home country because they feared death were acknowledged as refugees. The Swiss government considered asylum a humanitarian concession that it could refuse or revoke at any time (Bade 2003:

140). As Switzerland became a haven for revolutionaries, the government reacted by restricting refugees' activities, banning them from participating in organizations as long as they stayed in the country. Then Switzerland expelled Mazzini and other revolutionaries, and the focus shifted to England, which became the nineteenth century's most significant asylum-granting country (Bade 2003: 143). After 1851, France, Belgium, and Switzerland deported political refugees to Britain rather than back to their home countries. Sometimes the British government encouraged political refugees to go to the United States, and in 1858 it secretly financed the emigration of more than a thousand men, women, and children (Bade 2003: 146).

During the nineteenth century, Britain did not pass the kind of restrictive laws that made European countries increasingly inhospitable to refugees. Indeed, they could become British citizens after three years' residence, unless they were notorious troublemakers like Marx, whose petition for naturalization was denied in 1874. Nevertheless he lived unmolested in Britain until his death in 1883, and he rests in peace near several of his followers in Highgate Cemetery in London.

The life of political exiles in Britain was not easy unless they were wealthy. A few managed to become university professors or publish journals. Others struggled as tutors or governesses. Marx was a freelance journalist, writing mostly for US newspapers. He never earned enough money to support himself and his family, depending on the beneficence of his wealthy friend and fellow exile Friedrich Engels for many years.

On arriving in England, many exiles felt free, since no government spies shadowed them and they could associate with one another without constraint. After the post office opened Mazzini's correspondence in 1844, the government was criticized in the House of Commons for introducing "the spy system of foreign states . . . repugnant to every principle of the British Constitution and subversive of the public confidence" (quoted by Ashton 1986: 41). Certain activities classed as crimes in Europe, such as political conspiracy, propaganda, and incitement to revolution, were not criminal offenses in Britain. Furthermore, Britain boasted the right to assemble, freedom of the press, and an elected Parliament, which many European countries lacked. British asylum policies provided a humanitarian alternative to the repressive laws of the Continent.

Over time, however, the exiles suffered from penury, isolation, and disillusionment. In his journal, *The Star of Freedom*, G. J. Harney of the Association of Fraternal Democrats wrote in 1852, "The exile . . . is free to land upon our shores, and free to perish of hunger beneath our inclement skies" (quoted by Ashton 1986: 34). While the government did little or nothing to harm political refugees, it also did nothing to help them. The Association of Fraternal Democrats and other organizations provided limited financial assistance to refugees, but some disappeared into the morass of poverty, went mad, or subsisted by begging. In 1854, a London police report estimated that of almost two thousand exiles in the city, two-thirds were living in straitened circumstances (Ashton 1986: 226).

A few political exiles became famous in Britain. For example, Gottfried Kinkel, a university professor, was sentenced to life in prison for his involvement in the 1848 revolution in Prussia. He managed to escape to Britain with his family. Well connected with British intellectuals, who became his patrons, he was asked to deliver lectures all over the country. The press portrayed him as the victim of extreme punishment by an oppressive government (Ashton 1986: 155). As Britain admitted Italian political refugees in 1874, the Italian ambassador wryly observed, "England is very chary of making restrictions on the freedom of entry of foreigners to these shores. Deposed emperors and kings, princes in trouble, persecuted ecclesiastics, patriots out of work – all find an asylum in little England" (quoted by Winder 2004: 186).

Escaped slaves from the United States also fled to Britain, especially after passage of the Fugitive Slave Act in 1850. Even before that law went into effect, prominent abolitionist activists, such as Frederick Douglass and William Wells Brown, stayed in Britain until friends there bought their freedom so they could return home.

Codification of Asylum

In 1880 the British Institute of International Law passed the Oxford Resolutions, one of which stated, "Extradition shall not take place for political acts" (quoted by Grahl-Madsen 1980: 4). On the other hand, in an 1856 extradition law, Belgium declared that "murder, assassination or poisoning of the head of state of a foreign country or of members of his family shall not be considered a political crime or as an act connected with such a crime" (25). Governments generally agreed that political asylum could be given only to certain kinds of political dissidents – usually nonviolent ones – and political crimes were different from common crimes. Like medieval kings and popes, they wanted to restrict sanctuary to those they classified as deserving. But the essence of traditional sanctuary is openhandedness: anyone who sets foot on sacred ground must be admitted, no questions asked. It is too difficult to tell on the spot who might be innocent, who guilty. As a result, sanctuary has an ambiguous quality that makes it both compassionate and dangerous.

The United States became known as a country that welcomed immigrants and refugees, but it restricted entry in some ways. The Immigration Act of 1875 barred prostitutes and convicts. The Chinese Exclusion Act of 1882 was not repealed until 1943. Another 1882 law imposed a head tax on immigrants and prohibited entry of "idiots, lunatics, convicts and persons likely to become public charges" (quoted by Bau 1985: 40).

Immigration became a hot political issue in the United States and many other countries at the end of the nineteenth century, because of growing unemployment, poverty, industrial unrest, urban overcrowding, and abuses of the sweatshop system. At the same time, millions of people were leaving their home countries for economic, political, and religious reasons. About 2.5 million Jews fled persecution in eastern Europe and Russia from the 1880s to 1914. Only about 120,000 of them arrived in Britain during that period, and the 1901 census reported a total of 339,000 foreigners in a national population of 32 million. Nonetheless they were seen as invading hordes. In 1891 Sir

Howard Vincent, a member of Parliament from Sheffield, said they were arriving "in battalions and taking the bread out of the mouths . . . of English wives and children" (quoted by Stevens 2004: 34). There was a forceful anti-Semitic reaction: the British Brothers' League, a precursor of the far-right National Front, was established in 1901 in East London, where many Jewish refugees lived, to fight Jewish immigration. Their agitation inspired the Aliens Act of 1905, the first law since 1836 restricting immigration into Britain. As a result, many eastern European emigrants pushed on to America.

The 1905 Aliens Act did contain a provision protecting asylum seekers: "In the case of an immigrant who proves that he is seeking admission to this country solely to avoid prosecution or punishment on religious or political grounds or for an offence of a political character, or persecution involving danger of imprisonment or danger to life or limb, on account of religious belief, leave to land shall not be refused on the ground merely of want of means, or the probability of his becoming a charge on the rates" (quoted by Stevens 2004: 39).

This law could be the first in British history to recognize asylum, even though the words *asylum* and *refugee* were not mentioned. Nonetheless, the home secretary insisted at the time that there was "no such thing as a 'right' of asylum" (quoted by Price 2007). According to legal scholar Dallal Stevens, the home secretary mentioned the Huguenots as desirable immigrants because they had brought money and skills to Britain. He expressed willingness to protect refugees who brought tangible benefits and did not become a burden on the state. He also distinguished between genuine and bogus applicants (2004: 38). These attitudes have been constant features of government refugee and immigration policies in Britain and other countries up to the present.

The main purpose of the 1905 Aliens Act was to keep "undesirables" out of Britain. Only immigrants traveling in steerage (third class) were examined to determine their physical condition and means of support. Immigrant ships with more than twenty foreign passengers could be denied entry, and customs officers could turn back those unable to support themselves. Although aimed at Jewish migrants from the Baltic, the act could be used against any would-be immigrants. Throughout the twentieth century, immigration would be buffeted by shifting political alliances (Winder 2004: 259).

Before passage of the 1905 act, asylum was said to be "writ in characters of fire on the tablets of our Constitution"; after its passage, asylum became a privilege of the state, not an automatic right (quoted by Kushner and Knox 1999: 397).[1] The number of political refugees admitted to Britain decreased markedly. Yet, in the words of a government official ninety years later, "this country has a proud and consistent record in its treatment of refugees. Our humanitarian record is second to none" (quoted by Kushner and Knox 1999: 399). This is true only because other countries' treatment of refugees has been no better. The 1905 Aliens Act was significant in establishing administrative and legal procedures to decide refugee cases and linking asylum with immigration. Its limitation of foreigners' entry into Britain had grievous consequences for refugees for the rest of the century.

The tumult of war in the early twentieth century decisively ended Britain's long period of hospitality and sanctuary. The Aliens Registration Act of August 1914 (the month World War I started) included internment of "enemy aliens," a term that had not been heard in the country in almost a century. The right to appeal adverse immigration decisions was removed, as was the exception in the 1905 law benefiting political and religious refugees. In 1915, the British government made compulsory the presentation of a passport upon entry into the country; it had been optional since 1858. Also in 1915, the Germans erected a high-voltage electrical fence between occupied Belgium and Holland; about three thousand people died trying to cross it.

During World War I, thousands of foreigners were interned in Britain, and 24,000 were still in camps in November 1918. In Germany, 110,000 foreign civilians were interned in eighteen camps at the end of the war. About 400,000 enemy aliens were interned in all the warring countries during the war. The French government revoked the citizenship of all naturalized citizens who had been born in an "enemy state." After the war, a series of restrictive laws made entry into Britain a privilege. An overtly racist Special Restriction (Coloured Alien Seaman) Order, apparently aimed at East Indians, required all foreigners to register with the police (Winder 2004: 286). As an American graduate student in England in the 1970s, I had to register at the nearest police station.

Meanwhile the United States was closing its "golden door" to immigrants and refugees.[2] One late-nineteenth-century law authorized deportation of indentured workers. Bau comments, "This expansion of the deportation power reflected the slow but certain shift of U.S. immigration policy from one of open welcome to an increasingly complicated system of selection and exclusion" (1985: 41). The Immigration Act of 1917 imposed a literacy requirement, codified previous grounds for exclusion, extended exclusion to Asians, and allowed deportation up to five years after entry. After forty years of relatively easy entry by more than 23 million immigrants from all parts of Europe, the Emergency Quota Act of 1921 drastically "limited the annual immigration of persons of a given nationality to 3 percent of the number of such persons already in the United States in the year 1910" (quoted by Bau 1985: 41).[3]

The law was frankly racist: its intention was to keep southern and eastern European immigrants out and allow northern and western Europeans in. From 1917 on, the government used immigration laws to deport foreign-born political activists, antiwar campaigners, and trade unionists. The US National Origins Act of 1924 removed time limits for deportation of anyone who entered the country without a proper visa and restricted entry to 164,000 immigrants per year. In 1927, the annual quota was lowered still further to 150,000. As a result, Argentina and Brazil received more immigrants between 1925 and 1930 than the United States did. Thus did intolerance of the dangerous other become official policy.

5 Nineteenth-Century Sanctuary outside the Law

I will shelter, I will help, and I will defend the
fugitive with all my humble means and power. I will
act with any body of decent and serious men . . . in
any mode not involving the use of deadly weapons,
to nullify and defeat the operation of [the fugitive
slave] law.

– Rev. Theodore Parker, 1850

Among the many fugitives who have sought sanctuary in England over the years was Frederick Douglass, perhaps the greatest human rights advocate of the nineteenth century. In 1845, soon after the publication of his autobiography, he fled from the United States to avoid recapture by his owner in Maryland and became a wildly successful lecturer in England and Ireland. While he was there, British supporters purchased his freedom, enabling him to return to the United States in 1846.

For Douglass and a few other prominent runaway slaves, England was the most remote station of the Underground Railroad (UGRR), the last stop in a long and complex network that stretched from Florida to Canada and beyond. It operated successfully for about sixty years, between the turn of the nineteenth century and the beginning of the Civil War. Hundreds of escape routes ran from North Carolina to the Canadian border, and as many as ten thousand people, black and white, might have been involved in conducting forty thousand to one hundred thousand slaves to freedom.[1] Because the UGRR served as a model for many later sanctuary efforts that took place outside the law, it is worthwhile to examine its structure, participants, and operations.

The eighteenth-century roots of the UGRR lie in the decline of slavery in northern states. In Pennsylvania a law from 1780 mandated gradual emancipation, banned slave trading, and automatically freed slaves brought into the state after six months' residence. Although blacks were "excluded from most schools, denied the right to vote, barred from many public places, and relegated mostly to menial occupations," they were legally free in Pennsylvania (Bordewich 2005: 47). In addition, the national Ordinance of 1787 created five new "free" states on the western frontier – Ohio, Indiana, Illinois, Michigan, and Wisconsin – to which slaves could flee. However, the United States Constitution said in Article 4, paragraph 2: "No person held to service or labor in one state under the laws thereof, escaping into another, shall, in consequence of any law or regulation therein, be discharged from such service or labor, but shall be delivered up on claim of the party to whom such service or labor may be due." The Congress passed a fugitive slave law in 1793 to implement this provision. Slaves had no right to contest the law because they were considered to be property, not human beings.

Nevertheless, small communities of free people of color and escaped slaves established themselves in northern and western cities. Between 1765 and 1800, for example, the number of free blacks in Philadelphia grew from 100 to almost 6,500, about 9 percent of the city's population. In these cities fugitive slaves could disappear among friends and learn how to build new lives as free people of color (Bordewich 2005: 45).

Escape was extremely difficult and dangerous. Most slaves had little idea of how or where to flee. Vigilantes patrolled communities, steamboat captains searched for stowaways, and black travelers were subject to arrest if they could not present proof of their status on demand. If they failed, they could be beaten, tortured, mutilated, sold south, or killed. Most fled alone and emancipated themselves without help from anyone. Even if they did succeed, life in the north and west was precarious. Slave catchers, who operated with little or no interference even in northern cities, could invade black residences, terrorizing and seizing inhabitants with impunity. Blacks could not afford to trust any white person. Frederick Douglass himself received no help from whites, only from blacks, when he escaped to New York City from Maryland in 1838.

Yet a decentralized, grassroots network of black and white preachers, teamsters, peddlers, slaves, sailors, ship stewards, lawyers, business owners, family members, friends, and parishioners did aid and protect fugitive slaves. The "underground road" was started around Philadelphia, perhaps coordinated by Quakers, at the turn of the nineteenth century. (Only after the introduction of the railroad to the United States in the early 1830s did its name change to "underground railroad.") It did not operate "like a well-oiled machine. . . . There was never a network that began in the South and ran uninterruptedly all the way to Canada." Instead the UGRR was divided into small operations. Some stretched across a county and were well coordinated. Those regions were connected to other regions, and through them a fugitive could eventually reach the "promised land" of Canada (Switala 2004: 21).

The UGRR consisted of western, central, and eastern routes with myriad branches, and all ended in Canada. The western route went up the Mississippi River Valley through Kansas and Missouri to Iowa and Illinois, then through Michigan, usually via Detroit. The central route went from the heart of the South via Kentucky, West Virginia, western Maryland, Ohio, Indiana, and Pennsylvania. The eastern route started from the southeastern states via Maryland, Delaware, Virginia, Pennsylvania, New Jersey, New York, and New England. The Ohio River Valley was an especially important corridor. After crossing the river, runaways who made contact with the UGRR could hope to be conducted safely to the Great Lakes (Bordewich 2005: 196). Sometimes the journey to freedom could take hours or days – Douglass reached New York City from Maryland in less than twenty-four hours by train and boat – months if slaves traveled by foot all the way to Canada.

Of necessity the UGRR's operations were secret; after passage of the 1793 Fugitive Slave Act, helping slaves escape was a federal crime. Most of those who helped knew the names of collaborators who lived nearby, but they might not know anything about the network beyond twenty or thirty miles away. One of the participants, Isaac Beck of southern Ohio, described the organization: "The method of operating was not uniform but adapted to the requirements of each case. There was no regular organization, no constitution, no officers, no laws or agreement or rule except the 'Golden Rule,' and every man did what seemed right in his own eyes" (quoted by Bordewich 2005: 5). Most participants said or wrote nothing about their activities, and as a result few names of those involved were recorded. Family stories and folklore kept alive the memories of what Bordewich calls "the country's first racially integrated civil rights movement" (4).

The first history of the UGRR was by William Still, an African American freeman who worked for the Pennsylvania Anti-Slavery Society in Philadelphia from 1847 to 1861 and the Philadelphia Vigilance Committee from 1852 until the Civil War. He "coordinated the activities that made Philadelphia one of the nation's strongholds of abolition. He was also one of the Underground Railroad's most significant historians, maintaining meticulous records of the 649 fugitives who were sheltered in the city prior to the Civil War" (Blight 2004: 178). Still carefully hid the records, which included information about UGRR participants, routes, and safe-house locations, until after the war ended. In 1872 he self-published *The Underground Railroad* and sold it by mail for many years.

In 1898, historian Wilbur Siebert published *The Underground Railroad from Slavery to Freedom*, based on thousands of questionnaires sent to UGRR participants and other documentary materials. He collected the names of 3,211 "practical emancipationists" and said there were many more. (Bordewich notes that Siebert's list included only white men.) He recorded the work of many "conductors," including Daniel Gibbons, a Quaker farmer in Lancaster County, Pennsylvania, who helped fugitives for fifty-six years. Gibbons kept records of about a thousand slaves whom he assisted between 1824 and 1853.

The Role of the Quakers

Quakers were among the best-known UGRR conductors, not only in Pennsylvania but in North Carolina, Illinois, Indiana, and Ohio. A network of Quakers was helping runaway slaves in Philadelphia as early as 1786. Later, via their regional yearly meetings in Philadelphia and other cities, they collected and sent funds to coreligionists farther south who used the money to smuggle runaway slaves to free states. For the Quakers "the trek out of North Carolina . . . was not merely a geographical journey, but a spiritual one from the darkness of moral depravity into the light of redemption" (Bordewich 2005: 79).

Among the most effective and best-known UGRR organizers was Levi Coffin, a Quaker who lived and operated first in North Carolina and later in Indiana and Ohio. In 1819 he and his cousin created the earliest known operation to transport fugitives across hundreds of miles of unfriendly territory to safety. Of his work, Coffin said, "The dictates of humanity came in opposition to the law of the land, and we ignored the law" (quoted by Bordewich 2005: 63–64).

In 1826, when things got too hot for Coffin in North Carolina, he moved his family to southern Indiana. Later he moved to southern Ohio. Many other Quakers and some free blacks also settled in these border areas. As a prominent businessman and director of the Richmond branch of the Indiana State Bank, Coffin was able to operate openly. Willing to take risks, use trickery, and work under difficult conditions, he "represented a new, pivotal kind of figure in the clandestine network, sometimes called a 'general manager,' who exerted a combination of managerial efficiency and moral suasion to rationalize the operation of what had formerly been a fairly haphazard system" (Bordewich 2005: 219). Coffin declared: "I expressed my antislavery sentiments with boldness on every occasion. . . . I told the sympathizers with slave-hunters that I intended to shelter as many runaway slaves as came to my house, and aid them on their way, and advised them to be careful how they interfered in my work" (quoted by Bordewich 2005: 220). In his 1845 autobiography, Douglass criticized such boldness:

> I have never approved of the public manner in which some of our western friends have conducted what they call the Underground Railroad. . . . I honor those good men and women for their noble daring, and applaud them for willingly subjecting themselves to bloody persecution, by openly avowing their participation in the escape of slaves . . . while, upon the other hand, I see and feel assured that those open

declarations are a positive evil to the slaves remaining, who are seeking to escape. They do nothing toward enlightening the slave, whilst
they do much toward enlightening the master. (quoted by Bordewich
2005: 238–39)

A decade earlier, divisions among Quakers had led them to withdraw from leadership of the abolitionist movement. Some Quakers
objected to the movement's militant rhetoric and actions. Coffin and
seven other Quakers were expelled from the Indiana Yearly Meeting
for divisiveness in 1842. He protested, "We were proscribed for simply adhering to what we believed to be our Christian duty. We asked
only liberty of conscience – freedom to act according to one's conscientious convictions" (quoted by Bordewich 2005: 229). He continued
to help runaway slaves until the outbreak of the Civil War, later estimating that he had directly or indirectly assisted around a hundred
runaway slaves a year, some 3,300 fugitives in all. As a result, he was
widely known as the "president of the Underground Railroad." But
the UGRR was much more extensive than the sphere of his operations in the Ohio River Valley.

Other well-known UGRR organizers included Thomas Garrett and
Isaac Hopper, both Quaker businessmen. Garrett lived in the Wilmington, Delaware, area for many years. Around 1815, at age twenty-four
or twenty-five, he found out that one of his father's black servants had
been kidnapped. He traced a wagon track to Philadelphia, where he
found the abducted woman and set her free. After that, he dedicated
himself to rescuing slaves. Married to the daughter of a director of the
National Bank of Wilmington, he obtained funds for his work from
the wealthy DuPont family. In the early 1850s "he was the linchpin,
if not the formal director, of a diverse network that . . . included
Quakers and Catholics, farmers, whites within the law enforcement
establishment, black fishermen and watermen and, as he called her,
'that noble woman,' Harriet Tubman" (Bordewich 2005: 354). Tubman was said to have rescued some three hundred slaves from the
South and later served as a scout and spy for the Union army during
the Civil War.[2] Garrett estimated that by 1860 he had assisted about
2,750 slaves.

Isaac Hopper recounted that he had first helped a runaway slave in 1787, when he was sixteen years old:

> Soon after Hopper's arrival in Philadelphia, he encountered his first fugitive, an enslaved sailor who had jumped ship and was desperate to escape recapture. Wanting to help in some way, Hopper asked among his neighbors until he heard about a Quaker in rural Bucks County who was reputed to be "a good friend to colored people." He then found someone to provide the fugitive with a letter of introduction and directions to the man's house where, Hopper was later assured, the sailor was kindly received and provided with a job. (Bordewich 2005: 47)

Hopper and others passed fugitives among members of their extended family, personal friends, Abolition Society activists, and others until they reached safety, often somewhere in the countryside outside Philadelphia (Bordewich 2005: 59). This pattern of action became standard procedure for the UGRR. Hopper once told a magistrate: "I would do for a fugitive slave whatever I should like to have done for myself, under similar circumstances. If he asked my protection, I would extend it to him to the utmost of my power. If he was hungry, I would feed him. If he was naked, I would clothe him. If he needed advice, I would give him such as I thought would be most beneficial to him" (quoted by Bordewich 2005: 56). He received death threats, his family members were attacked, and his house was burned down. But for him working against slavery was a religious act; nothing could stop him from continuing it (Bordewich 2005: 52).

Philadelphia, where William Still, Isaac Hopper, and other UGRR participants worked and lived, was the center of the Society of Friends or Quakers, many of whose members opposed slavery. The city also had a sizable community of free blacks and escaped slaves; some were prosperous business owners who financially supported the UGRR. The mother church of the African Methodist Episcopal Church was located there, and AME churches in the vicinity became UGRR "stations." Nevertheless, race riots, antiabolitionist disturbances and antiblack pogroms took place in Philadelphia, and slave catchers operated there for many years. In response, Pennsylvania became a sanctuary state in 1820, when its legislature passed a law making it a felony to kidnap blacks, in defiance of the Fugitive Slave Act of 1793.

During the 1830s, the UGRR steadily expanded as the abolitionist movement grew. Some antislavery campaigners were also UGRR conductors or organizers, but the antislavery societies did not endorse the activities of members who carried out illegal actions. Many committed abolitionists were unwilling to break the law; others eventually decided to go underground, as the "slave power" gained influence and its representatives wielded increasing clout in Congress. Blacks formed their own "vigilance committees," which cooperated with white allies or acted independently. For example, the New York Vigilance Committee started operating in 1835 with David Ruggles, a courageous twenty-five-year-old black journalist, as its secretary. It became the nexus of UGRR operations in New York, with links extending south to Philadelphia and north to central New York state, New England, and Canada (Bordewich 2005: 172). It gave direct assistance to fugitives such as Frederick Douglass. During its first year, the committee helped 335 men and women. Composed of about a hundred members and a steering committee of five or six men, it raised funds in the local black community. Prominent New York abolitionists might also have given it financial support.

A determined new generation of activists, black and white, started to make its mark in the 1830s and 1840s. In 1834, white students at an evangelical seminary in Cincinnati debated slavery and came out against it. Some went into the city's black neighborhoods to work with residents on an equal basis. Shocked, the seminary's trustees ordered the students to stop discussing slavery. Many of the students moved to Oberlin College, a known center of abolitionist fervor, where they became part of one of the most active UGRR communities west of the Appalachians (Bordewich 2005: 131).

Rev. John Rankin was an agent of the Ohio Antislavery Society who became an important UGRR operative in the 1830s and 1840s, one of a hundred to two hundred abolitionists in Ripley, Ohio, a town overlooking the Ohio River and the border with Kentucky. Rankin was a "moral entrepreneur" who worked with Presbyterian churches and black communities. In that part of Ohio blacks acted as conductors and agents, and black hamlets provided refuge before fugitives traveled further north (Bordewich 2005: 199).

Harriet Beecher Stowe, who lived nearby in Cincinnati and hid fugitive slaves in her home, based the character of Eliza in her novel *Uncle Tom's Cabin* on a woman who escaped across the partly frozen Ohio River in 1838 with her baby in her arms. After collapsing on the riverbank, she was discovered by a slave catcher who had watched her make her way across. He directed her to Rankin's house at the top of the hill. Rankin sent her to the next UGRR station without learning her name. A few years later, Levi Coffin sent her north.

Rankin's UGRR work was very risky, endangering his entire family. In 1841, his house and barn were attacked in the middle of the night, but the family fought off the attackers, including one they shot dead. After this attack, Rankin published an announcement in the local newspaper that he would shoot anyone who came onto his property after dark. This warning did not apply to runaway slaves, who arrived at all hours. His four sons, who all became Presbyterian ministers, took care of the new arrivals. "At least one of the Rankin boys was expected to be on call at any given moment to saddle up and hasten his charges to the next friendly home." The UGRR stations were fifteen to twenty miles apart, "the maximum distance for mounted riders or a wagon to travel at night and return before dawn" (Bordewich 2005: 207).

Rankin's example shows how the UGRR and the abolitionist movement existed "in a symbiotic relationship with the societies serving as a fertile recruiting ground for clandestine activists, and the Underground Railroad in turn supplying abolitionist lecture halls and fundraisers with a steady stream of flesh-and-blood fugitives who . . . were living proof of slavery's inhumanity" (Bordewich 2005: 162). Echoes of this kind of relationship may be seen in the US sanctuary movement of the 1980s, described in chapter 7.

Women's contributions to the UGRR received little recognition, but they were essential to its operation. They did the unsung work of feeding, sheltering, and nursing runaways. The wives of escaped-slave activists, such as Harriet Hayden in Boston and Anna Douglass in Rochester, cared for them in their homes. Some did much more.

In a Michigan community women sounded the alarm when slave catchers arrived. Four of nine members of Cleveland's all-black vigilance committee were women. Both white and black women served as conductors (Bordewich 2005: 369). Women's antislavery societies and committees specialized in helping escaping female slaves.

The Road to Canada

Although the new free states provided refuge to fugitives, they also passed laws discouraging them from settling there. Northern states also passed discriminatory ordinances, the "black laws," which made life difficult for free people of color. No part of the United States was a truly welcoming place for blacks. But in Canada slavery was in steep decline by 1800, and after the War of 1812, Canada welcomed blacks to help defend its underpopulated southern borders from invading Americans.[3] As an incentive, blacks were given the right to vote there. By the 1820s, black runaways were building settlements in Canada opposite Buffalo, New York, and Detroit, Michigan. These modest towns – Amherstburg, St. Catherines, Buxton, and others – became the northern terminuses of the UGRR.

Also in the 1820s, the United States and Britain were at odds over the flight of slaves to Canada. US secretary of state Henry Clay, a professed opponent of slavery who owned dozens of slaves, tried to negotiate extradition agreements guaranteeing the return of escaped slaves. But Britain "steadfastly refused . . . on the ground that the British government could not 'depart from the principle recognized by the British courts that every man is free who reaches British ground'" (quoted by Siebert 1968: 193).

Canada may have been legally hospitable to escaped slaves, but the situation there was very difficult. The climate was poor, diseases – including tuberculosis – were rife, and the settlements had few resources. Quakers, Indians, and philanthropists tried to help. Josiah Henson, who had escaped to Canada in 1830 from slavery in Maryland, founded a settlement called Dawn that struggled to provide subsistence for about five hundred inhabitants. By 1860 between twenty thousand and sixty thousand black refugees had settled in

Canada, moving from rural areas to towns where they could find employment more easily.

When the US Congress passed the Fugitive Slave Law (FSL) of 1850, Canada became the only secure destination for runaway slaves. The law was passed because it had become so difficult during the 1840s to apprehend runaways in the free states. Part of the Compromise of 1850, the new law was draconian:

> Anyone who hindered a slave catcher, attempted the rescue of a recaptured fugitive, "directly or indirectly" assisted a fugitive to escape, or harbored a fugitive, was liable to a fine of up to $1,000 and six months' imprisonment, plus damages of $1,000 to the owner of each slave that was lost. Commissioners were to be appointed by the federal circuit courts specifically to act on fugitive slave cases, and provided with financial incentives . . . to facilitate the recovery of runaways: the commissioner would receive a fee of $10 each time he remanded a fugitive to the claimant, but only $5 if he found for the alleged slave. Commissioners could be fined $1,000 for refusing to issue a writ when required, and they were personally liable for the value of any slave who escaped from their custody. (Bordewich 2005: 318)

Slave catchers could arrest slaves without a warrant, and slaves had no way to contest their seizure. The federal government undertook to pay the costs of returning the escaped slave to his or her owner, on a federal vessel if necessary.

Resistance to the FSL throughout the free states was immediate and tremendous. The city council of Syracuse, New York, "voted that if the Central Railroad, which ran through the middle of the town, ever carried a recaptured fugitive back toward slavery, its rails should be physically taken up from the streets" (Bordewich 2005: 412). Vigilance committees took direct action to prevent escaped slaves from being arrested, hearings from taking place, and apprehended slaves from being returned to their masters. Armed bands of rescuers invaded courtrooms, seized slaves from custody, and sent them to Canada.

One of the first such rescues took place in 1851 in Christiana, Pennsylvania, a district where Congressman Thaddeus Stevens and many others hid slaves in their homes. William Parker, a fugitive slave, ran a secret black militia in Lancaster County, where Christiana is located. When slave catchers attacked the town, Parker and his men killed a slave owner and wounded his son in a confrontation. Parker and a slave escaped to Rochester, New York, where Frederick Douglass helped them get on a boat to Canada at great risk to himself. Canada's governor-general personally granted Parker asylum.

The federal government sent forty-five troops to Christiana, whereupon thirty-five blacks and three white Quakers surrendered. A grand jury indicted them for treason, but the presiding judge at their trial found that "the efforts of a band of fugitive slaves in opposition to the capture of any of their number . . . was altogether a private object, and could not be called 'levying war' against the nation" (quoted by Siebert 1968: 281). The defendants were acquitted. During the first year after passage of the FSL, at least sixty rescues of more than one hundred fugitives took place. As such rescues proliferated in the free states during the 1850s, it became almost impossible to find a northern jury that would convict anyone of defying the FSL.

The Myth of Uncle Tom

In 1852 Harriet Beecher Stowe published *Uncle Tom's Cabin*, which portrayed the UGRR as "a Homeric endeavor that was part Christian drama of self-sacrifice, part frontier saga ripped from the pages of James Fennimore Cooper" (Bordewich 2005: 370). An international best-seller, the book sold 300,000 copies in its first year of publication and effectively inflamed public sentiment against slavery. Its powerful message can be found in a passage describing the private debate over the FSL between a US senator and his wife. Here a woman strongly expresses a religious argument for giving sanctuary and breaking the law, opposing the legalistic position of her husband.

> "Now John, I want to know if you think such a law as that is right and Christian?"
>
> "You won't shoot me, now, Mary, if I say I do!"
>
> "I never could have thought it of you, John; you didn't vote for it?"

"Even so, my fair politician."

"You ought to be ashamed, John! Poor, homeless, houseless creatures! It's a shameful, wicked, abominable law, and I'll break it, for one, the first time I get a chance; and I hope I *shall* have a chance, I do! Things have got to a pretty pass, if a woman can't give a warm supper and a bed to poor, starving creatures, just because they are slaves, and have been abused and oppressed all their lives, poor things!"

"But, Mary, just listen to me. Your feelings are all quite right, dear, and interesting, and I love you for them; but then, dear, we mustn't suffer our feelings to run away with our judgment; you must consider it's not a matter of private feeling, – there are great public interests involved, – there is such a state of public agitation rising, that we must put aside our private feeling."

"Now, John, I don't know anything about politics, but I can read my Bible; and there I see that I must feed the hungry, clothe the naked, and comfort the desolate; and that Bible I mean to follow."

"But in cases where your doing so would involve a great public evil –

"Obeying God never brings on public evils. I know it can't. It's always safest, all round, to *do as He* bids us. . . . Turning a woman out of doors in a snow-storm, for instance; or, maybe you'd take her up and put her in jail, wouldn't you? You would make a great hand at that!"

"Of course, it would be a very painful duty," began Mr. Bird, in a moderate tone.

"Duty, John! Don't use that word! You know it isn't a duty – it can't be a duty! If folks want to keep their slaves from running away, let 'em treat 'em well – that's my doctrine. If I had slaves (as I hope I never shall have), I'd risk their wanting to run away from me. . . . I tell you folks don't run away when they are happy; and when they do run, poor creatures! They suffer enough with cold and hunger and fear, without everybody's turning against them; and, law or no law, I never will, so help me God!"

"Mary, Mary! My dear, let me reason with you."

"I hate reasoning, John – especially reasoning on such subjects. There's a way you political folks have of coming round and round a plain right thing; and you don't believe in it yourselves, when it comes to practice." (Stowe 1952: 78–79)

At that moment a runaway slave carrying a baby arrives fainting at their door, and of course they take her in.

Fighting the Law

In 1852, Isaac Hopper died at age eighty after more than fifty years of helping fugitives. By that time, spurred by the FSL and having overcome widespread disapproval, radical abolitionism had become a powerful social movement (Bordewich 2005: 341). Opposition to slavery that had been covert became overt. Abolitionists thundered that the law violated the biblical injunction in Deuteronomy 23:15–16 "not to deliver unto his master the servant that hath escaped." The abolitionist movement became violent and revolutionary, as some of its members took drastic action that went beyond civil disobedience. Rev. Jermain Loguen, a fugitive slave living in Syracuse, New York, publicly declared: "What is life to me if I am to be a slave in Tennessee? I have received my freedom from heaven, and with it came the command to defend my title to it. . . . [M]y ground is taken. I have declared it everywhere. I don't respect this law [FSL] – I don't fear it – I won't obey it! It outlaws me, and I outlaw it. I will not live a slave, and if force is employed to re-enslave me, I shall make preparations to meet the crisis as becomes a man" (quoted by Bordewich 2005: 325). At about that time the mayor proclaimed Syracuse a sanctuary city.

During the 1850s, as the nation moved toward civil war, the UGRR stepped up its activities, helping tens of thousands of runaway slaves to reach Canada. Loguen, who handed out business cards describing himself as an "Underground Railroad Agent," helped about 1,500 fugitives escape to Canada via Syracuse. As a result, widespread opposition to the FSL led to prosecutions of underground workers that brought slavery to public attention across the country, despite some politicians' attempts to bury the issue (Siebert 1968: 317). For example, from the 1830s on, Calvin Fairbank, who worked with Levi Coffin, helped forty-seven slaves escape. He served seventeen years in prison for his UGRR work. In 1852 he was kidnapped from Indiana to Kentucky, convicted of stealing a slave from the latter state, and sentenced to fifteen years, of which twelve years were spent in harsh

conditions that broke his health. Other UGRR workers were prosecuted and fined heavily. In some cases, their friends raised funds to
save them from destitution. As a result of their sacrifice, the work of
thousands of other activists, and the courage of the self-emancipat-
ing slaves, during and after the Civil War the United States outlawed
involuntary servitude and mandated equal protection of the law for
"all persons," including former slaves.

Estimates of the number of runaway slaves helped by the UGRR
between 1800 and 1860 vary from forty thousand to one hundred
thousand, a small percentage of more than 4 million persons in
bondage at the beginning of the Civil War. But the UGRR's significance goes far beyond the number of slaves it rescued. It was "the
greatest movement of civil disobedience since the American Revolution, engaging thousands of citizens in the active subversion of federal law and the prevailing mores of their communities" (Bordewich
2005: 438). As such, it was the forerunner of the labor, civil rights,
antiwar, sanctuary, and women's movements of the late nineteenth
and twentieth centuries.

The UGRR was also "the seedbed of religious activism in American politics" (Bordewich 2005: 438). Its rhetoric and principles were
biblical. Churches providing sanctuary did not claim a legal privilege
but rather tried to respond to religious injunctions regarding hospitality (Bau 1985: 160). Rev. Leverett Griggs of Bristol, Connecticut,
preached after the Supreme Court's Dred Scott decision of 1857: "Fugitives from American slavery should receive the sympathy and aid of
all lovers of freedom. If they come to our door, we should be ready
to feed, clothe and give them shelter, and help them on their way. If
we make the Bible our rule of life, if we are willing to do unto others as we would they should do unto us, we can have no difficulty on
this subject" (quoted in Bau 1985: 160). But in this statement Griggs
went beyond "religious commands regarding hospitality" by expressing political as well as religious convictions. He addressed himself to
"lovers of freedom," and what he proposed was illegal.

Likewise, in its Declaration of Sentiments, the first national conference of abolitionists in 1833 used evangelical language, saying
opponents of slavery had "the highest obligation" to "remove slavery

by moral and political action" (quoted by Bordewich 2005: 146). The declaration expressed support for nonviolent action and did not call on abolitionists to break the law. The UGRR applied such principles but carried out acts of civil disobedience to secular law in the name of a higher law.

Abolitionism and the UGRR flourished in the places where the evangelical revival of the early and mid-nineteenth century was strongest. As evangelical Methodists, Presbyterians, Scotch Covenanters, Congregationalists, and Quakers moved west, they took along their religious beliefs, their antislavery convictions, and the determination to resist slavery. Preachers not only inveighed against slavery in their sermons, they also helped slaves to escape. Churches put into practice traditional religious mandates to give sanctuary to escaped slaves. Laypersons extended the meaning and reach of sanctuary to their own homes. Armed with religious conviction, this widespread social movement developed in spontaneous but coherent resistance to constituted legal authority. It acted both secretly and publicly, informally but effectively. After sixty difficult years of iron-willed struggle, it attained its objective. No wonder, then, that it has provided the template for American political movements ever since.

Asylee in Toryglen housing estate,
Glasgow. Photo by Linda Rabben © 2008.

"Be welcome," Ticuna indigenous
village, Brazilian Amazon.
Photo by Linda Rabben © 1993.

Durham Cathedral sanctuary knocker,
used with kind permission, copyright ©
Angie Morton ArtyAnge Photography 2012.

The nineteenth century's most
notorious asylum seeker, Karl Marx.

Principal routes of the Underground Railroad.
James Oliver Horton and Lois E. Horton, *Hard
Road to Freedom: The Story of African America*.
Copyright © 2001 by James Oliver Horton and
Lois E. Horton. Reprinted with permission of
Rutgers University Press.

Trocmé family tomb with
remembrance stones,
Le Chambon-sur-Lignon, France.
Photo by Linda Rabben © 2007.

Hungarian refugees taking a train to
Switzerland, their new country of asylum.
UN 52161/1956–1957. UN Archives.

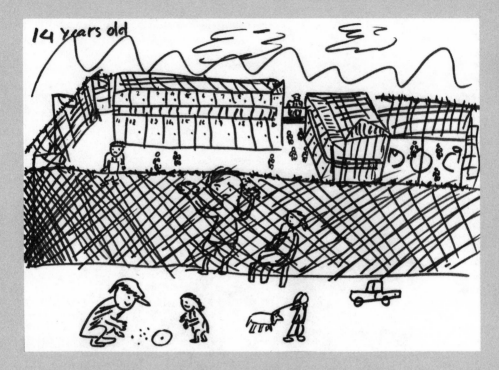

An image drawn in July 2014 by a fourteen-year-old asylum seeker detained at the Christmas Island detention center. Photo: Australian Human Rights Commission/AAP Image.

A young girl from the Syrian Arab Republic waits in a queue to board a train from Macedonia to the Serbian border, August 2015. © UNICEF/UNI195367/Georgiev.

The end of the border fence, Arizona/Mexico.
Photo by Linda Rabben © 2014.

"Solidarity with the Sans-Papiers, demonstration," Nantes, France, 2010. http://nantes.indymedia .org/article/19493, downloaded October 2010.

Rosa Robles Loreto in sanctuary
at Southside Presbyterian Church,
Tucson, Arizona, November 2014.
Photo by Linda Rabben © 2014.

6 The Pleasures of Holocaust Rescue

And above all, I beg of you – don't make me and my
wife into heroes. What we did we could not have
done otherwise! That's all!

– French Protestant pastor who
sheltered Jews during World War II

Sanctuary was and is a predominantly religious institution,
and it often flourishes outside the law; modern asylum came into
existence and continues as a secular institution hedged by legal constraints. The conductors of the Underground Railroad (and many of
the slaves who freed themselves) saw their actions as divinely inspired
and protected. They provided and sought sanctuary and freedom. But
the officials who granted asylum to political refugees acted in accordance with policies and regulations. Since the seventeenth century,
governments have given or denied refuge primarily as an assertion
of their rights and sovereignty. Asylum seekers tried to fit into the
categories the governments created. The typical nineteenth-century
asylum seeker was "a European leader of a nationalist movement
forced to flee after losing a round in his prolonged battle against
the ruling order" (Stastny 1987: 294). Twentieth-century refugees, by
contrast, were "attacked for what they are: a pariah group marked by
a separate religion, 'race,' etc. Refugees now come wholesale rather
than retail." Unlike earlier asylum seekers, they often had no political involvement and were forced to flee for their lives merely because
of their identity. Genocide accounted for millions of deaths at a time
and triggered a general exodus from danger by anyone and everyone
who could escape.

In the face of massive population movements caused by economic, political, and social upheavals in the late nineteenth and early twentieth centuries, governments sought to control the large-scale entry of strangers. Restrictive laws closed the open door of immigration, especially after World War I, leaving tens of millions of refugees wandering about Europe in desperate conditions. The British government, which had accepted thousands of Belgians during the war, tried to force them to return home in 1919. Britain's Aliens Restriction (Amendment) Act of 1919 merely extended provisions of the 1914 Aliens Act. Renewed annually until 1971, it had no provisions benefiting refugees or asylum seekers and allowed no appeal of negative decisions. One member of Parliament explained the reason for the restrictions: "We have been the dumping ground for the refugees of the world for too long" (quoted by Stevens 2004: 54). The Conservative politician Lord Hailsham later commented that Britain had "one of the least liberal and one of the most arbitrary systems of immigration law in the world" (quoted in Stevens 2004: 55).

Refugees between the Wars

The new League of Nations established the so-called Nansen Office after World War I, to help refugees overcome the obstacles that governments placed in their way. Its most notable achievement was introducing the principle of *non-refoulement* to international law. Non-refoulement is a prohibition on sending asylum seekers back to a country where they might be persecuted, tortured, or killed. The League of Nations also named a high commissioner for refugees, who had to raise funds to run his office and repay money the League lent him to start operations. Governments gave him little help.

In 1930 the British home secretary stiffly told a Jewish delegation that it was up to "the sovereign state to admit a refugee if it thinks fit to do so" (quoted by Kushner 2006: 146). Three years later, after Hitler came to power, hundreds of thousands of German Jews began applying for asylum in Britain and other countries. With no formal refugee policy, Britain resisted providing permanent refuge to Jews escaping Germany (Kushner 2006: 41). The British government insisted that British Jews guarantee the maintenance of Jewish refugees so they would not become charges of the state. Only a few were admitted under these conditions from 1933 to 1938. By 1933 most Western countries had severely restricted the entry of foreigners.

The home secretary had absolute discretion to deport aliens. In the mid-1930s, a committee was set up to advise him, but it lapsed in 1939. Because of the dire economic situation, the Aliens Act was enforced more rigidly as the 1930s went on. In a 1938 memo, the Home Office candidly said that the point of a visa system for Germans and Austrians was "to prevent potential refugees from getting here at all" (quoted by Stevens 2004: 58). Kushner estimates that of 500,000 Jews who applied for entry to the United Kingdom in the 1930s, only 80,000 were admitted, most on temporary visas. In deciding who could enter, officials overtly discriminated by age, sex, and class.

As Europe drifted toward world war, refugees from various conflicts came desperately knocking. Millions fled Spain during and after the civil war (1935–38). Some 500,000 fled to France; in 1939, two camps held 180,000 on the French Mediterranean coast. By the end of that year, more than 300,000 Spanish refugees had left France for Latin America, especially Mexico.

In 1938, under pressure from his wife, President Roosevelt convened the Evian Conference of twenty nations to discuss "the refugee problem in Europe." It came to no firm conclusion, but far-off Australia offered to accept 15,000 Jewish refugees from Germany and the Sudetenland. Half of them arrived, but the other half did not make it. Meanwhile thousands of left-wing politicians and activists were fleeing Germany and Italy for other European countries. Like their nineteenth-century predecessors, many tried to stay in Europe to continue their political work from outside their home country (Bade 2003: 203). Some were interned and deported to Germany or the death camps; others, like the literary critic Walter Benjamin, committed suicide when they despaired of escaping from the Nazis.

Meanwhile the United States was also closing its doors. The story of the *St. Louis* is emblematic of the late 1930s. In 1939, almost one thousand Jews fled from Germany to Cuba on the ship. More than seven hundred of the passengers were waiting for US visas to be processed: "For reasons that are not entirely clear, the Cuban Government refused to let the refugees land. . . . [T]he vessel proceeded to Miami, but it was refused permission to dock. For a time it was so close to Miami Beach that the passengers could hear dance music being played at the resort's luxury hotels. . . . The Treasury Department even assigned a Coast Guard cutter to shadow the *St. Louis* to make sure that no one tried to swim ashore" (Daniels 2004: 79–80).

As the boat went from one East Coast port to another, Eleanor Roosevelt tried to intervene on the refugees' behalf, to no avail. The liner had to turn back to Europe with its refugee passengers still aboard. Many later fell into the hands of the Nazis and perished, but some survived to observe the fiftieth anniversary of their journey at a reunion in Miami.

The exact number of emigrants who left Germany before the war is unknown. Bade estimated that 280,000 to 330,000 of the refugees were Jews. Emigrants from central European countries under German control numbered 450,000 to 600,000. More than eighty countries gave them refuge. Relatively few of those who tried to flee Germany and Austria – only about 100,000, of whom 80 percent were Jews – found refuge in the United States. Half of them arrived in 1938 or later. One reason they did not flee earlier was that emigration was expensive, time-consuming, and difficult. The German government put up so many bureaucratic obstacles that most people who wanted to leave could not get out before the war started. The Nazis extorted money and property from those who were trying to get out, so that only the well-off could afford to leave. As soon as hostilities commenced, it became impossible to escape from Europe. The British government, for one, stopped issuing entry visas in September 1939, as the war began.

Governments' reluctance to rescue European Jews continued during the war. "Unwillingness to offer refuge was a central cause for the Western world's inadequate response to the Holocaust," writes historian David Wyman, who calls the US and British governments "callous" for their failure to rescue Jews before and during the war (1984: 98).

Concerned individuals and organizations did not let the British and American governments' reluctance to admit refugees deter them from trying to rescue German Jews. In 1933, Sir William Beveridge and Lionel Robbins founded the Academic Assistance Council (AAC) with Lord Rutherford as president. Its mission was to help Jewish academics whom the Nazis had dismissed from German universities (Seabrook 2009: 2). Among the hundreds of academics the AAC rescued before World War II were eighteen Nobel Prize winners, seventy-one Royal Society fellows, and fifty British Academy fellows. They included Max Born (physicist), Ernst Gombrich (art historian), Hans Krebs (biochemist), Max Perutz (molecular biologist), Sir Nikolaus Pevsner (art historian), and Karl Popper (philosopher). The AAC paid the refugees' travel expenses and helped them find academic positions in Britain whenever possible. Some of them repaid the favor by helping the Allies win the war (Seabrook 2009).

The Kindertransport

British activists founded the Inter-Aid Committee for Children from Germany in 1936. It arranged for 471 children to be admitted to Britain, providing "a model of Jewish-Christian cooperation in refugee matters" (Kushner and Knox 1999: 154). The Refugee Children's Movement (RCM) grew out of the earlier body in 1938. Former prime minister Stanley Baldwin made a radio appeal for funds and raised £500,000 for the RCM. This was the seed money for the Kindertransport, which ferried almost ten thousand children from Austria, Germany, and Czechoslovakia to Britain from late 1938 to September 1, 1939.

The RCM's leaders believed it would be impossible to obtain the government's permission to rescue Jewish adults from central Europe because of widespread anti-Semitic sentiment in Britain; therefore they concentrated on helping children. Likewise, the government justified its refusal to grant asylum to foreign Jews by pointing to public anti-Semitism, thus creating a self-fulfilling prophecy. Similar attitudes can be seen today in Britain regarding people of color, as the government justifies its draconian restrictions on asylum by pointing to racist sentiments among the public.

The British public did support rescuing refugee children, however. Especially after the shocking events of the *Kristallnacht* pogrom in November 1938, British people became more welcoming to refugees. The originator of the Kindertransport was a son of German Jewish immigrants to Britain, Nicholas Winton, a clerk at the British Stock Exchange. Raised as a Christian, he later said he had been motivated by humanitarian rather than religious feelings. In 1938, Winton traveled to Prague and was horrified by the plight of its Jews. Back in London, he lobbied the Home Office and charitable agencies (both Jewish and Christian) to send as many endangered children as possible to Britain (Kushner 2006: 147). For his efforts, he received an MBE (Member of the British Empire, a royal decoration) in 1983 and a knighthood in 2003, when he was ninety-three years old. In 2014, the Czech government bestowed its highest honor on him at age 105. He insisted, "I wasn't heroic because I was never in danger" (quoted by Moss 2014). Others who helped set up the Kindertransport included Frank Foley, a civil servant, and Anglican bishop George Bell of Chichester.

Bertha Bracey, a Quaker, was part of the committee that successfully lobbied the Home Office for establishment of the Kindertransport. She went to Germany to meet with Jewish women's groups to set up the rescue. As secretary of the British Friends' Committee on Refugees, she supervised eighty caseworkers and volunteers, mostly women, who worked with fourteen thousand German, Austrian, and Czech refugees in 1938. In 1945, she persuaded the British government to transport three hundred child survivors of the Theresienstadt concentration camp to Britain in ten bombers. For her work, she was named one of the "Righteous among the Nations," memorialized at Yad Vashem, and designated a Hero of the Holocaust by the British government.

More than 160 local committees in England, Scotland, and Wales formed to place the children in homes and hostels. The RCM chose children from a pool of sixty thousand whose parents applied to private, British-run groups in Berlin, Vienna, Prague, and other central European cities. The British government did not want to be directly involved in arranging for transport and resettlement. Anyone who wanted to take in a child had to pay a cash deposit, show that his or her financial situation was stable, and prove that the proposed home was suitable (Kushner and Knox 1999: 155). The required deposit amounted to £50, the equivalent of about £1,500 (about US$2,250) today and far beyond the capacity of most British people. The children received temporary transit visas, not permanent leave to remain in the country. Apparently the government expected that once the war ended, the foreign children would leave. Kushner comments bitterly, "Guilt (and an attempt to compensate for it) has been the motivating force for most of the generous moments of British refugee policy in the twentieth century" (2006: 147). In this instance and many others, ordinary people, not policy makers, were the ones showing generosity. At the same time as the Kindertransport was being organized, the British government closed Palestine to European Jews. And the US Congress defeated a bill to accept twenty thousand German children in early 1939.

In Britain, the RCM took responsibility for the children's maintenance, education, religious instruction, and training for "useful work which will fit them to become self-supporting and responsible citizens, whether in this country or abroad" (Curio 2004: 54). The children were supposed to be dispersed around the country so that they would not be conspicuous in any one place. They were told not to speak German and "not [to] draw attention to themselves by complaining." Those considered mentally or physically abnormal were not permitted on the trains and boats to Britain. Sometimes the committees made mistakes; a refugee told Karen Gershon in 1966: "I came to England at the age of 15, seven days before the war. On arrival it was discovered that my sister should have come instead. I was nearly sent back, but it was too close to the war. My sister perished at Auschwitz" (Gershon 1966: 45).

The first train left Prague on December 1, 1938. Eight more trainloads departed from Prague in 1939. At the height of the transport, three hundred children were arriving in Britain each week; their ages ranged from two to seventeen. Many were sent to reception centers where conditions varied from bad to intolerable. Sometimes prospective foster parents would arrive at a center and pick a child out of the crowd of new arrivals. Cute little blond-haired, blue-eyed girls stood a better chance of being chosen than gangling teenage boys, who were the most difficult to place.

Some of the children had to use initiative to gain refuge. One boy found out where Baron Rothschild lived and hiked to his palatial country home. He asked Rothschild to help get his father out of Germany. Rothschild asked, "Can your father work on a chicken farm?" The boy replied, "He'll do anything," and it was arranged (Harris 2000). A few parents, such as newspaper correspondent Hella Pick's mother, did manage to accompany their children on condition that they work as domestic servants. But most of the *kinder* went unaccompanied to Britain, never saw their parents again, and found out what had happened to them only after the war.

One of the Kindertransport organizers wrote an account of his work for Gershon's 1966 collection of refugees' stories. Trevor Chadwick recounted that he was teaching at his family's preparatory school in 1938 when he heard about the children in Prague. He went there to pick up two children and returned later to pick up more, bringing out twenty. When he went back to Prague for a third time, "I felt depressed. . . . Only 20!" By March 15, 1939, when the Germans marched triumphantly into Prague under the Munich agreement, he was ready to take one hundred children out by air but could not find a plane to accommodate them. So he arranged for special trains to take them to Britain. In Prague he had two helpers, and the three spent all night writing begging letters to guarantors in England. Chadwick wrote, "I can't say how many children were on my books, but it must have been in the thousands. Nor can I say how many I eventually got away, but it was only hundreds, alas" (Gershon 1966: 22–23).

Chadwick tactfully remarked that the Home Office must have taken so long to send him visas for the children because "they just didn't realize. If only the Home Secretary could have spent a few days with me, seeing brutality, listening to, not arguing with, young Nazis, as I often did, he would doubtlessly have pushed the whole thing along fast. If he had realized that the regulations were for so many children the first nudge along the wretched road to Auschwitz, he would, of course, have immediately imported the lot" (Gershon 1966: 24). When the visas did not arrive, he made some up himself. A message from the Home Office "contained a threat to send [the children] back, but I figured the mob of legally accepted guarantors would stop that one," Chadwick said (25).

The children arrived at British ports traumatized or bewildered, usually speaking and understanding no English. A refugee who was seven years old at the time told Gerson almost thirty years later: "We were in a room facing a man and a woman and were told that they were Mr. and Mrs. Smith. . . . They put us in their car and we set off to drive some miles to their home. We sat in the back, my sister and I, clutching hands, tired with all that had gone before, and confused with all the babble of English that we had heard, of which we could understand not a word" (47).

Most of the prominent figures and backers of the RCM were upper-class men, but women also played a prominent role in managing the organization and other refugee agencies. Eight of the twelve organizing secretaries of RCM's regional committees were women, as well as all eight department heads of the Quaker refugee relief organization. Eleanor Rathbone, an independent member of Parliament, was active in refugee work from 1933 on. She spoke out in Parliament against the government's restrictive refugee policies, criticizing its obstruction, stinginess, and lethal delays (Oldfield 2004: 58). During the 1930s she spoke in favor of asylum for Basque children, communist and socialist Czechs, and Austrian and German Jews. After *Kristallnacht* she founded the Parliamentary Committee for Refugees. In an article in the *New Statesman* in 1939, she castigated the government for overloading voluntary organizations with rescue work it should have been doing or supporting. She protested the internment of Kindertransport refugees as enemy aliens in 1940. Known as the "MP for refugees," she had "incalculable" influence on public sentiment before and during the war (Oldfield 2004: 59).

Other important women included Anna Essinger, an educator who moved her progressive school from Germany to England in 1933 with the help of the Academic Assistance Council. She gave shelter to Kindertransport children in 1939 and convinced the RCM to make its placement strategy more humane. Greta Burkill, a German married to a British academic, was "a one-woman rescuer of Jewish youngsters" who fought with university officials, local education committees, the Education Ministry, and the International Student Service to grant aid to deserving university applicants (Oldfield 2004: 63). As chair of the Cambridgeshire Refugee Children's Committee, she had responsibility for eight hundred to two thousand children.

Other women involved in helping Jewish refugee children included Edith Morley; Ruth Simmons and her mother, Hama Simmons; and Elaine Blond and her friend Lola Hahn-Warburg, both of whom worked on refugee issues until their deaths in the late 1980s. Dorothy Hardisty, RCM's general secretary until 1948, was an eloquent advocate for the children. She said they had "endured over a long period of time and in increasing severity such physical and mental suffering as had stolen their childhood from them" (quoted by Oldfield 2004: 67).

The RCM came into conflict with British Orthodox Jews who wanted the children to be raised in Orthodox homes. Solomon Schonfeld's mission was to save this remnant of the Jewish people and preserve their religious identity at all costs. An uncompromising and difficult man, he personally arranged for about a thousand children to enter Britain. He was furious when Parliament gave legal guardianship of the kinder to the chairman of the RCM in 1944.

Many of the kinder lived with Christian families, and their experiences varied considerably. Some told Gershon they had felt happy, accepted, and loved. Others were haunted by fears for their relatives in Europe or placed with unsympathetic or even abusive families. Barriers to their progress included "the determination of some refugee committees to keep their charges under control, the rigid class and ethnic stratification of British society and the financial and psychological burdens which many refugees carried with them" (Kushner and Knox 1999: 156). One said, "I was 10 years old when I arrived and found it difficult to accept that life in England was 'normal,' that one could walk in the street, go into a shop or get onto a bus without fear of attack or insult" (Gershon 1966: 48).

Quakers played a prominent role in the Kindertransport and resettlement of Jewish children in Britain. Ruth David collected stories from about fifty kinder who had received help from Quakers in Germany and England. Lore Jacobs of Ontario, Canada, wrote that she was fifteen years old when the Northampton Society of Friends helped her find a family to live with. Records from that Friends Meeting showed that the group had paid the £50 surety for her. Quakers also helped kinder with school fees and found places for them at Quaker schools and colleges. In general, the survivors reported, the Quakers did not try to convert the children to Christianity but respected their beliefs and practices.

One survivor said that her mother had jumped on the last Kindertransport train out of Vienna in 1939. "Without the Quakers," she wrote, "my mother would not have made it to England" (David 2003). Another said her parents had escaped to Venezuela, but she was not allowed to travel alone on a ship to join them. Quakers in Britain helped her during the war, and she reunited with her parents in 1947. Filmmaker Karol Reisz had a happy memory of receiving a bicycle as a gift from the principal of a Quaker school in Britain. For their relief work on behalf of millions of people during both world wars, the American Friends Service Committee and the UK Friends Service Council received the Nobel Peace Prize in 1947.

Some of the kinder had a harder time, struggling to overcome negative stereotypes and hidebound attitudes to achieve success in Britain. John Grenville, born in Berlin in 1928, was sent to a private school, where he did well. But the Cambridge RCM committee insisted that he leave school at sixteen. He became a gardener at Peterhouse College, Cambridge University. When he told the college he was leaving to attend London School of Economics, the bursar asked if he was sure, "because . . . we have you in mind for our head porter" (quoted by Kushner and Knox 1999: 157). They wanted him to fill a working-class role for the rest of his life. Grenville later became professor of history at Birmingham University.

The older kinder were classified as "enemy aliens" and sent to internment centers after the fall of Holland, Belgium, and France in 1940. Prime Minister Winston Churchill famously retorted, "Collar the lot!" when a press campaign whipped up public hysteria against foreigners. Though the internment of refugees violated international law and had no basis in British law, political pressure prevailed for a time. More than twenty thousand people, including children, were interned on the Isle of Man and in hastily arranged camps for more than a year. Some Jewish refugees were detained along with Nazi sympathizers.

About 2,500 detainees were put on a ship to Canada that was torpedoed by a U-boat but did not sink. A Kindertransport survivor told Gershon that the prisoners were treated like animals on the boat for two long months before they finally arrived in Australia, where they were interned. He later returned to Britain to join the army. Eventually public support for internment dropped significantly, and most of the detainees were let go. Several thousand left Britain for the United States and other countries or joined the British armed forces and served with distinction. A Kindertransport refugee said she had joined the army at age eighteen "to thank England for saving my life" (quoted by Harris 2000). In the military, she finally "felt like everybody else."

Although the British government allowed the children to enter the country in 1939 with the proviso that they would leave at age eighteen, thousands stayed after the war ended and became naturalized citizens. Despite its negative attitude toward refugees, the government did eventually make it possible for the kinder to remain permanently in the country.

The first popular account of the Kindertransport was published in 1944. *A Great Adventure: The Story of the Refugee Children's Movement* portrayed it in a wholly positive light, as part of an ancient British tradition of hospitality. But Kushner insists that the British public showed ambivalence, "followed after 1945 by several decades of silence, indifference and obscurity before the recent (largely) celebratory approach has emerged" (Kushner 2006: 10).

Most of the Kindertransport survivors kept silent about their experiences during the war, in some cases for as long as fifty years. They went on to lead fairly normal lives for the most part, although some had sustained severe emotional damage. Some of the children expressed intense survivor's guilt in Gershon's book. One of the contributors defined a refugee as "someone who is not wanted in one place and given shelter in another out of pity. He is therefore forced to choose between death and charity" (Gershon 1966: 150). When

Gershon's book was published in 1966, no organization of Kinder-transport children existed and the Holocaust was not discussed. It was almost taboo to dwell on the tragic past, so the refugees suffered in silence. But the consequences of the trauma they experienced have affected at least two generations.

The fiftieth anniversary of the Kindertransport, celebrated in 1989 with great fanfare, led to the founding of the Kindertransport Asso-ciation. Its members were mostly British, but almost one thousand members lived in Canada, the United States, and Israel. A flood of Holocaust books, articles, films, and commemorations followed. A collection of 243 essays by Kindertransport survivors, I Came Alone, appeared in 1990. The first history of children in World War II was published in 1991. During the 1990s, the focus was on children who had hidden or been hidden, so the Kindertransport received less atten-tion than harrowing stories from the Continent.

In 1999, a plaque commemorating the Kindertransport was unveiled at the House of Commons, and in 2003 a memorial sculp-ture was installed at Liverpool Street Station in London, where many of the kinder had disembarked. "By this stage," Kushner writes, "the campaign against asylum seekers had reached a fever pitch" in Britain, but the kinder were respectable after sixty years (Kushner 2006: 165).

Kushner offers no comfort to anybody who would like to see the Kindertransport as a triumph of humanitarianism: "Self-contained and self-congratulatory, the story [of the Kindertransport] becomes cut off from the messiness of modern refugee movements, includ-ing the existence of enormous numbers of unaccompanied refugee children today who can be counted not in the thousands but in the millions." He also believes that the Kindertransport story has been used to legitimate discriminatory refugee policies that have existed in Britain since the early twentieth century. In his view, "the fatalism towards the (non-)rescue of the parents and other adults during the 1930s is replicated in the paralyzed response to the millions suffering in the world today who we convince ourselves we cannot help" (167).

In the face of the murder of 6 million Jews, of whom 1.5 million were children, the Kindertransport may be seen as a well-intentioned but inadequate rescue effort whose symbolism grossly outweighed its effectiveness. Nevertheless, it saved almost ten thousand children who probably would have been killed otherwise. It would be impossible to weigh the value and meaning of those ten thousand lives against the tragedy of the millions who were lost. As the Talmud says, "Whoever saves a single soul, it is as if he had saved the whole world" (quoted by Fogelman 1994: 18).

The rescuers amounted to a tiny proportion of the 700 million Europeans, Asians, and Africans who witnessed World War II, but they provided powerful proof of the reality of reciprocal altruism as a universal human practice. Perhaps that is why many of them, like the pastor quoted in this chapter's epigraph or Nicholas Winton, felt they had done nothing special in sheltering Jews and other persecuted people. Eva Fogelman, a psychologist, did extensive research on the rescuers and found that most "were not loners or people who felt alienated from society. But the secret of rescue effectively isolated them from everyone else. Neighbors viewed people who harbored Jews as selfish and dangerous because they risked their lives and the lives of those around them" (1994: 68). Fogelman theorizes that a "rescuer self" emerged, helping rescuers "re-center" themselves around their transformed social role. She sees rescue as "an expression of the values and beliefs of the innermost core of a person. It is a core nurtured in childhood. . . . This rescuer self was, and over the years has continued to be, an integral part of their identity" (Fogelman 1994: xviii). The rescuer had to be alert, quick-witted, a skilled liar, and a good actor. Rescuers questioned their own motivations and consulted their conscience about the lying, deception, and illegal acts they had to commit. Religious belief also helped them: "In moments of extreme danger, turning to God often alleviated their fear. Spiritual transcendence of the terrifying present made it possible to withstand regular brushes with death" (87).

Rescue Networks across Continents

Many rescuers did not operate alone, but formed networks that extended over dozens, hundreds, or even thousands of miles. Saving one Jew in France, wrote Elisabeth Maxwell, involved ten or more people. Gilbert documented one incident in which more than fifty people helped a Jew escape from Antwerp to Switzerland via France, not including those who looked the other way and said nothing.

Coordinating rescue was complex, expensive, dangerous work, and it involved people of every class, occupation, age, sex, educational level, and nationality. A few prominent rescuers, such as Oskar Schindler, Varian Fry, Aristides de Sousa Mendes, and Raoul Wallenberg, were able to help thousands of people. Schindler saved 1,200 Jews with the help of a small group who probably did not know of one another's activities. Fry and eight helpers saved 1,500 to 4,000 Jews. Mendes, the Portuguese consul general in Bordeaux, single-handedly signed visas for 30,000 refugees during a five-week period in 1940. Wallenberg saved at least 30,000 Hungarian Jews with a network of four hundred people.

Most rescuers could save only a few people. Many had witnessed Nazi atrocities or knew someone who had been a victim, so they could not deny or ignore what was happening. Although they faced many difficulties and dangers in sheltering Jews, they believed they could help. Numbering in the thousands, they hid Jews in "attics, cellars, sewers, ditches, pigsties, haystacks, brothels, closets, pantries, space behind double walls, monasteries, convents, orphanages, schools and hospital quarantine rooms" across Europe. "Network rescuers' actions infused their lives with meaning and purpose. Rather than just talking about their values and beliefs, network members had an opportunity to act on them," comments Fogelman (1994: 210).

Networks of rescuers sometimes "organized around a leader whose charismatic personality and forceful presence attracted those seeking ways to express their anti-Nazi rage" (Fogelman 1994: 211). But leaders could be denounced or killed, and they were difficult to replace. Like participants in the Underground Railroad, most network members knew only a few other members and may have been unaware of the extent of the network beyond their vicinity. It was safer for them not to know any more than they had to. A few wide-ranging networks did become known after or even during the war. For example, the "Dutch-Paris" network included three hundred people who forged identity papers, found temporary shelters for fugitives,

obtained money, and escorted people across borders. Networks operating between France and Switzerland and involving Catholic clergy
sheltered Jewish children in abbeys and churches. They saved some
seven thousand Jewish children.

About twenty thousand Danes formed six independent rescue networks composed of students, physicians, taxi drivers, clergy, and many
others as part of the general resistance to German occupation. The
networks carried out the famous rescue of most of Denmark's Jews
over a two-month period in 1943. A German official had warned that
deportations of all of the country's Jews would start in three days'
time. Ordinary citizens warned their Jewish friends and neighbors.
Fishing boats and other craft transported the Jews to Sweden, a two-
to three-hour trip, under intense German surveillance.

Similar networks formed in other occupied countries, such as Holland. They comprised Protestant and Catholic church groups, liberal
political groups, and anarchist university students. Individuals also
operated as rescuers under extremely perilous conditions. Johtje and
Aart Vos hid thirty-six people – up to fourteen Jews at a time – in their
house. The local police chief warned them when the Nazis were coming, and they would escort their Jewish guests through a tunnel to
the nearby woods. The obituary of Mrs. Vos, who died at age ninety-
seven in 2007, recounted: "Mr. and Mrs. Vos resisted the notion that
they had done something out of the ordinary. . . . Mrs. Vos said, 'I
want to say right away that the words "hero" and "righteous gentile"
are terribly misplaced. I don't feel righteous. . . . We didn't sit at the
table when the misery started and say, OK, now we are going to risk
our lives to save some people'" (Hevisi 2007).

Miep Gies was a better-known Dutch rescuer because of her association with the family of Anne Frank. She estimated that

> she was one of 20,000 Dutch men and women who helped shelter Jews.
> Some acted alone; others were part of an organized network effort
> whose work and safety depended on secrecy and anonymity. These
> nameless forgers, businessmen and homeowners provided false iden-
> tity papers, food coupons, money and shelter. Caution dictated that
> people should know as little as possible about one another. Families

who opened their homes to people the resistance sent avoided intro-
ductions. Over a three- or four-year period, Jews might stay in as many
as 40 different places. Some of these unknown rescuers were caught
and killed. (Fogelman 1994: 15)

Many networks grew spontaneously without formal structure or
rules. In Utrecht, for example, students started helping fugitives during their summer vacation. Hetty Dutihl Voute told Fogelman, "[Of
those] who were left, we knew who we could trust and rely on. That
same core group stayed together until the end." In Amsterdam, Tina
Buchter, her mother, and her grandmother hid more than a hundred
Jews, five at a time, on the top floor of their house. They were part
of a network that helped fugitives escape to Switzerland by walking
at night for three months. Before expected raids, someone at Gestapo
headquarters would phone to warn them, and they would hide their
visitors. They set up a special bell that rang on the third floor, and
"when the Germans rang the front doorbell, Tina and her mother
rang the second bell – and the Jews on the third floor left the house
through the back doors and back windows to the roof. If there was
no time to leave, the Jews would crouch in a tiny secret attic com-
partment that had been built by a carpenter who was a member of
the Dutch underground" (Gilbert 2003: 332).

Dutch rescuers hid Jews in homes, on farms, and at children's
holiday camps. The Dutch constitute the second-largest group of rescuers, after the Poles, who are honored at Yad Vashem, the Holocaust
memorial in Jerusalem. Nonetheless, most of Holland's Jews – 107,000
out of 140,000 – were deported to death camps and killed during the
war (Gilbert 2003: 332). Many, like the Frank family, were denounced
by Dutch collaborators. But the high toll of treachery makes the
examples of the rescuers all the more noble and daring.

Among the most unusual rescuers were Muslim peasants who hid
Jews after the Nazis invaded Albania in 1939. They acted in accordance with *besa*, a strict honor code. The word means "to keep one's
word and includes a moral imperative to offer one's home to protect
and shelter any guest in need," the Raoul Wallenberg Foundation
explained in honoring these rescuers. "At the start of the war, the

Jewish population of Albania numbered about 200. As persecution increased, Jews from other European countries sought refuge in Albania. By war's end there were some 2,000 Jews living there, making it the only nation in Europe where the Jewish population increased during those years" (Dunn 2008).

At a commemorative ceremony in Connecticut in 2008, Arian Myrto "explained how his father rescued a Jewish brother and sister. . . . The guests shared a room with family members, he said; they were dressed in traditional Albanian costumes and passed off as extended family" (Dunn 2008). Another family sheltered four Jewish families. A son recounted that his father had told the Jewish guests, "Now we are one family. You won't suffer any evil. My sons and I will defend you against peril at the cost of our lives." According to the daughter of another man who gave refuge to Jews, "Our home is first God's house, second our guest's house, and third our family's house. The Quran teaches us that all people, Jews, Christians, Muslims, are under one God." Among the 22,000 non-Jewish rescuers honored at Yad Vashem are sixty-six Albanians.

One of the most illustrious rescuers was Bishop Angelo Roncalli, later Pope John XXIII, who interceded with the king on behalf of Bulgarian Jews, persuaded the Turkish government to take in Jews who reached that country, and did his utmost to prevent the deportation of Greek Jews (Fogelman 1994: 37).

In Italy, cycling champion Gino Bartali

> transported counterfeit identity papers to Jews who were at risk of being deported to concentration camps. The papers were hidden in the frame of his bike. Giorgio Goldenberg, the son of a Jewish survivor, said in 2010 that Bartali had also taken him and his family in, hiding them in his cellar until the liberation of Florence in 1944. Bartali never spoke publicly of his clandestine wartime activities, which he is believed to have carried out at the behest of the archbishop of Florence, and only told parts, gradually, to his son, Andrea. [In 2013] he was awarded the title Righteous among the Nations by Yad Vashem, the Holocaust memorial centre in Jerusalem. "When I asked my father why I couldn't tell anyone, he said: 'You must do good, but you must

not talk about it. If you talk about it you're taking advantage of others' misfortunes for your own gain,'" Andrea Bartali told the BBC [in 2014]. (Davies 2014)

In Italy, Jews were hidden at farms and in houses, monasteries, convents, and abbeys. The abbot of the Assisi Franciscan monastery, Bishop Giuseppe Placido Nicolini, sheltered three hundred Jews. Catholic religious establishments in several other countries independently decided to shelter Jews. In Poland some 189 convents hid more than 1,500 Jewish children (Fogelman 1994: 173).

In eastern European countries under Nazi rule, entire families, including children, were hanged in town squares for sheltering Jews. Yet despite the ubiquity of anti-Semitism, Christian individuals and networks saved Jews for religious reasons. Fogelman recounts the story of a Polish woman who decided to rescue a four-year-old Jewish girl after asking herself, "What if this was my child, my mother, or me needing shelter? What would Christ have done?" (quoted by Fogelman 1994: 173). Of the Polish family that sheltered him for three months, Moshe Smolar said, "When I ask myself what were their motives, I can only attribute their good deeds to their humanitarian feelings originating both from their compassionate feelings toward the Jews, deep emotional empathy with the persecuted, and truly deep and pure religious feelings" (quoted by Gilbert 2003: 21).

Two social workers in Warsaw set up a secret network that forged documents to get Jews food, medicine, and clothing. Irena Sendlerowa used a Jewish-Christian network to smuggle 2,500 children out of the Warsaw ghetto and hide them with families in the city. Sanctuaries in Poland included convents, orphanages, and "a trapdoor, covered with straw and manure [that] led to a tunnel that was connected to a pit, a cave-like space beneath and beyond the house, with an air shaft consisting of a hole beneath a cherry tree" where four Jews were hidden (Gilbert 2003: 6).

Varian Fry's organization, which stretched from America to France, exemplifies a long network of rescuers. In June 1940, Fry and a few friends raised $3,500 in New York to rescue prominent European intellectuals, politicians, unionists, and artists who were trying to leave France in the wake of the German occupation. They then met with Eleanor Roosevelt and asked for help in obtaining visas to go to France to arrange for the refugees' escape. In their presence, she telephoned President Roosevelt and persuaded him to authorize their visas. Fry headed to Marseille in August 1940 with a list of two hundred refugees. He intended to stay in France for three weeks and came home after thirteen months. Within two weeks of arriving in France, he was sending refugees (without visas) across the Spanish border on their way to New York.

Fry's network included Hiram Bingham, the US vice-consul in Marseille, who hid refugees in his villa; the American Federation of Labor, which pressured the US government to issue visas; a Corsican gangster in Marseille, who laundered money sent from the United States; the American Friends Service Committee office in Marseille; sympathetic French mayors and border guards; and eight American and French helpers in Marseille. His chief assistant was Albert O. Hirschman, later a prominent social scientist who taught at the Institute for Advanced Study and Yale, Columbia, and Harvard Universities. According to his 2012 obituary, Hirschman "rustled up fake identification documents for refugees and, having studied in detail the vagaries of black markets, devised new ways to smuggle money into France" (Langer 2012: C8).

Each night Fry would cable a list of refugees to the Emergency Rescue Committee (ERC) in New York. The ERC then pressured the State Department to issue transit visas (Marino 1999: 124). Meanwhile Fry would distribute funds to the refugees so they could subsist. By the end of 1940, the ERC raised $100,000, a substantial sum at the time, for this and other purposes.

As the German and Spanish governments cut off escape routes, the danger for Fry and his confederates kept increasing. Much of what they were doing was illegal. Fry kept their work secret to protect network members who were not involved. He believed that they had to be shielded from the details, because he was also risking death by helping British flyers escape from France (Marino 1999: 293).

Fry made civilian refugees his first priority. The State Department disapproved of his actions and kept ordering him to leave France, but Fry ignored the orders. The Vichy government finally expelled Fry as an "undesirable alien" in September 1941, and Hirschman walked across the Pyrenees into Spain, "carrying extra socks and a two-volume collection of the works of Montaigne" (Langer 2012: C8). In his thirteen months in France, Fry and his helpers engineered the escape of two thousand Jews and other refugees, including the artists Marc Chagall and Max Ernst.

Although the French government gave Fry the Croix de Chevalier of the Legion of Honor shortly before his death in 1967, the United States did not recognize his work until 1991, when the Holocaust Memorial Council posthumously awarded him the Eisenhower Liberation Medal. In 1996, Yad Vashem named him as one of the Righteous among the Nations. But for Fry during his lifetime, virtue had to be its own reward.

Cities of Refuge

From 1940 on, efforts to shelter Jews went on in many parts of France. Sanctuaries included children's homes, farms, convents, schools, and private homes. Networks of rescuers included Catholic and Orthodox priests, nuns, and bishops, Protestant pastors, mayors, police, peasants, and many others. For example, Pierre-Marie Théas, the bishop of Montauban, near Toulouse, issued a pastoral letter denouncing "'the uprooting of men and women, treated as wild animals,' and calling on Catholics to protect Jews" (Gilbert 2003: 267). A nun, Marie-Rose Gineste, traveled by bicycle throughout the diocese for two days, twelve to fourteen hours per day, distributing the letter. It was read aloud in forty churches the following Sunday. Resistance forces smuggled the bishop's letter to London, where it was broadcast to France over the BBC. Sister Gineste continued her work by arranging safe houses in the Montauban diocese and stealing food ration cards for Jews.

In August 1942, Cardinal Pierre-Marie Gerlier of Lyon and his secretary found hiding places for five hundred adults and more than a hundred children threatened with deportation. This action led to the establishment of the "Circuit Garel," the first network to protect

Jewish children in southern France. Both Jews and Christians participated in this network. At about the same time, Germans ordered all
Catholic priests who sheltered Jews to be arrested in both occupied
and unoccupied France. In response, Cardinal Gerlier refused to surrender Jewish children who were sheltered in Catholic homes after
their parents had been deported. Eight Jesuits were arrested in Lyon,
and the papal secretary of state protested.

In Paris, a Russian Orthodox nun, Mother Maria, hid Jews in her
convent. She and an Orthodox priest, Father Klepinin, smuggled
Jewish children out of the Drancy internment camp in garbage bins.
They supervised the production of false documents and made contact
with rescue groups. Father Klepinin issued fake baptism certificates
for Jews who took on new identities (Gilbert 2003: 268). Both were
arrested and died in concentration camps.

It is well known that the Vichy government cooperated enthusi-
astically with the Germans to round up and deport Jews to the death
camps in eastern Europe. Nonetheless, more than two-thirds of France's
wartime Jewish population of 300,000 survived. Josephine Levy, one
of the survivors, commented, "That could not have been done without the help of many French people, who perhaps sheltered a Jew for
one night, or transmitted a message, or performed some similar act
of decency" (quoted by Gilbert 2003: 292).

One French village in particular has become famous for sheltering Jewish refugees from 1940 until Liberation in 1944. Le Chambon-
sur-Lignon, in a remote part of the mountainous Haute Loire region
not far from Lyon, hid more than three thousand Jewish children and
adults on farms and in hostels, children's homes, and private homes.[1]
Protestant pastors André Trocmé and Edouard Theis and their wives,
Magda Trocmé and Mildred Theis, were honored by Yad Vashem for
spearheading these efforts. Although the Trocmés and Le Chambon
gained international recognition, about a dozen other communities
and pastors in the region also took in Jews. These predominantly
Protestant communities, descendants of Huguenots who had hidden fugitives since the seventeenth century, felt impelled by religious
sentiment to risk their lives by helping Jews, even after the Germans
took control of the area from the Vichy government.

The people of the Vivarais-Lignon Plateau and the Cévennes Mountains near Le Chambon were mostly poor peasant farmers for whom reticence was an ingrained virtue, the result of centuries of religious persecution. In general they believed that those who did good deeds kept their mouths shut, and those who talked about what they did could not be trusted to be telling the truth. The documented history of sanctuary on the plateau goes back to the French Revolution, but the area developed as a refuge prior to the beginning of World War II. During World War I, refugees stayed in Le Chambon. In 1938, some two thousand refugees from the Spanish Civil War were living in a mining area nearby. These farmers believed that in sheltering Jews, whom they regarded as God's chosen people, they were merely doing their duty. Twenty-three Protestant pastors of thirteen parishes, including a former mayor of Le Chambon, Charles Guillon, coordinated and supported their efforts. A few Catholic communities on the plateau also sheltered Jews. Historian Patrick Henry writes, "No other communal effort on this scale ever occurred for this length of time anywhere else in Occupied Europe" (2002: 3).

After the fall of France, the Vichy government took over the southern half of the country and set up internment camps for refugees across the south. In response, international organizations, such as the American Friends Service Committee (AFSC), and national groups, such as CIMADE (Comité Inter-Mouvements auprès des Evacués), OSE (Organisation de Secours aux Enfants), and Secours Suisse aux Enfants, set up regional offices and began visiting the camps, providing humanitarian relief and helping some of the inmates, especially children, to escape. CIMADE, run entirely by women, started in 1939. Philip Hallie, the best-known (though not necessarily the most accurate) chronicler of Le Chambon, wrote of CIMADE: "At first they tried to relieve some of the suffering in the terrible, disease-ridden internment camps of southern France, and they made careful records of the horrors there in order to mobilize world opinion against them. . . . [T]hey developed a web of *équipes* (teams) in the summer of 1942 . . . and with these teams they took through the mountains of France to neutral Switzerland the refugees who were most dangerous to their hosts and most endangered themselves, the Jews" (1979: 135). Guillon, who was part of CIMADE's network, brought YMCA funds to Le Chambon and facilitated the escape of Jews to Switzerland. Others involved in these efforts included Mireille Philip, Dora Rivière, Madeleine Dreyfus, and Simone Mairesse, all of whom risked their lives.

In 1940, the AFSC asked Reverend André Trocmé to help refugees in the camps, and particularly to assist children of deportees who had been sent to Germany for forced labor. Burns Chalmers, who ran the AFSC office in Marseille, encouraged Trocmé to create a city of refuge in Le Chambon, hidden in the mountains. It was a summer resort town with numerous hotels, *pensions,* and children's homes, as well as a secondary boarding school, the École Nouvelle Cévenole, founded by Trocmé and his copastor, Edouard Theis, in 1938. So it had plenty of places to house refugees and educate their children. Funds to support Trocmé's work came from the AFSC, the Fellowship of Reconciliation, the Swiss Red Cross, the Swedish government, and other outside sources.

Trocmé sermonized against the Nazis indirectly and with some subtlety. On June 23, 1940, he and Theis declared from the pulpit:

> The duty of Christians is to resist the violence that will be brought to bear on their consciences through the weapons of the spirit. . . . We appeal to all our brothers in Christ that no one agree to collaborate with this violence. . . . To love, to forgive, to do good to our enemies, this is our duty. . . . We will resist whenever our adversaries will demand of us obedience contrary to the orders of the Gospel. We will do so without fear, but also without pride and without hate. (Trocmé 2004: vi)

He was more direct in refusing to cooperate with Vichy authorities. When a French police commander came to Le Chambon demanding the names of Jews he was sheltering, Trocmé replied, "I don't know the names of those people, but even if I did have the list you're demanding I wouldn't give it to you. They have come seeking asylum and protection from the Protestants of this region. I am their pastor – that is, their shepherd. It's not the place of a shepherd to give up the ewes in his charge" (Trocmé n.d.: 365). On the following Sunday, he preached to a packed church that it was the congregation's duty to hide Jews.

Vichy police took him, Theis, and Roger Darcissac to a concentration camp, but they were released unharmed about three weeks later. In 1943–44, Trocmé and Theis became refugees themselves when they went underground for ten months in flight from the Gestapo.

Whether Trocmé was at home or in hiding, his wife, Magda, was instrumental in coordinating rescue efforts. Her daughter, Nelly Trocmé Hewett, called her "a social service agency by herself" (interview with the author, 2007). In an interview published in 1986, Magda Trocmé said:

> Those of us who received the first Jews did what we thought had to be done – nothing more complicated. It was not decided from one day to the next what we would have to do. There were many people in the village who needed help. How could we refuse them? . . . When a problem came, we had to solve it immediately. . . . The lesson is very simple, I think. The first thing is that we must not think that we were the only ones who helped during those times. Little by little, now that we speak of these things we realize that other people did lots of things too. . . . It is important, too, to know that we were a bunch of people together. . . . If you have to fight it alone, it is more difficult. But we had the support of people we knew, of people who understood without knowing precisely all that they were doing or would be called to do. None of us thought that we were heroes. We were just people trying to do our best. (Rittner and Myers 1986: 100–107)

Many other people who sheltered Jews on the plateau remain nameless. (In recognition of this fact, Yad Vashem honored all the plateau's communities.) There was, strictly speaking, no organization, no office, no files, and no leader – just a network. The approach was simple but effective: Members communicated at Bible study group meetings or during visits to one another's homes. Strangers would arrive and be taken in, no questions asked. A skilled refugee and several local people created false identity documents for them. Before a police raid, the telephone in the parsonage would ring, and someone – nobody was sure who – would say, "They're coming." Then someone would run out to the surrounding farms and hamlets and warn the refugees to hide in the forest for a while. One Catholic rescuer in Le Chambon remarked, "It happened by itself." Nelly Trocmé Hewett quoted her mother to the effect that "you can't plan something like that." Yet the people of the plateau managed to hide about 3,500 Jews between 1940 and 1944, and CIMADE spirited scores of them to Switzerland, two hundred miles away. Thus rescue on the plateau was both an individual and a social activity.

Le Chambon still regards itself as a *terre d'asile*. A local historian tells the story of a family of Iranian refugees that arrived in the village in 2005. Eventually the French government issued a deportation order for the family. But local residents spirited them away so the authorities could not find them. The village is still steeped in memories of the war years; an exhibit in the railway station documenting the wartime rescue operation is a modest tourist attraction. The local post office proudly sells first-day covers commemorating Le Chambon's recognition by Yad Vashem. A plaque donated by grateful Holocaust survivors hangs on a wall across the street from the Protestant church where André Trocmé and Edouard Theis preached. In the village cemetery, on top of the Trocmé family tombstones, lie memorial pebbles left by Jewish visitors. At the Cévenole School founded by Trocmé and Theis, students from around the world still learn the lessons of nonviolent resistance.

Appropriately enough, Le Chambon and surrounding villages are not easy to find, hidden on a high plateau at the end of a long journey along precipitous, winding roads. For anyone seeking to wrest positive meaning and inspiration from the horrors of the Holocaust, this remote area provides both a refuge and a proof of the enduring reality and inherent power of altruism that underlie sanctuary and asylum. The example of its heroes, who refused to consider themselves heroic, quietly renews one's battered faith in simple decency, if only for the few hours it takes to walk the well-worn village streets. Le Chambon and surrounding villages are monuments to the elemental pleasures of sheltering, being sheltered, and surviving.

However, some of those who survived the war in hiding could not bring themselves to return to the places where they had hidden or even to think about what had happened there. They joined millions of other refugees – some of whom spent years after the war in displaced people's camps – who eventually found permanent homes far from the temporary sanctuaries that had saved their lives. Many of their stories were not retold for decades, if at all. Nevertheless, by the end of the twentieth century, thousands of books, articles, films, broadcasts, and other accounts of the Holocaust rescuers had appeared. They became archetypal figures who would inspire people around the world to imitate their example. Their success restored moral authority to sanctuary and challenged governments to recognize and establish asylum as a universal human right.

7 The Twentieth-Century Heyday of Asylum

> Any human being is a sanctuary. Every human being
> is the dwelling of God. . . . Any person, by virtue of
> being a son or a daughter of humanity, is a living
> sanctuary whom nobody has the right to invade.
>
> – Elie Wiesel, 1985

The twentieth century has been called "the century of the
refugee" (Rabbi Hugo Gryn, quoted in Kushner 2006: 232), as hundreds of millions of human beings fled their homes in the wake of civil
conflicts, revolutions, genocide, and total war. In 1945, an estimated
40 million people were displaced in Europe. Many spent months or
years in camps, while others left for other continents. The facts of
the Holocaust became widely known as the leaders of the losing side
stood trial for war crimes and crimes against humanity. In response,
the Allies created the United Nations as the implementer and the
Universal Declaration of Human Rights as the basis of revivified
international law. In the process, the asylum seeker became globally
recognized as worthy of government protection.

Earlier international agreements had mentioned asylum seekers
and refugees. In 1889, the Montevideo Treaty on International Penal
Law laid down principles governing asylum in Latin America. Additional Latin American treaties on asylum were signed in 1928, 1933,
and 1939. The League of Nations had set up the office of High Commissioner for Refugees in 1921, and the Convention Relating to the
International Status of Refugees of 1933 established non-refoulement
as a principle of international law. In this convention, signatories
agreed not to return individuals to their country of origin if they
faced persecution there (Bau 1985: 48).

Even so, the United States and the United Kingdom failed to codify asylum in their immigration statutes during most of the twentieth century. Instead they made entry as difficult as possible by relying on old restrictive laws to exclude outsiders. From 1920 on, the United States kept many categories of immigrants out through quotas and other restrictions. In 1940, the Alien Registration Act required registration and fingerprinting of all aliens living in or seeking to enter the United States. Until 1950, there was no such thing as refugee status in the United States. The government admitted refugees only on an ad hoc basis in extraordinary situations. The 1950 Internal Security Act mandated the exclusion and deportation of politically dangerous noncitizens. All aliens were required to report their address yearly to the Immigration and Naturalization Service. However, this and other laws also authorized the attorney general to withhold or stop the deportation of anyone who would be subjected to physical persecution in the home country (Bau 1985: 44–45).[1]

Although the law did not allow admission of refugees, only withholding of their deportation, this was the first time the United States recognized their need for special treatment under immigration law. In general, the United States did not welcome outsiders. The 1952 Immigration and Nationality Act (also called the McCarran-Walter Act) "provided that total annual immigration should not exceed one-sixth of 1 percent of the number of inhabitants in the United States in 1920," a very small figure indeed (quoted by Bau 1985: 43).[2]

On the international level, the United Nations Relief and Rehabilitation Administration was established in 1943, and the International Refugee Organization was founded in 1946. Both organizations helped millions of refugees during and after the Second World War. In 1950, the United Nations set up an office of High Commissioner for Refugees.

During the war, the British government closed its doors to most refugees. Nonetheless, it created an official definition of refugees that found its way into later international agreements: "All persons, wherever they may be, who, as a result of events in Europe, have had to leave, or may have to leave, their countries of residence because of the danger to their lives or liberties on account of their race, religion or political beliefs" (quoted by Stevens 2004: 119). After the war, the government accepted more than one hundred thousand refugees from the Eastern bloc, but British authorities excluded most Jewish survivors of the Holocaust (Kushner and Knox 1999: 398). British historians Tony Kushner and Katharine Knox observe that "belief in the fundamental justice of granting asylum to the oppressed has rarely been enough on its own to change restrictionism" (399). They attribute the British government's occasionally generous asylum policies since 1945 to guilt, economic self-interest, and the workings of international power politics. Other governments operate in the same way.

In this ambivalent atmosphere, the Universal Declaration of Human Rights was promulgated on December 10, 1948. Article 14 of the declaration simply says, "Everyone has the right to seek and to enjoy in other countries asylum from persecution." It does not give anyone the right to be *granted* asylum. Governments still saw giving asylum as the right of states in the exercise of their sovereignty. The UK delegate to the United Nations argued in 1948 that "the right of asylum was the right of every state to offer refuge and to resist all demands for extradition" (quoted by Stevens 2004: 136).[3] A historian employed by the Home Office to write its history in 1950 denied that Britain had a meaningful tradition of granting asylum or allowing refugees to settle there (Kushner 2006: 30).[4]

The resettlement or return of refugees continued to be a problem in Europe long after the end of World War II. In response, the United Nations adopted the Convention Relating to the Status of Refugees in 1951. This agreement was limited to refugees displaced "as a result of events occurring before 1 January 1951" and only in Europe (quoted by Bau 1985: 49). Not until 1966 did the Protocol Relating to the Status of Refugees extend the convention to the entire world and declare it to be a "universal instrument" (quoted by Kushner 2006: 409).

Article 1(A)(2) defines a refugee as someone who, "owing to a well-founded fear of being persecuted for reasons of race, religion, nationality, membership of a particular social group or political opinion, is outside the country of his nationality and is unable or, owing to such fear, is unwilling to avail himself of the protection of that country; or who, not having a nationality and being outside the country of his former habitual residence as a result of such events, is unable or unwilling to return to it" (Center for the Study of Human Rights 1992: 58). Economic migrants, victims of natural disasters, those displaced by military or civil conflict, or those judged not to have a well-founded fear of persecution were excluded from the protection of the convention. The intention of the agreement was as much to exclude as to admit people who had fled their homes.

The convention reinforces the concept of non-refoulement in article 33(1): "No contracting state shall expel or return ('refouler') a refugee in any manner whatsoever to the frontiers of territories where his life or freedom would be threatened on account of his race, religion, nationality, membership of a particular social group or political opinion" (Center for the Study of Human Rights 1992: 65). However, article 33(2) limits the effect of the preceding article: "The benefit of the present provision may not, however, be claimed by a refugee whom there are reasonable grounds for regarding as a danger to the security of the country in which he is, or who, having been convicted by a final judgment of a particularly serious crime, constitutes a danger to the community of that country" (65).

The drafters did recognize that those fleeing persecution might not have time to apply for a visa or take their passports with them. Article 31(1) states: "The contracting states shall not impose penalties, on account of their illegal entry or presence, on refugees who, coming directly from a territory where their life or freedom was threatened . . . enter or are present in their territory without authorization, provided they present themselves without delay to the authorities and show good cause for their illegal entry or presence" (65). Overall, however, legal scholar Patricia Tuitt points out that international refugee law privileged the sovereign interests of Western states over the needs of refugees (1996: 1–2).

The 1951 convention is a very limited and flawed document. It has no viable enforcement mechanism. It does not guarantee refugees the benefits of permanent resettlement but says only that they may stay indefinitely in the country of asylum. It provides the bare minimum of protection. In many ways it is a half-measure. The 1966 protocol addresses some of the problems with the convention, but governments could always find ways to circumvent these and other agreements. As a result, the most insistent enforcers of international law are ordinary people and organizations that pressure governments to abide by their commitments.

Nevertheless, as the Cold War became the dominant feature of postwar life, the US government found it strategically useful to admit refugees, especially from the Eastern bloc. The Refugee Relief Act of 1953 gave emergency admission to victims of racial, religious, or political persecution who fled a Communist, Communist-dominated, or Middle Eastern country and to victims of natural disasters (Bau 1985: 46).[5] Up to 214,000 refugees could be admitted, and a US citizen had to sponsor each one. Some 189,000 refugees were admitted under this act. With each East-West confrontation, Congress passed special laws to admit specific groups of refugees. In 1956, for example, 31,915 Hungarians were admitted to the United States after the unsuccessful revolt against Soviet domination in their country. They were allowed to adjust their status after two years, but most of the refugees who came in under these laws "remained in a legal limbo, with few rights or privileges . . . , only a temporary status and an uncertain future" (Bau 1985: 47).

In 1956, the British government reluctantly proposed accepting two thousand Hungarian refugees. After much public outcry, the government admitted twenty thousand Hungarians (out of two hundred thousand who fled Hungary). Its attitude was clear in a statement by the home secretary:

> On arrival the refugees are taken to barracks. . . . At these barracks the refugees are registered by the police and provided with any necessary clothing and equipment. They are then moved to hostels in different parts of the country where every endeavor is made to familiarize them with the British way of life and to find employment for them or to place them in accommodation offered by the public. A considerable number of these refugees wish to emigrate to other countries and it is hoped that early arrangements will be made accordingly. Canada, in particular, has offered priority to Hungarian refugees. (Quoted by Kushner and Knox 1999: 250)

The government provided £355,000 (about US$8 million today) for the Hungarians' transportation and resettlement. A public appeal by the Lord Mayor of London raised £895,000 in a few weeks and more than £2.5 million (about US$56 million today) in all. Local voluntary organizations cared for the new arrivals. But, Kushner says, all measures taken on their behalf were temporary, and many were put to work in coal mines. (The British government usually justified admitting asylum seekers and refugees during the Cold War as a means of addressing labor shortages.)

After a few years, the Hungarians were forgotten and the memory of their experience was lost. There was always a new group of refugees to command public attention, usually through negative coverage in the tabloid press and provocative statements by ambitious politicians. The experience of despised outsiders who gradually and quietly integrated into British society was repeated many times.

In 1968, not long after the United Nations adopted the Protocol Relating to the Status of Refugees, Enoch Powell, a Conservative member of Parliament, made an inflammatory speech against immigrants that became notorious as the "rivers of blood" speech. In it he predicted a race war if "coloured" immigrants continued to arrive in Britain in large numbers. Journalist Roy Greenslade observes: "For many people there is no difference between the grandchild of a 1950s West Indian immigrant, a refugee granted permission two years ago to stay under the terms of the 1951 UN Convention or a person newly arrived and in the process of applying for asylum. All are deemed to be aliens and underpinning this viewpoint is, of course, racism" (2005: 21).

While Britain and other Western nations were admitting refugees and asylum seekers from Eastern bloc countries, the press and politicians were calling for other immigrants to be expelled or refused entry. Among the results were considerable confusion about the various categories of migrants and the frequent expression of xenophobic sentiments, which became commonplace and went mostly unchallenged.

Nevertheless, the 1951 convention was considered a "powerful weapon in the Cold War armory of the Western powers," which scored many propaganda victories by giving asylum to Eastern bloc artists, intellectuals, sports stars, spies, and other famous defectors (Gibney

and Hansen 2005: 2:503). Over time, refugee laws and policies soft-
ened somewhat. In the United States, the 1962 Migration and Refugee
Assistance Act allowed refugees to adjust their status after arrival and
stay permanently in the country. Amendments passed in 1965 to the
repressive McCarran-Walter Act abandoned national quotas in place
since 1924 and ended the wholesale exclusion of Asians. Reuniting
families and addressing labor shortages became the stated goals of
US admissions quotas.

Denial as National Policy

Adjusting to the influx of refugees and asylum seekers from former
colonies was difficult for the United Kingdom. In the late 1960s and
early 1970s, Parliament reacted to the arrival of 23,000 Asians with
British passports who had been forced to leave Kenya by passing a
law that "restricted entry to those who had a patrial connection with
the UK, that is, those with a parent or grandparent born, adopted or
naturalized in the UK" (quoted by Price 2007: 1). The effect of the law
was to make Commonwealth citizens of color with British passports
into second-class citizens. Accordingly, when Idi Amin expelled 80,000
Indians, more than half of whom had British passports, from Uganda
in 1972, Britain accepted only 28,000 (Kushner and Knox 1999: 270).

The British Immigration Act of 1971 did not include provisions
regulating asylum, which was left to the discretion of the home secretary. According to Kushner and Knox, "The Uganda crisis came in
a context of increasingly vocal hostility towards nonwhite immigrants
and their descendants and an ongoing political campaign which used
the excuse of popular antipathy to tighten immigration laws in Britain" (1999: 269). After the Labour Party came to power in 1974, the
Ugandans' status was adjusted. But fifteen years later British immigration officers were still making entry decisions with no knowledge
of the political conditions in the countries that asylum seekers were
fleeing. No law including provisions on asylum was enacted in Britain before 1993. Until that time, the government applied the Aliens
Restriction (Amendment) Act of 1919, which contained no due process for asylum decisions and generally ignored the Refugee Conven-

tion. Asylum seekers who entered Britain without documents could be classed as illegal entrants and deported, in clear violation of the convention (Stevens 2004).

Chileans fleeing political persecution in the 1970s similarly tested the British government's capacity to give refuge. In 1973, when left-wing opponents of General Pinochet sought sanctuary in the British Embassy in Santiago, the Conservative government's ambassador refused to let them in. At the time Britain was selling arms to Pinochet. The Labour government that came to power in 1974 was somewhat more hospitable but still refused to expedite entry visas for Chileans. The new government grudgingly agreed to accept "some applications on an individual basis from those who express as their first choice their wish to be resettled in the United Kingdom and who have some ties with the United Kingdom" (quoted by Kushner and Knox 1999: 294).[6]

By 1975, about a third of the Chileans who had applied for visas had been admitted. Between 1974 and 1979, some three thousand Chileans arrived in Britain. Most were middle class, and more than 50 percent were university educated. While the government contributed only £150,000 to the UN High Commissioner for Refugees for Chilean resettlement in Britain, a Joint Working Group for Refugees from Chile set up a private resettlement program and reception centers in London and Birmingham. As with previous groups of asylum seekers, the government was reluctant to help; a public campaign bullied it into offering scant assistance. By 1987, about two hundred thousand Chilean exiles were scattered around the world, along with Uruguayans, Argentineans, Brazilians, Paraguayans, Bolivians, Guatemalans, Hondurans, and Salvadorans fleeing right-wing dictatorships. Very few managed to enter Britain.

From 1975 to 1979, tens of thousands of Vietnamese, Laotian, and Cambodian refugees sought entry into Britain. The anti-communist Thatcher government mounted a campaign to persuade people to accept them (Pirouet 2001: 19). Once again the government offered no long-term help with language instruction or resettlement. Pirouet notes, "In typical British fashion, this was left to the churches and other voluntary groups," whose efforts she calls "piecemeal" (2001: 19).

Thousands of refugees from the Commonwealth countries of Cyprus in the mid-1970s and Sri Lanka in the mid-1980s placed additional strains on the British government. In response, Parliament passed the Carriers' Liability Act of 1987, which fined airlines and shipping companies that transported anyone without proper documents to the United Kingdom. In 1987, scores of Tamils from Sri Lanka stripped to their underwear in protest at the airport as British authorities tried to deport them. They were detained in a disused car ferry while the Home Office processed their asylum applications. Most were deported but later quietly allowed to return. From then on, when asylum applications from a specific country increased, the home secretary would introduce a new visa requirement (Stevens 2004: 93).

From the late 1980s onward, increasing numbers of Kurds from Iraq, Iran, Syria, and Turkey arrived in Britain seeking refuge from political persecution. The Conservative government dismissed them as economic migrants. A Labour MP denounced the "cynicism and meanness on the part of the Home Office" in its treatment of the Kurds (quoted by Kushner and Knox 1999: 342).[7] Of the desperate Kurds who paid traffickers to smuggle them into Britain, the government said it had "no special responsibility for those people who are not refugees coming here as part of a government program," thus violating the Refugee Convention's asylum provisions (quoted by Kushner and Knox 1999: 343).[8] As the Thatcher government moved toward its end in 1991, Conservative MP Jeffrey Archer organized a pop concert for the Kurds, then suffering severe privation in so-called safe havens after the Gulf War, and raised £1 million (about US$22,500,000 today). The Kurds stayed, and by the early 2000s some twenty thousand Kurds, mostly from Turkey, lived in well-established communities in several British cities.

In the 1980s, although asylum applications were rising sharply in Europe, the number of asylum seekers to Britain remained relatively low. Many more people were emigrating out of Britain than immigrating into the country during that decade. Nevertheless the government held onto long-standing xenophobic policies and attitudes, continuing to ignore the Refugee Convention and other international agreements that might have eased the entry of asylum seekers.

Asylum as an Instrument of US National Interests

The United States government took a more flexible approach, including the United Nations' definition of refugees in the Refugee Act of 1980 and setting a yearly quota of fifty thousand refugee admissions. Subsequent immigration laws sought to maintain the number of asylum seekers at a relatively low level while the government selectively used refuge as an instrument of foreign policy. In practice, asylum seekers from countries that the United States defined as enemies, such as Cuba and the Soviet Union, had an easy time gaining entry, while those fleeing friendly regimes, such as El Salvador and Guatemala, were usually denied asylum. In 1984, during the wars in Central America, 20 percent of all asylum applications were successful. Of these, 60.9 percent came from Iran, 40.9 percent from Afghanistan, 32.7 percent from Poland, and 12.3 percent from Nicaragua. All these countries had governments that the United States considered hostile. Also in 1984, only 2.45 percent of Salvadoran applicants and 0.39 percent of Guatemalan applicants gained asylum in the United States, which was supporting their right-wing governments in violent conflicts with left-wing opponents (Bau 1985: 217).

The US government's negative attitude toward Central American asylum seekers began getting public attention in the early 1980s, as opposition grew to US involvement in El Salvador, Honduras, Nicaragua, and Guatemala. But asylum was already a precarious institution. Asylum seekers lacked legal representation, were not informed of their rights, were held in remote detention facilities if they entered the United States without documents, had no access to legal materials, and were not even permitted to have paper and pencils in detention. Their personal communications were routinely confiscated, and their attorneys (in the unlikely event they had them) were not notified of hearings. In subtle and overt ways, authorities pressured asylum seekers to agree to "voluntary" departure. A series of federal court decisions in the 1980s found such practices routine and widespread but illegal (Bau 1985: 162–69).[9]

The Revival of Sanctuary

In 1981, Immigration and Naturalization Service (INS) agents pursued an undocumented migrant into a downtown Los Angeles church, chased him down the aisle, and arrested him in the gallery. The negative repercussions of this incident led the INS to order agents not to pursue "aliens" into churches, schools, or hospitals (Bau 1985: 218). Sanctuary would be paid lip service. At the same time, however, the Border Patrol was arresting, detaining, and deporting thousands of Central Americans who might have been asylum seekers if they had known that they could request asylum. By chance their plight came to the attention of a few good Samaritans in and around Tucson, Arizona.

One of the first to get involved in what became known as the Sanctuary Movement was Jim Corbett, a Quaker rancher in southern Arizona. One day in May 1981 a friend of his picked up a hitchhiker from El Salvador on the road to Corbett's house. The Border Patrol stopped the car and arrested both men, accusing Corbett's friend of alien smuggling. The friend told the story after arriving late for dinner at Corbett's house. Corbett's biographer later wrote: "A war was going on in El Salvador, which in itself would be reason to leave. Corbett had also read about random murders and disappearances. . . . Central American politics weren't a particular concern of his, and he didn't know too much about the causes of the war. But he did have compassion for its victims. His friend's experience affected him more than any news story he had read." The next day he "woke up knowing he had to do something" (Davidson 1988: 16, 19).

Corbett set out to rescue the Salvadoran hitchhiker. He called the Border Patrol and the INS. When they refused to give him any information, he contacted a local activist group called the Manzo Area Council which referred him to a Catholic priest, Father Ricardo Elford, who was helping Salvadorans in the Tucson area. Elford and a Presbyterian pastor, John Fife, had been organizing regular vigils protesting US policies in Central America since the murder of four American churchwomen in El Salvador in December 1980.[10] Corbett was too late to find the hitchhiker, who had been deported, but he did discover that many more Salvadorans were arriving in Arizona.

He, Elford, Fife, attorney Margo Cowan, and a few others began to respond to what they saw as "a deliberate effort to deny these people access to legal aid and to ship them, as quickly as possible, back to El Salvador. . . . Corbett knew that the situation required him to act. He had to try to save as many refugees as he could" (22). He and his wife started sheltering refugees in their house. So did others in southern Arizona.

One of Corbett's friends told a story about a planeload of deported Salvadorans who were murdered on arrival in San Salvador. He said the killings were to serve as an example to anyone else who might consider leaving the country (Davidson 1988: 18). The US government denied that any deported Salvadorans were being killed when they arrived home. That year a federal district court ordered that the INS must inform Salvadorans in immigration detention of their right to seek asylum. The court found that the government was acting illegally, but the INS kept pressuring detained Salvadorans to agree to deportation. Corbett's sense of urgency grew, although he did not view his actions as political activity. He later said the Sanctuary Movement "began as a day-to-day response to arriving refugees. None of us realized what we were getting into" (Corbett 1988: 1).

Corbett mostly worked independently on the issue. He sent letters to Quakers and Quaker meetings around the country, explaining the refugees' need for legal and social services. Although he did not ask for donations, people sent them. Corbett used the money to post bonds and pay the expenses of refugees staying at his house (Davidson 1988: 28). Every day he would drive across the Mexican border, pick up Salvadorans, and take them to his home. He was not afraid to break the law. His father had been a lawyer and a New York state legislator who talked to his children about international law and the Nuremberg trials at the dinner table.

In late 1981, John Fife read a statement by Corbett to his superiors in the Presbyterian Church. It shows the religious and political arguments that underlay the actions of the movement's founding activists.

Because the U.S. government takes the position that aiding undocumented Salvadoran and Guatemalan refugees in this country is a felony,

we have no middle ground between collaboration and resistance. . . .
For those of us who would be faithful in our allegiance to the Kingdom, there is also no way to avoid recognizing that in this case collaboration with the government is a betrayal of our faith, even if it is
a passive or even loudly protesting collaboration that merely shuts out
the undocumented refugee who is at our door. . . . We can take our
stand with the oppressed, or we can take our stand with organized
oppression. We can serve the Kingdom or we can serve the kingdoms
of this world – but we cannot do both. . . . When the government itself
sponsors the crucifixion of entire peoples and then makes it a felony
to shelter those seeking refuge, law-abiding protest merely trains us
to live with atrocity. (quoted by MacEoin 1985: 20)

Meanwhile a local grassroots group, the Tucson Refugee Support
Group, was already bringing Salvadorans across the border, and the
Tucson Ecumenical Council (TEC), a clergy group, was trying to help
Salvadorans gain refuge in the United States. By the end of 1981, TEC
decided to announce publicly what it was doing, to "claim moral high
ground and maybe even rally support before the INS had them all
branded as alien smugglers" (MacEoin 1985: 66).

Rev. Kenneth Kennon of Tucson became aware of the situation of
Salvadoran refugees in INS custody in late 1980. With several other
members of TEC, he visited the El Centro detention camp to interview Salvadorans. In a 2001 memoir he recalled: "'My God, we sent
Jews back to the Holocaust. Are we doing it again?' I wondered as
we talked. . . . I was stunned by their stories of systematic state terrorism, imprisonment, torture and the death of family members and
neighbors at the hands of the Salvadoran military and death squads"
(30–31).

The sanctuary activists self-consciously modeled themselves after
precursors such as the conductors of the Underground Railroad. In
a 1991 memoir, Corbett wrote, "Sometimes our neighbors count on
us to obey the law rather than the government, as in the case of the
efforts by the community of Le Chambon to save Jews from Vichy
officials and the Nazis" (Corbett 1991: 101). Perhaps some of the
activists remembered sanctuary efforts that had taken place ten to

twenty years earlier, during the Vietnam War, when conscientious objectors sought refuge in churches, divinity schools, and university student unions.

For example, ten churches in the San Francisco Bay Area had declared sanctuary in 1971. The next day, the Berkeley City Council voted to provide sanctuary to "any person who is unwilling to participate in military action" (quoted by Bau 1985: 168).[11] Local police were forbidden to investigate or arrest sanctuary seekers. This was the first known instance since the mid-nineteenth century of a government body offering sanctuary in the United States.

Some of the Tucson activists, including Gary MacEoin, had helped Chilean refugees during the 1970s, and several local churches had set up a support network (Cunningham 1995: 15). MacEoin told Hilary Cunningham that this support system was the basis of the Sanctuary Movement and the model for its operations in Arizona.

At the suggestion of a Lutheran pastor in Los Angeles, in early 1982 John Fife proposed to his congregation that the church serve as a sanctuary for Central Americans. TEC asked other churches around the county to sign a declaration of sanctuary, and Fife wrote to the US attorney general that his church would "publicly violate the Immigration and Nationality Act, Section 274(A)" (quoted by Crittenden 1988: 74). On March 24, 1982 (the second anniversary of the assassination of Salvadoran archbishop Oscar Romero, who, like Thomas Becket, had been killed at the altar), Fife, Corbett, Elford, and others publicly announced their intention to offer sanctuary to Central Americans. A rabbi quoted Leviticus: "If a stranger lives with you in your land, do not molest him. You must count him as one of your own countrymen. Love him as yourself, for you were once strangers yourselves, in the land of Egypt." Churches in five US cities also announced their intention to provide sanctuary. The press conference on the steps of Southside Presbyterian Church received national coverage. The INS sent undercover agents to attend the press conference, a procession, and an ecumenical service that day. Fife later recalled, "We couldn't stop. We'd already made the decision when we got involved in that whole effort that the life-and-death needs of the refugees overrode any other set of risks that we might encounter here in the United States.

The conclusion we came to is the only other option we have is to give public witness to what we're doing, what the plight of the refugees is, and the faith basis for our actions" (quoted by Bau 1985: 11).

Cunningham argues that sanctuary activism in Tucson did not start out as a coherent, ideologically motivated movement (1995: 187). Sanctuary Movement theoreticians such as Jim Corbett cited the separation of church and state to justify offering sanctuary on religious grounds and claimed that giving sanctuary was part of the right to free exercise of religion guaranteed in the Constitution. Corbett and others also claimed that the US government was violating national and international law by refusing to grant asylum to Central Americans. He called his actions "civil initiative" rather than "civil disobedience." In 1985, when the Sanctuary Movement was at its height, Bau commented, "The contemporary invocation of sanctuary is not simply a legal or a political phenomenon but rather the revival and continuation of an ancient tradition" (124).

Typically sanctuary activists would drive about ten hours into Mexico to pick up refugees from a church with which they were in contact. They would drive the refugees to the Mexican side of the border, give them Mexican clothing, and instruct them to identify themselves as Mexicans if caught, so they would not be deported to Central America. Once the refugees had crossed the border, they would go to a nearby church and wait to be picked up. A sanctuary worker would take them to Tucson on back roads where the Border Patrol was less likely to find them. Sometimes sanctuary workers would hike with the refugees through the Sonoran Desert. They called this procedure "crossing" (Otter and Pine 2004).

Soon not just dozens but hundreds and then thousands of Central Americans were arriving in Tucson and other cities near the US-Mexican border. By December 1982, Southside Presbyterian Church had given refuge to 1,600 Salvadorans. What had started as a cottage industry became an industrial operation. Overwhelmed, Corbett and other Arizona sanctuary workers asked for help from contacts around the country.

Between 1982 and 1987, some four hundred to five hundred churches decided to offer sanctuary to Central Americans. They provided legal services, social services, transportation, and resettlement help. The churches were equipped for such work because many already fed and housed the homeless or helped legal refugees through church-related agencies. To shelter undocumented people, they had to redefine their mission and priorities. "There is a new urgency about being a genuine community; the person in the next pew is no longer a stranger but now a potential co-felon," Bau observed (1985: 15). Some churches did not actually shelter refugees but provided other services. And some took in refugees without publicly declaring themselves sanctuaries.

In 1982, Reverend David Chevrier, pastor of Wellington Avenue United Church of Christ, a sanctuary congregation in Chicago, remarked, "This is the time and we are the people to reinvoke the ancient law of sanctuary, to say to the government, 'You shall go this far and no further'" (quoted by Bau 1985: 9). But Bau cautioned, "While it is inevitably a political act to break the law—an act of civil disobedience—law-breaking is not the primary motivation for sanctuary." He quoted a sanctuary church member: "By offering sanctuary, we can at least stop supplying these death squads with their victims" (20).

A network of church members, clergy, lawyers, and social workers coordinated the movement, but there was no defined hierarchy, organization, or rules. The churches did not join a formal structure—they simply declared themselves to be sanctuaries. Bau called it a "profoundly democratic movement" of people transporting, housing, feeding, and assisting refugees.

In 1982, Corbett visited the Chicago Religious Task Force on Central America, which was organizing a nationwide movement against US policy in the region. He asked the Task Force to undertake coordination of the burgeoning Sanctuary Movement. The Task Force agreed, but its priorities and philosophy were fundamentally different from Corbett's. He saw his mission as humanitarian rescue; it saw sanctuary as a political tactic in the larger struggle to change US foreign policy. The Task Force wanted the refugees to become public figures in the antiwar movement, but the Arizona people opposed "using" the refugees, especially if public appearances could endanger them. On one occasion, the Task Force sent a mentally ill refugee back to

Tucson because sanctuary workers could not cope with him, infuriating the Arizona activists.

The Chicago churches did not have the resources to provide private sanctuary, recalled Michael McConnell, who managed the Task Force from 1984 to 1988 (interview with the author, 2007). They believed it would help more people to send refugees out into the community as witnesses and victims to inform the public about the real nature of the Central American wars. The Task Force, which was dominated by Catholic clerics, nuns, and lay persons, wanted to set up a centralized structure for the movement, while the Tucson activists were Quakers and Presbyterians who traditionally rejected creeds and hierarchical decision making (Cunningham 1995: 42).

A clash erupted when the Task Force refused to give Corbett its mailing list. Thereupon Corbett wrote a report in which he backed away from "an active role in shaping the future of the movement," in Bau's words (1985: 30). The movement and its politics seemed to get in Corbett's way. He continued to work with a few friends and organizations in southern Arizona, discussing each case and seeking consensus about when to help (Davidson 1988: 82). They did not base their decisions on the refugee's political ideology but on their definition of need and their interpretation of the 1966 Protocol Relating to the Status of Refugees. Meanwhile, in Chicago, the Task Force was organizing antiwar marches, demonstrations, canvassing, and other public actions that often featured refugees who told stories of persecution, torture, murder, and genocide.

By 1983, some thirty thousand Salvadorans had been killed and a million displaced, of whom one-third to one-half were said to be in the United States. US military assistance to the far-right Salvadoran government totaled $500 million per year. In Guatemala, which received much less public attention, tens of thousands were dead and two hundred thousand had fled to the United States or refugee camps in Mexico. A 1984 Supreme Court decision refused to define "a well-founded fear of persecution" in deportation cases, so the INS continued to deny asylum to Salvadorans and Guatemalans. In 1985, a thousand refugees were being deported to Central America each month. A congressional bill to protect Salvadorans from deportation languished in committee (Davidson 1988: 76).

By 1983, it was clear that the INS would not arrest members of sanctuary-providing communities, making it easier for churches to give refuge to undocumented refugees (Davidson 1988: 75). During 1983 and 1984, the movement grew steadily across the country. The conservative Rabbinical Assembly passed a resolution: "Whereas millions of Jews were murdered by the Nazis because nations, including the United States, would not open their gates, the National Assembly endorses the concept of sanctuary and urges the government of the United States to grant extended voluntary departure status to those fleeing the violence in Central America" (quoted by Bau 1985: 187).

Progressive Catholic bishops and the National Assembly of the Conference of Major Superiors of Men endorsed the movement, as did Reverend Jesse Jackson. Some conservative Catholic bishops opposed it, and the National Association of Evangelicals refused to endorse it, but more than seventy-five American and Canadian churches created an "overground railroad" to Canada (Bau 1985: 188). When the Canadian government began deporting Guatemalan refugees, a United Church of Canada congregation in Quebec declared sanctuary, and the government stopped the deportations.

As the movement grew, local groups struggled to coordinate their efforts. Gary MacEoin put together a guidebook for local sanctuary providers, in which he advised, "Selection of an appropriate refugee family should begin as soon as the decision to declare sanctuary has been made. The role of this family will involve active and continuing dialogue with the host community, educating as many North Americans as possible about the situation in Central America, about the plight of the refugees there and here, and about U.S. policy toward Central America and toward refugees from Central America" (1985: 202). A committee of six to ten people, at least one of whom should be fluent in Spanish, was to coordinate sanctuary provision and facilities. During the first two weeks of the refugees' stay, monitors were to stay on church premises. Then the refugees should be moved to a house or apartment. He quoted Reverend David Chevrier's recommendation that volunteers spend six to ten hours each week for the first two months "on coordinating, food, furniture, clothing and monitoring." The sponsoring congregation was to be responsible for the refugee family until it became "economically and emotionally independent." But community support was to decrease after three months. MacEoin's instructions resembled the policy the federal government took toward the refugees it brought to the United States: "It is important to avoid the development of dependency by not providing anything the refugees are able to provide for themselves" (202). But it was difficult to insist that traumatized torture survivors, peasants who spoke no English, and small children become self-sufficient in a matter of months.

Who carried out all this work? According to Robin Lorentzen, women outnumbered men by about two-thirds on all levels of the movement. They were mainly housewives and nuns who used family, church, and community resources to reconstruct the refugees' lives (1991: 3). Women not only organized local sanctuary provision; they also participated in advocacy, outreach, and direct action, including travel to Central America on fact-finding missions. They saw the church as women's territory and themselves as part of a venerable religious tradition that stretched from ancient and medieval sanctuary to the Underground Railroad and Holocaust rescuers. During their travel to Central America, they discovered that the Catholic Church played an important role in the liberation movements targeted by repressive governments. They picked up the rhetoric of liberation theology, and they came to see themselves as allies of Third World social movements in their defiance of US policy.

By the mid-1980s, about two million Central Americans had fled their home countries, and about 42,000 Americans had pledged to resist US policies in Central America. Sanctuary became the largest grassroots civil disobedience movement in the United States since the 1960s (Lorentzen 1991: 14). The movement spanned thirty-four states. At least one state (New Mexico), twelve to twenty-seven cities, five hundred churches and synagogues, and thousands of organizations declared themselves sanctuaries. Eventually participants numbered about seventy thousand North Americans and two thousand to three thousand Central Americans out of the half million who were entering the United States each year.

The Movement on Trial

For a time the US government chose not to prosecute the principal figures of the Sanctuary Movement. The INS apparently followed the advice of the undercover agent who attended the March 24, 1982, launch of the movement in Tucson: "It seems that this movement is more political than religious but that a ploy is going to be Border Patrol 'baiting' by that group in order to demonstrate to the public that the U.S. government via it's [sic] jack-booted Gestapo Border Patrol Agents think [sic] nothing of breaking down the doors of their churches to drag Jesus Christ out to be tortured and murdered. I believe that all political implications should be considered before any further action is taken toward this group" (quoted by Crittenden 1988: 75–76).

The Border Patrol arrested a few activists while they were transporting Salvadorans in Texas in 1984. Then the FBI sent professional human smugglers to infiltrate the movement, tape sanctuary meetings, and provide evidence that participants were breaking the law. Corbett claimed that the government launched the operation under pressure from Arizona senator Barry Goldwater, "who was outraged that 60 Minutes, People magazine, USA Today and numerous documentaries, newspaper series and TV news reports were covering my border crossings, with no apparent intervention or deterrence by the government" (Corbett 1991: 166). According to Rev. Kennon of the TEC, "Our witness provoked a governmental attempt to repress us. It engaged in intimidation, clandestine infiltration, electronic surveillance, and finally, federal prosecution. To their chagrin, these tactics did not diminish the movement. On the contrary, they spurred us on. In holy defiance of outrageous policies, hundreds of religious congregations across the nation publicly declared themselves sanctuaries for Central American refugees, as did colleges and universities, cities, and even states" (2001: 33).

In January 1985 the government's undercover campaign (ironically called "Operation Sojourner") against the movement reached its climax with the indictment of sixteen activists, including Jim Corbett and John Fife, for smuggling of illegal aliens and conspiracy, which were federal felonies. The defendants included two Mexican nationals who had helped Central Americans in Mexico; they voluntarily traveled to Arizona to participate in the trial. Several of the defendants made deals with the prosecutors or had charges dropped. Eleven stood trial: two Catholic priests, one nun, a Presbyterian minister, a Methodist missioner, a Catholic director of religious education, the director of TEC's refugee services, a Unitarian volunteer, a Mexican lay worker from Nogales, and two Quaker volunteers. There were also scores of "unindicted co-conspirators," and fifty-five Guatemalans and Salvadorans were subpoenaed as prosecution witnesses.

On the day the indictments were issued, Border Patrol arrested undocumented Central Americans in Phoenix, Seattle, Philadelphia, and Rochester. None was in a church – according to one Sanctuary Movement activist, no refugee in sanctuary in the 1980s was ever arrested. Also on that day, an international symposium on sanctuary convened at a Tucson synagogue. More than 1,300 people attended. They took the opportunity to discuss legal and fundraising strategies for the upcoming trial.

"The arrests breathed new life into the movement," Miriam Davidson wrote (1988: 96). Numerous church groups, Catholic bishops, the Presbyterian Church, the American Baptist Church, the Mennonite Central Committee, the American Friends Service Committee, the National Council of Churches, the Rabbinical Assembly, and many other organizations spoke publicly in support of the defendants.[12] Meanwhile, at a Senate subcommittee hearing in April 1985, Reagan administration official Elliott Abrams insisted that Salvadorans were economic refugees. There was no evidence that they had been persecuted, he said, and asylum decisions were fair and impartial. In his testimony, the INS commissioner raised the specter of a refugee "invasion" from Central America.[13]

The sanctuary trial began in federal court in October 1985, lasted six months, and cost the government about $1.2 million. It was a circus. Almost every defendant had his or her own lawyer, and the defense strategies sometimes clashed. From the beginning, the judge prohibited the defense from mentioning conditions in Central America, international law, human rights, or religious or political reasons for giving sanctuary. As a result, the defendants were unable to gain the jury's sympathy, and the defense rested without presenting any case. Defense attorneys did manage to discredit one undercover prosecution witness and force the government to withdraw taped evidence. In addition, the government presented almost no evidence against the pivotal figure in the case, Jim Corbett.

In his instructions to the jury, the judge said, "Good motive is not a defense to intentional acts of crime. So, if you find beyond a reasonable doubt that the acts constituting the crime charged were committed with the intent to commit the unlawful act and bring about the prohibited result, then the requirement that the act be done knowingly and willfully as defined in these instructions has been satisfied, even though the defendant may have believed that his conduct was politically, religiously or morally required, or that ultimate good would result from such conduct" (quoted by Davidson 1988: 146). The jurors must have been mystified by this instruction, since the judge had forbidden the defendants to explain their motives. They deliberated for nine days, finally finding eight of the eleven defendants guilty of one felony or another. Jim Corbett was among the three who were acquitted of all charges.

After the trial, the INS commissioner said, "Above all, this case has demonstrated that no group, no matter how well-meaning or highly motivated, can arbitrarily violate the laws of the United States" (quoted by Davidson 1988: 154). But some jurors said they did not feel good about the verdict. One commented, "I didn't want to do it but we had to." Another explained, "We followed the [judge's] instructions to the letter."

Arizona senator Dennis DeConcini and forty-seven members of the House of Representatives wrote to the judge in support of the sanctuary workers. Amnesty International promised to designate the defendants as prisoners of conscience if they were sent to prison. The judge might have disappointed the government when he sentenced all the convicted defendants to five years' probation in May 1986. He demanded that the defendants sign a statement agreeing to stop their sanctuary activities, but when they refused, he dropped the statement as a condition of probation.

In his sentencing statement, John Fife declared: "From the Declaration of Independence to the trials at Nuremberg, our country has recognized that good citizenship requires that we disobey laws or officials whenever they mandate the violation of human rights. A government agency that commits crimes against humanity forfeits its claims to legitimacy. . . . Sanctuary depends . . . on the capacity of the human spirit to respond to suffering" (quoted by Davidson 1988: 154). Perhaps as a result of his leading role in the Sanctuary Movement, Fife was elected moderator of the General Assembly of the Presbyterian Church (USA) in 1992. He was still helping sanctuary seekers in Arizona in 2014.

After the trial, Corbett informed the INS that some undocumented people were coming across the border to apply for asylum. The Tucson INS office processed their asylum requests without arresting the migrants (Davidson 1988: 160). In mid-1987, four sanctuary workers – Rev. Kenneth Kennon, a rabbi, a Presbyterian elder, and a Lutheran layman – were apprehended as they shepherded refugees across the border, but the Border Patrol let them go. "As long as sanctuary operated without a lot of publicity, the government seemed content to look the other way" (Corbett 1991: 160).

Rev. Kennon recounted that he coordinated sanctuary efforts from 1986 to 1989 without hindrance and "participated in the ongoing sanctuary work in a variety of regional and national forums, speaking tours, educational engagements and church-related groups. I also continued my involvement in sanctuary border work assisting refugees to arrive safely in Tucson, get legal representation, apply for asylum and make contact with family members" (2001: 36). Corbett wrote in his memoir: "Since [1986], there has been no further challenge by federal officials to our practice of sanctuary in Tucson. The Border Patrol has agreed not to pursue suspected 'aliens' into a place of worship" (1991: 177).

The Immigration and Naturalization Service waited until 1989 to arrest America Sosa, a prominent sanctuary seeker and campaigner against US involvement in El Salvador who had been living unmolested in Washington, DC, since 1985. She was taken into custody in a church office and charged with illegal entry into the United States. Hundreds of supporters rallied outside the immigration court during her deportation hearing in August 1989. The government dropped the case, and Sosa later became a US citizen (Mahanta 2014).

Some historians have claimed that the guilty verdicts caused the movement to decline, but the number of churches giving refuge to Central Americans actually increased after the 1986 trial:

> The courtroom drama . . . heightened public awareness of the Sanctuary ministry and prompted several hundred churches, a few synagogues and 22 city councils to declare themselves public sanctuaries for Central American refugees. . . . [B]y 1987–88 there were three semiautonomous Sanctuary Movements – in South Texas, southern Arizona and southern California. . . . Each of these groups established its own independent network of church groups and funding resources. . . . Each region also developed its own style of sanctuary. . . . [S]everal Salvadorans formed their own sanctuary communities (mainly in San Francisco and New York). (Cunningham 1995: 62)

Meanwhile public opinion gradually turned against the Reagan administration's support for murderous right-wing regimes in Central America, especially after the Iran-Contra Affair in 1987 and the murder of six Jesuits in El Salvador in 1989. As a result, the incoming George H. W. Bush administration began backing away from overt involvement in the region. In 1990, the government stopped deporting Salvadorans already in the United States and granted them temporary protected status. At that time, an INS official stated: "If sanctuary is feeding and clothing persons in distress, then the INS does that. The immigration service feeds more and clothes more Salvadorans than anybody in the Sanctuary Movement" (quoted by Cunningham 1995: 35–36). Corbett concluded, "In effect, we'd won" (1991: 181). By 1993,

Central American refugees and human rights organizations were no longer asking the sanctuary underground for help (Cunningham 1995: 189). More than twenty years later, hundreds of thousands of people who had fled Central America in the 1980s were still living in the United States, although many were caught in the limbo of temporary protected status, which provides no pathway to citizenship.

A civil suit, *American Baptist Churches v. Thornburgh*, brought during the sanctuary trial and decided in 1990, established the ABC Agreement, an important precedent in US asylum law. According to Corbett,

> Because there was "a real and immediate threat of prosecution of sanctuary providers," the court had ruled that the plaintiffs had standing to bring the suit. . . . [T]o avoid having the evidence of federal violations of refugee law presented in court, the Department of Justice agreed to halt the deportation of in-country Guatemalans as well as Salvadorans and to re-adjudicate any Guatemalan or Salvadoran political asylum application that had been rejected during the 80s. At least 500,000 undocumented Salvadorans and Guatemalans would be eligible for temporary safe haven, and more than 100,000 asylum cases could be re-adjudicated under new, reformed procedures. (quoted by Cunningham 1995: 181)

To Corbett, however, ABC was "just an agreement signed by a government that continues to sponsor gross violators of human rights in Central America and that routinely violates its own statutes and treaties." He considered "the sanctuary movement's real victory" to be "the development of sanctuary as an enduring institution. . . . For these churches, synagogues and meetings, providing sanctuary has become integral to being faithful" (quoted by Cunningham 1995: 182). From the beginning of his involvement in 1981 until his death in 2001, Corbett was faithful to his conception of sanctuary as both a religious institution and a civil initiative. His legacy is a faith-based sanctuary movement that continues to operate quietly in Arizona and beyond.

The women activists whom Lorentzen interviewed believed that the Sanctuary Movement had been successful and credited it with preventing a US invasion of Nicaragua. They also saw their resistance to the Central American wars as part of a long-term struggle against US imperialism that they expected to continue for many years. One said, "Sanctuary was fighting for 'the salvation of the soul of America'" (quoted by Lorentzen 1991: 199).

Although the Sanctuary Movement presented itself as religious in character, it operated in the secular realm, and it used political strategies to gain political objectives. Even Corbett sought to do something much more ambitious than sheltering individuals fleeing persecution. Challenging the inequitable implementation of asylum policies, he called upon the US government to live up to its obligations under the Constitution and international law. The churches and faith-based organizations that supported the Sanctuary Movement not only offered refuge, they also advocated for the human rights of asylum-seekers, refugees, and migrants by carrying out a variety of public activities, pressuring the government, bringing legal actions, organizing local and national groups, and building coalitions.

Placing the movement in historical context, historian Gervase Rosser writes: "Unrecognized by the law, the modern sanctuaries owe the grudging respect with which they have been viewed by public authority largely to the strength of community feeling. . . . [N]eighborhood action clearly retains a potential independent force as a mitigator or critic of the policies of government" (1996: 79). Since the 1980s, sanctuary activists in the United States and other parts of the world have used similar strategies to defend and advance the right to asylum wherever it is threatened. And without a doubt it *is* threatened.

8 Asylum Now in Canada, Australia, and the United Kingdom

Still Human Still Here

– British campaign on behalf of destitute asylum seekers

The Commonwealth nations of the United Kingdom, Canada, and Australia have shared cultural, economic, and political traditions for more than two hundred years. During much of that time British migrants played a predominant role in the development of Canada and Australia. In the twentieth century the Canadian and Australian governments adopted similar policies to encourage immigration from diverse countries, while the British government went to great lengths to keep migrants out or severely limit their entry. All three societies have signed international agreements that oblige them to give refuge to the persecuted, and they have implemented varying migration policies in response to international developments, crises, and wars. Their histories as receiving countries show similarities and divergences that make for interesting comparisons and contrasts.

Canada's Migration Conundrum

Canada has hosted millions of immigrants throughout its history. Sanctuary is also a venerable tradition in Canada, going back to the American Revolution (when loyalists found refuge there) and the Underground Railroad of the nineteenth century. During the Vietnam War in the 1970s and the Sanctuary Movement in the 1980s, Canada gave shelter to young men fleeing conscription in the United States and to refugees from civil conflict and genocide in Central America. A comprehensive history of Canadian immigration points out that its refugee program expanded in 1982 to include Salvadorans facing deportation to El Salvador from the United States because the US government refused to recognize them as asylum seekers (Kelley and Trebilcock 2010: 399). After the end of the Vietnam War, more than sixty thousand Vietnamese, Laotian, and Cambodian refugees resettled in Canada from 1978 to 1980. During a brutal civil war in the 1980s, thousands of Lebanese refugees were allowed into Canada.

Like other receiving countries, however, Canada's immigration policies mixed welcome with rejection. Kelley and Trebilcock observe, "For most of its history, Canada's immigration practices have been racist and exclusionary" (2010: 466). Entry of thousands of refugees, asylum seekers, and immigrants from unfamiliar countries in the 1980s and 1990s strained the immigration system to its limits. Canada drew back from its self-identification as a welcoming nation as the Cold War came to an end in the late 1980s.

The case of Sami Durgun illustrates the changes that were taking place at that time. A Kurd, Durgun arrived in Canada from Turkey in 1988 and applied for asylum in 1989. Two years later, the government rejected his claim. The Immigration and Refugee Board suggested that he could pretend he was not Kurdish and be safe in Turkey (Cunningham 2013: 163). Perhaps because Durgun was well known in Toronto as a Kurdish activist and local organizations spoke up for him, he was granted protected status in 1993. By 2000, he still had not received the documents he needed to live a normal life, study, or work in Canada. The security services could not seem to convince themselves that he was not a terrorist, despite repeated, extensive investigations that found no evidence Durgun had been involved in violent activities. Also during the 1990s, the Canadian immigration authorities focused on identifying fraud and abuse and were suspicious of those who might take advantage of Canada's "generosity" (165).

At this time, US officials were pressuring the Canadian government to do something about its relatively open borders. The government gave Canadian immigration officials greater authority to limit access to the refugee determination system. As a result, asylum was denied more often, and deportation notices increased. The general trend was to make all immigration policies more restrictive. Nevertheless, Canada's government acknowledged its humanitarian responsibilities and constructed a framework for appealing negative asylum decisions. During the 1990s, Canada's immigration system was characterized by "a widely shared commitment to a relatively high and constant level of immigration; . . . a dramatically more diverse, multiethnic, multicultural immigration intake; fragile consensus of the moral and legal imperative for a relatively generous refugee policy; a stronger consensus on the need to preserve a generous family reunification policy; and a broad recognition that the major features of future immigration policy should be determined through open public and political debate" (Kelley and Trebilcock 2010: 416). Durgun was caught up in these contradictory currents.

From 2000 to 2008, 1.6 million immigrants arrived in Canada, and foreign-born residents increased to 18 percent of the total population. Yet the Immigration and Refugee Protection Act of 2002 marked a reversal of legislative accountability in earlier statutes. Deportation became easier, detention was extended, and appeals were limited. Lawyers and advocacy groups argued that "the relatively broad grounds for denying access went far beyond what was actually needed to ensure the security and integrity of the system . . . [and] did not accord with acceptable international standards" (Kelley and Trebilcock 2010: 441). Legal actions challenging negative asylum decisions proliferated, but courts became increasingly reluctant to question executive decisions.

Since 2010, new laws and policies have made asylum in Canada increasingly difficult to obtain. A 2013 Harvard Law School report states that "through the Safe Third Country Agreement [with the United States] and the Multiple Borders Strategy, Canada is systematically closing its borders to asylum seekers and circumventing its refugee protection obligations under domestic and international law. . . . [T]hese measures deter, deflect and block asylum seekers from lawfully making refugee claims in Canada in arbitrary and unprincipled ways" (Arbel and Brenner 2013: 1).

Another strategy used to prevent asylum seekers from arriving in Canada (and other receiving countries) is the imposition of visa restrictions on nationals of certain countries. For example, Canada began requiring that Mexicans and Czechs apply for visas in the mid-2000s. Between 2008 and 2012, asylum applications from Mexico dropped from 9,471 to 321; between 2009 and 2012, asylum applications from the Czech Republic (where Romani were experiencing discrimination and violent attacks) dropped from 2,085 to 28 (Arbel and Brenner 2013: 6).

Meanwhile government ministers have tried to gain political advantage and turn public opinion against asylum seekers by characterizing them as "bogus refugees," "scroungers," "queue-jumpers," "system abusers," "visa cheaters," and "terrorists" – terms apparently borrowed from British right-wing politicians and tabloid newspapers (Chan 2014).

As a result of these actions, the number of refugee claims made at Canadian borders has declined sharply in recent years. In 2013, Canada accepted about 7,800 out of some 20,000 asylum claims (35 percent of all claims received, rejected, abandoned, or withdrawn), down from 77 percent accepted of 14,000 claims on record in 1990 (Immigration and Refugee Board of Canada 2013). By the end of 2014, only 200 Syrian refugees had been admitted. The government had pledged to accept 1,300 Syrians, of whom 1,100 were to be funded by private organizations, but red tape stalled the effort (Burman 2014). Yet when the government changed in 2015, the new prime minister saw to it that 10,000 Syrian refugees were admitted before the end of the year, with 15,000 more expected by early 2016. This modest expression of official hospitality puts Australia, the United Kingdom, and the United States to shame.

On the other hand, as in Britain and Australia, asylum seekers in Canada may be detained indefinitely in medium-security prisons with convicted felons. The Red Cross has been refused access to monitor immigration detention centers. Under recent regulations, asylum seekers who are not detained are denied full public health and other services. Refugees, however, are treated humanely. For about a decade

Canada's government seemed to abandon its tradition of welcoming the stranger, following the example of countries that were closing their doors to migrants. It remains to be seen if the new government will repeal restrictive laws and implement more-generous refugee and asylum policies across the board.

Australia's Asylum Pendulum

Like Canada, "Australia has developed a proactive approach to immigration – actively recruiting and selecting prospective newcomers. Immigration has been utilized as a mechanism of nation-building by successive governments," sociologist Claudia Tazreiter writes (2004: 126). As a result, by 2001 a quarter of Australia's population was foreign-born. But Australia had kept in place its 1901 Immigration Restriction Act, which excluded nonwhites from the country for seventy years. Despite its adoption of multiculturalism in the 1970s, the government's recent policy of mandatory, nonreviewable detention of mostly nonwhite or non-Western asylum seekers echoed older racist attitudes and actions toward Aborigines, the indigenous inhabitants of the country.

Since the 1990s, Australia has had quotas for admission of refugees, reserving twelve thousand to twenty thousand places for "humanitarian" cases and women at risk.[1] When the number of arriving asylum seekers increases, admissions of other humanitarian cases decrease.

As it became increasingly difficult to gain asylum in Australia and other countries in the 1990s, desperate people fleeing persecution, civil conflicts, and genocide began paying smugglers to transport them to safety. Human trafficking and smuggling now constitute a huge global industry, worth $12 billion to $30 billion annually (estimates vary; see, for example, Al Jazeera 2015). Migrants may have no idea where smugglers are sending them. For example, Caroline Moorehead (2005) describes an Iraqi-Iranian Christian family fleeing religious persecution in the Middle East. The smugglers they hired dictated the destination, sending them to Australia via Malaysia. Sectors of the Australian press contemptuously refer to such people as "queue jumpers," because they enter the country without visas. The Australian government's response has been to try to exclude asylum seekers smuggled in by boat summarily on arrival. Those who do manage to land have difficulty finding legal advice, permission to work, health care, and other assistance if they decide later to apply for asylum. They have to wait six months before becoming eligible for help from the Immigration Advice and Application Assistance Scheme, administered by the Red Cross. Numerous restrictions and deadlines tend to exclude many asylum seekers from consideration.

Australia's asylum policy has been fraught with contradictions. During the 1990s, refugees from nearby East Timor had considerable difficulty obtaining asylum in Australia. The Australian government was trying to deport them to Portugal, which had controlled East Timor until 1975. In response, a sanctuary movement developed among Australian Catholic organizations. More than fifteen thousand Australians provided safe houses that became available when deportations were imminent (Tazreiter 2004: 147).

Finally, in 1999, after Indonesian troops and their collaborators ravaged East Timor and thousands of Australians demonstrated in support of its independence, the Australian government offered temporary safe haven to Timorese refugees. Also that year, the government transported four thousand refugees from Kosovo at a cost of $100 million while trying to prevent ten thousand Asian boat people from landing. Whereas they warmly welcomed the Kosovars, the public responded negatively to other asylum seekers, especially those who arrived by boat (Tazreiter 2004: 148).

From 1992 on, the government passed increasingly restrictive laws, including mandatory, nonreviewable detention for unauthorized arrivals, to prevent asylum seekers without documents from entering the country. As the use of detention increased in the 1990s, the media exposed sensational cases of inhumane conditions in immigrant detention centers or instances of refoulement. For example, in 2000 the government deported a Chinese woman who was eight and a half months pregnant after her asylum claim was denied. On arrival in China, she was forced to undergo an abortion. In 2014 the Australian Coast Guard handed over thirty-six Sri Lankan asylum seekers, including six children, to the Sri Lankan Navy. Police later charged them with "illegally leaving the country." Human rights advocates noted that Sri Lankan authorities reportedly torture people in their custody (Bourke and AAP 2014).

The hardening of Australian asylum policy may go back to the notorious 2001 *Tampa* incident, when 433 asylum seekers rescued from a sinking boat by a Norwegian container ship were denied entry to Australia. Most were sent to the independent island nation of Nauru, which Australia paid to detain them. (New Zealand granted asylum to 149 of the refugees.) To gain public support for their actions in this case, government officials made the false claim that Iraqi refugees on the *Tampa* had thrown their own children overboard. Parliament then passed laws that some advocates believed repudiated Australia's responsibilities under the 1951 Refugee Convention. From 2001 to 2003, the government spent more than $500 million on offshore refugee detention, which it called the "Pacific Solution." The mandatory, indefinite detention of asylum seekers, both offshore and in remote locations in Australia, continued until 2008, when a newly elected Labor government ended the policy.

For more than fifteen years, Australian nongovernmental organizations worked closely with the government while protesting its asylum policies. Church and other groups provided services to torture survivors, visited asylum seekers in detention, and published reports about detention conditions while receiving government funds to provide social services to immigrants. In 1996, the Asylum Seekers' Centre set up a forum for refugee organizations to coordinate activities and meet with government agencies and the UN High Commissioner for Refugees. The forum, called Interagency, had more than a hundred member groups, an international e-mail network, and an e-mail newsletter. But the effectiveness of its advocacy was constrained by its members' ties to the government.

According to Tazreiter, "Under the Howard Government (1996–2007) many NGOs were defunded, particularly those who were primarily advocacy focused. But some organizations (the Red Cross for example) still have a 'service delivery' role for asylum seekers which gains government funding. It is often the completely independent organizations, such as Amnesty International, that are the most prominently vocal in criticism of government policy" (personal communication, 2015). For example, an independent body, the Australian Human Rights Commission, did not hesitate to declare that detention of asylum seekers should be used only as a last resort. The commission insisted that detention was undesirable for single women, children, unaccompanied minors, or those with special medical or psychological needs (Tazreiter 2004: 204).

Caroline Moorehead comments that the government's Pacific Solution was "an immense sledgehammer to crack a very small nut" (2005: 128). In 2001, the year of the *Tampa* incident, 1,640 asylum seekers arrived in Australia, while about 50,000 overstayers, who had arrived legally from Europe and the United Kingdom but remained after their visas expired, were living quietly, undisturbed, in the country.

Despite the expense and opprobrium its asylum policies caused, the right-wing government of John Howard repeatedly fomented a moral panic among Australia's citizenry, manipulating fears of an "invasion" of desperate Asian terrorists to win election three times over an eleven-year period. And yet, each turn of the political screws generated more public opposition to those policies.[2] A sanctuary movement without a name insistently challenged the government in the name of Australian values, basic fairness, and human decency.

Finally, in mid-2008, the new government announced a more humane asylum policy. The Pacific Solution of offshore detention ended. Asylum seekers would no longer be locked up on arrival in the country. The government also pledged not to detain migrant children and families. Migrants who did not pose a threat to the community could remain in the country until their status was resolved. After trying out pilot programs modeled on Sweden's asylum system, which emphasizes case management, alternatives to detention, and work rights for asylum seekers, Australia's government announced in May 2009 that it would reform the asylum system across the entire country.

Yet in 2013, some 2,800 asylum seekers were in "community detention" with freedom of movement, while more than 8,500 remained under guard in detention facilities and "alternate places of detention." The government funded community and church-based organizations to provide services to community detainees, who had access to welfare services, health care, and housing but were not allowed to do paid work. Over time the government cut back their access to benefits. They remained in legal limbo, sometimes for years (Marshall et al. 2013: 55–57).

The new system lasted about four years. In mid-2012, as a national election approached, the government announced that it was reinstituting the Pacific Solution, explaining that "increasing numbers of refugees pay Indonesian smugglers to ferry them to Australia in overcrowded boats, resulting in hundreds of deaths. Almost 1,000 asylum seekers, often from war-torn Middle Eastern and South Asian nations, have drowned in the waters between Indonesia and Australia since 2001. . . . Fatalities have accelerated in the past three years, with 604 people losing their lives since October 2009" (Withers 2012). Under the new (old) policy, "only refugees who arrive by boat will be barred from obtaining a visa and settling in Australia" (A. Chen 2014: 53). Boat people would be sent to detention in the neighboring countries of Papua New Guinea and Nauru for possible resettlement there.[3] Reaction by migrant and human rights advocates was swift and loud. The Australian Human Rights Commission said the policy threatened the Refugee Convention; the Human Rights Centre said it set an "alarming global precedent" (A. Chen 2014: 54). Many groups protested that offshore detention conditions were hellish. Organizations including Amnesty International, the UN Working Group on Arbitrary Detention, and the Australian Human Rights Commission were not permitted to visit Nauru's detention centers, which operated without independent oversight or accountability.

James Hathaway, an expert on international refugee law, commented: "We created the market for human smuggling. If asylum seekers could lawfully come to Australia and make a refugee claim without the need of sneaking in by boat, they would do it. But we make it illegal and create the market that smugglers thrive on" (quoted by Hewett 2012). At that time some four thousand migrants were detained. The government's draconian response to the arrival of a few thousand boat people seemed disproportionate to outside observers but effective in winning votes.

In November 2014, the immigration minister announced that Australia would no longer resettle refugees who had registered with the UN High Commissioner for Refugees in Indonesia after June 30, 2014. This decision, which some critics said violated Australia's obligations under international law, aroused the ire of the Indonesian government and the outrage of human rights and immigrant advocates.

The following week, the UN Committee against Torture (CAT) called on the Australian government to "stop putting asylum seekers into mandatory detention, and to make sure that asylum seekers on Manus Island and Nauru are treated more humanely, and their claims are promptly and properly addressed." CAT pointed to "harsh conditions, the protracted periods of closed detention and uncertainty about the future [that] reportedly creates serious physical and mental pain and suffering." The committee chair said that Australia had not provided evidence of compliance with the Torture Convention and had failed to show that it was not sending asylum seekers back to countries where they faced "substantial risk of torture." The government's mandatory detention of immigrants and children violated the Torture Convention, CAT found. The committee criticized harsh conditions in the detention centers: "overcrowding, inadequate health care and allegations of sexual abuse and ill-treatment" (quoted by Miller 2014).

On the same day, the Australian Parliament passed the Migration and Maritime Powers Amendment. It fast-tracked asylum decisions, reintroduced temporary (three- to five-year) protected status for asylees, and overrode any high-court decisions against mandatory offshore detention. The immigration minister secured its passage by promising to release hundreds of children detained on Nauru and other islands. The president of the Human Rights Commission said the amendment was "a very deliberate attempt to exclude international law" that would "bring Australia into disrepute" (quoted by Farrell 2014a).

In late December 2014, the immigration minister announced that one hundred adults and ninety-four children in family groups had been transferred from Christmas Island to a detention center in Darwin, on the Australian mainland. Arrangements were being made, he said, "to transfer them into the community." They would receive temporary protection visas (TPVs), good for three years and renewable. TPV-holders may work but cannot bring family members to Australia. They are permitted to travel outside the country "only in special circumstances." Few were expected to clear "a very high bar" to a permanent visa. The government was also setting up "safe haven enterprise zones," where refugees could work or study for up to five years (quoted by Safi 2014).

The transfer came after the Australian Human Rights Commission reported that conditions on Christmas Island were poor, and children detained there were suffering from "hopelessness and helplessness." Self-harm among children in all detention facilities was "shockingly high," the commission wrote. More than 150 children were still detained in Nauru, but the minister said nothing about their fate (Safi 2014).

The Australian Human Rights Commission then published "The Forgotten Children," a 324-page report that recounted the findings of the National Inquiry into Children in Immigration Detention. Released in February 2015, the report exhaustively documented and strongly criticized the wretched conditions in which children were detained indefinitely on the Australian mainland and offshore. Although the number of detained children had decreased markedly since 2012, in November 2014 Australia still held about eight hundred minors "in mandatory closed immigration detention for indefinite periods, with no pathway to protection or settlement," the report said.[4] "Some children of parents assessed as security risks have been detained for over two years without hope of release," the report charged (Triggs 2014: 13). Detained children had elevated rates of mental illness, were vulnerable to physical assault, and were denied education for a prolonged period. Furthermore, 167 babies were born in detention between 2012 and 2014, and about twelve of these were stateless, citizens of no country. "Australia is the only country in the world that imposes mandatory and indefinite immigration detention on asylum seekers as a first action," the report pointed out (10).

The commission's president concluded, "Both the former and current Ministers for Immigration agreed that holding children for prolonged periods in remote detention centers does not deter people smugglers or asylum seekers. There appears to be no rational explanation for the prolonged detention of children. . . . It is imperative that Australian governments never again use the lives of children to achieve political or strategic advantage. The aims of stopping people smugglers and deaths at sea do not justify the cruel and illegal means adopted. Australia is better than this" (Triggs 2014: 13, 15). The prime minister called the report a "blatantly partisan exercise" and said the Human Rights Commission "should be ashamed of itself." Asked "if he felt any guilt over the findings, the prime minister said 'none whatsoever'" (quoted by Medhora and Doherty 2015).

Despite public protests and legal challenges, the government's harsh asylum policies remained in place in 2016; the days when Australia won international praise for sheltering tens of thousands of refugees were long gone.

British Attitudes toward Immigrants

Britain has received immigrants for at least two thousand years, since settlers from the Roman Empire reached its shores. Yet it does not consider itself a country of immigrants. Indeed, the British government tries to ensure through its restrictive policies that net immigration is kept below 100,000 persons per year. These policies have consistently failed. In 2014, net migration into the United Kingdom increased by around 33 percent from the previous year, to 298,000, but only 24,914 people sought asylum, down from more than 84,000 in 2002 (United Kingdom Home Office 2015).[5] Forty-one percent of first applications for asylum were granted in 2014.[6] The reasons for the long-term decrease in asylum applications are unclear, but surely they include measures implemented to prevent asylum seekers from gaining refuge.

According to several studies, the British public has a negative attitude toward asylum seekers. "The assumption that most people seeking asylum are frauds shapes much of the debate," a 2013 study found (Philo et al. 2013). A poll by the British Red Cross in 2012 found widespread confusion about the differences between refugees, asylum seekers, and illegal immigrants. The media's coverage of asylum seekers was consistently and overwhelmingly negative, characterized by "conflation of forced and economic migration"; exaggerated estimates of the number of asylum seekers; their alleged burden on social services and the job market; their perceived illegality and criminality; and the need for "immigration control" (Thomas 2012).

In his groundbreaking 2005 study of the British media's portrayal of asylum seekers, journalist Roy Greenslade pointed out that asylum seekers "have been made into scapegoats for a variety of society's current ills, or alleged ills, such as the level of crime, the liberalism of the welfare state, the housing shortage and an apparently overcrowded island" (5). They were "cast as interlopers who have little or nothing in common with settled migrant communities. But, despite editors' success in having demonized the concept and practice of asylum-seeking, and turning the very phrase into a term of abuse, the casual misuse of terminology reveals an underlying anti-immigrant mindset. . . . [I]n reality, popular newspapers remain opposed to all immigration" (5).

The principal purveyors of anti-asylum-seeker sentiment for more than twenty years, Britain's top-selling tabloid newspapers, the *Sun*, *Daily Mail*, *Daily Mirror,* and *Evening Standard*, sold an average of some 6 million papers a day in 2014. Greenslade estimates that three people read each purchased copy of the top four tabloids, so that some 18 million people – more than 25 percent of the country's adult population – read them each day. As a result the tabloids are tremendously powerful formers of public opinion. The more respectable papers tend not to challenge the tabloids directly. Even the BBC repeated some of their claims, often referring incorrectly to asylum seekers as "illegal immigrants." Distorted statistics and exaggerated, sometimes fabricated, stories published by the tabloids have incited fears of a "flood" or "mass influx" of migrants and portrayed them as threats to the British way of life.

In the late 1980s, Greenslade writes, intolerance and reckless disregard for the truth in the tabloids "tipped over into an aggressive and unpalatable nastiness" (10). Even after the establishment of a Press Complaints Commission, the tabloids continued to stoke moral panics about asylum seekers and illegal migrants. In 2004, the *Express* carried on a vicious campaign against the Roma, forecasting a "huge gipsy invasion" from eastern Europe.

Greenslade concludes, "People want to believe what they are reading because it confirms their prejudices" (29). Ten years later, migrants in general, disabled people, and "welfare cheats" had become the tabloids' preferred targets, but politicians continued to cite public prejudices as justification for draconian asylum measures. So the cycle went on and on, feeding on itself.

Supposedly the British government set up its asylum policies to fulfill international obligations, but its real intention may be to make asylum as difficult as possible to obtain in the United Kingdom. Since 1993, when the 1951 Refugee Convention was incorporated into British law, at least ten statutes have regulated and restricted asylum, making the system ever more complex and convoluted. Court decisions have declared parts of these measures unlawful, but the government has found ways to get around them.

For example, in 2010 a British high court ruling lifted a work ban on 45,000 asylum seekers. In reaction, the UK immigration minister announced that the Home Office would allow asylum seekers to "apply only for vacancies among 400,000 skilled jobs in shortage occupations. . . . Asylum seekers would have to be qualified maths teachers, chemical engineers, high-integrity pipe welders or even experienced orchestral musicians or ballet dancers." The Refugee Council replied that "the shortage occupation list is not designed for asylum seekers but rather economic migrants needing sponsorship to come to the UK" (quoted by Travis 2010). Advocates saw the new policy as a transparent attempt to prevent asylum seekers from escaping destitution while they waited for their claims to be decided.

The Immigration Act of 2014 cut the number of immigration decisions that can be appealed from seventeen to four; allowed deportation of "certain harmful individuals" while their appeals were being heard; overrode the European Convention on Human Rights by restricting migrants' right to family life; required landlords and banks to check tenants' and customers' immigration status; and required "temporary" migrants to pay for medical treatment under the National Health Service (United Kingdom Home Office 2014b).

Although these provisions were not necessarily aimed at asylum seekers, the UN High Commissioner for Refugees expressed concern that they could "result in asylum-seekers, refugees and beneficiaries of subsidiary protection being stigmatized in the public mind and in their being denied access to housing or bank accounts. . . . Such measures could contribute towards a climate of misunderstanding and ethnic profiling. . . . [They] may have unintended consequences such as the denial of housing and other services to asylum-seekers, refugees, beneficiaries of subsidiary protection that result in their marginalization and inhibit their integration in the United Kingdom" (quoted by Mason 2013).

On and on rolled the rules and regulations, apparently disconnected from the realities of asylum seekers' situations, high court decisions, and international law. Asylum law, writes anthropologist Anthony Good, "occupies a solipsistic parallel universe" (2007: 96). The judicial system rigidly construes words and narrows the application of sanctuary to a few highly circumscribed types of entrants. Casuistic interpretation of the law severely limits access to asylum. In the United Kingdom, Good concludes, authorities systematically use the Refugee Convention to exclude people from asylum.

The asylum process set up by the immigration acts became dysfunctional over time. The UK Border Agency (UKBA) was set up in 2008 to replace the Immigration and Nationality Directorate (IND) in the Home Office, partly because of the IND's failings but also to deal with a huge backlog – as many as 450,000 undecided cases. Four years later, the media reported serious problems in the UKBA.

In response to a Freedom of Information Act request by the *Guardian*, the British government acknowledged that it had unlawfully tried to "remove" tens of thousands of migrants between 2008 and 2013.[7] Almost half of the forced removals had to be canceled because of court rulings. The administrative costs of canceling almost 49,000 removals totaled about £10 million over five years (L. Taylor 2013).

Private companies contracted by the government carried out dawn raids on the houses and apartments of refused asylum seekers, breaking down doors and taking whole families to detention centers before forcibly removing them from Britain. These raids attracted so much negative publicity, especially in Scotland, that the Home Office suspended them for a while.[8] Despite repeated public protests, they were still going on in some parts of Britain in 2014.

The chief inspector of borders and immigration testified to a parliamentary committee in 2013 that he had discovered hundreds of thousands of abandoned case files and correspondence from asylum seekers and members of Parliament that had never been opened. That year the government shut down the UK Border Agency and reincorporated it into the Home Office, transferring its functions to three new departments and letting go more than 120 experienced caseworkers in the process. In October 2014, the *Guardian* reported that the Home Office's immigration operation was "in chaos" again (Doward 2014a; Syal and Travis 2014).

How in practice does the asylum system work in the United Kingdom? An asylum seeker makes his way to the country, either with the help of a people smuggler or alone. As Good observes, asylum seekers "may be wholly unfamiliar with the UK – indeed, may not even know it *is* the UK – and are often exhausted and terrified, yet any delay in claiming asylum is seized on by the Home Office as undermining their credibility" (99). The asylum seeker is required to present himself at an office, Lunar House in Croydon, a southern suburb of London, as soon as possible after arrival.

Asylum seekers must fill out a twenty-page form and return it to the Home Office within fourteen days. They are then supposed to receive an interview notice, but these notices have been known to go to the wrong address. Or perhaps a female asylum seeker is in the hospital, giving birth, on the day of the interview. If asylum seekers do not appear or cannot convince the caseworker that they have a strong claim, they will be lodged temporarily in an accommodation center before dispersal or detained in one of eleven centers scattered around the country pending a fast-track hearing and possible removal.

In the course of a year, some thirty thousand migrants are detained in Britain, for periods ranging from a few days to months or years. Detention, which may be indefinite, has been described as "the black hole at the heart of British justice," because most detainees have not committed any crime and do not know when they will be released

(Owen 2015).[9] Ironically, almost half of detainees are not removed, raising the question, Why detain them then? Advocacy groups contend that by making them as miserable as possible, the government hopes to persuade detainees to agree "voluntarily" to return to their home countries. If this is the strategy, it does not work very well. Apparently refused asylum seekers prefer the prospect of a miserable life in Britain's destitution underground to torture, disappearance, or death at home.

Torture and trafficking victims, children, pregnant women, and people with serious mental or physical illnesses are not supposed to be detained, but they often are, sometimes for prolonged periods. In 2010, after a five-year legal battle, the government paid £2 million in compensation to forty minors who had been detained as and with adults. Twenty-five were between the ages of fourteen and sixteen when detained. Some had survived torture in their home countries; others had survived rape or other forms of sexual abuse (D. Taylor 2012). Children continued to be detained, even after the Conservative–Liberal Democratic government promised to end the practice in 2010. Ninety-nine children were detained in 2014. They were placed with their parents in family detention centers, so that the whole family could be expeditiously removed (Medical Justice 2014).

Detention often leads to deportation or removal. In late 2013, detainee Isa Muazu was gravely ill after spending a hundred days on a hunger strike to protest his upcoming deportation. He was forcibly removed to Nigeria after the high court ruled that he and thirty-one other hunger strikers could be detained until death was "unavoidable" (Medical Justice 2014). Flown in a private jet to Nigeria, he was returned to Britain after the plane was denied entry to Nigerian airspace. The flight cost between £95,000 and £110,000.[10] A House of Lords debate a few days later led to a stay of removal pending the outcome of an urgent hearing.

The subsequent campaign against Muazu's deportation was "massive." Forty parliamentarians signed a letter to the home secretary, and more than a hundred organizations called for clemency. About 120 people protested silently outside the Home Office. To no avail. The emaciated Muazu, who was suffering organ failure and had been found to be mentally ill by a psychiatrist, was removed again to Nigeria. On arrival he was taken to a hospital, and there his story ended. Many deportations end obscurely, and the Home Office does not track what happens to deportees after they are returned home.[11] NGOs report from time to time on a deportee's subsequent arrest, torture, disappearance, or death.

Also in 2013, the high court ruled in five cases that mentally ill detainees' human rights had been violated. The court called the government's failure to treat them humanely "willful or grossly negligent," and the Royal College of Psychiatrists opposed the detention of mentally ill people. However, "none of this attention appears to have led to change – mentally ill detainees are still detained for long periods of time, often without adequate assessment and care" (Medical Justice 2014: 7).

Torture victims, women, LGBT people, and children have special difficulties in detention. They are vulnerable to mental and physical illnesses, including tuberculosis, sexually transmitted diseases, hepatitis, HIV, malaria, post-traumatic stress disorder, even chicken pox. According to government regulations, people claiming to be torture victims should undergo a special medical examination by a physician affiliated with the Medical Foundation for the Care of Victims of Torture during their first twenty-four hours in detention. The findings determine whether the individual will be released from detention. But in practice this examination often does not take place or its results are ignored.

Sexual abuses occur before, during, and after detention. Women's reports of rape or harassment are often disbelieved. Other complaints by detainees include assault by guards; denial of antiretroviral medication to HIV-positive people; denial of appropriate food and blood-sugar monitoring kits to diabetics; handcuffing, even of disabled detainees, during outside medical appointments; failure to monitor hunger strikers; failure to transport detainees to hospital appointments; failure to disclose medication records; denial of physicians' right to photograph injuries and torture scars; poor responses to complaints about conditions.

While in detention, asylum seekers struggle to find legal representation, without which they have little chance of gaining asylum. Because of repeated government cutbacks in legal aid since 2004, they are unlikely to find a lawyer. According to Women for Refugee Women, 63 percent of asylum seekers were unrepresented when they appealed negative fast-track decisions. At one detention center, officials routinely refused applications for more time to present cases by women who had suffered rape or torture or were suicidal (Webber 2012: 61).

As abuses at detention centers multiplied, advocacy organizations brought cases before the courts to challenge government asylum policies. And so a pattern has been established since the 1980s: The government institutes a policy that harms migrants and asylum seekers. Advocacy groups and human rights law firms sue the government. The judge rules the policy unlawful, and a few plaintiffs benefit. The government then pushes a law through Parliament that perpetuates the policy. Under the British system, judges cannot overrule acts of Parliament. Thus the effects of the judge's decisions are limited; the struggle to make the immigration system more humane continues on a case-by-case basis and through campaigns that usually have only short-term success (Webber 2012).

Despite the fast-track process carried out in detention centers, asylum cases may take months or even years to be decided. According to testimony at the 2013 parliamentary inquiry, 49 percent of women asylum seekers waited more than two years for a decision, compared to 22 percent of men, perhaps because the women's cases were more complex and fit less easily into outdated Refugee Convention categories.

Until the mid-1990s, British authorities often ignored or misconstrued the special problems of women asylum seekers. After all, the words *sex*, *gender*, and *rape* did not appear in the Refugee Convention or UN High Commissioner for Refugees guidelines. Although the UN passed the Convention on the Elimination of All Forms of Discrimination against Women (CEDAW) in 1979 and Britain ratified it in 1986, British immigration judges often did not recognize rape as grounds for asylum. They seemed to see sexual aggression as a private act of lust rather than a political act of violence. One judge denied asylum to a fifty-year-old woman, saying, "Without wishing to appear unchivalrous, we have to say that there can be no significant risk of rape at her age" (quoted by Good 2007: 95).

Some judges appeared to discriminate against women asylum seekers on the basis of ethnic or national stereotypes, finding rapes of Bosnian women to be acts of "politically motivated ethnic cleansing" while denying that Tamil women in Sri Lanka were raped for political reasons (Good 2007: 95). Women's reluctance to talk about rape or their failure to discuss it immediately was used to discredit them. Instead of investigating cases of trafficked women as they were required to do, authorities detained them and placed them in fast-track removal proceedings.

Landmark legal cases were intended to change treatment of women in the asylum system. In *Fathi and Ahmady* (1996), "refusal to conform to gender norms in Iran was seen as a political act within the definition of the Convention at the appeals stage" (Information Centre about Asylum and Refugees 2007: 11). In the *Shah and Islam* case of 1999, "the appellants, both Pakistani women, had suffered domestic violence and were at risk of being accused of adultery, with all its consequences, if returned to Pakistan" (Stevens 2004: 329). On appeal, the House of Lords found that under the Refugee Convention, "women, who share an immutable characteristic, can constitute a social group if they face persecution in a country for being a member of that group" (Information Centre about Asylum and Refugees 2007: 11; Girma et al. 2014). These decisions led the Asylum and Immigration Tribunal (AIT) to issue gender guidelines in 2000. The 2005 *Fomah* decision by the House of Lords reinforced these guidelines by finding that women in Sierra Leone constituted a social group under the terms of the Refugee Convention because of their perceived inferiority and subjection to male domination.

The gender guidelines declared that "rape and other forms of sexual violence clearly amount to persecution in the same way as do other acts of serious physical abuse" (Black Women's Rape Action Project 2006: 7). They also pointed out that women might delay reporting rape in their asylum applications. Yet Women for Refugee Women reported in 2014 that the UKBA had failed to follow a Home Office asylum policy instruction, "Gender Issues in the Asylum Claim." As a result, some women who said they had been sexually assaulted or had fled the threat of genital mutilation were disbelieved. A 2013 parliamentary inquiry found that "women are less likely than men to receive a correct initial decision on their asylum claim," and the grounds for rejection were "arbitrary, subjective and demonstrated limited awareness of the UK's legal obligations under the Refugee Convention" (House of Commons, Home Affairs Committee 2013: 22). Half of these negative decisions were overturned on appeal.

Female genital mutilation (FGM) was a particularly difficult issue for asylum caseworkers and immigration judges. Afusat Saliu arrived in Britain from Nigeria in 2011 with her daughter and sought asylum after the birth of a second daughter. Saliu claimed that if she returned to Nigeria her daughters would be mutilated at her family's insistence.[12] An FGM survivor and a Christian convert, she also said she feared retaliation by the terrorist group Boko Haram, which, she alleged, had killed her father. Her application and subsequent appeals were denied. She was detained at Heathrow Airport for deportation in the midst of a UK campaign against FGM, spearheaded by the home secretary who was seeking to remove her. More than 125,000 people signed a petition on her behalf on Change.org, and her member of Parliament wrote twice to the immigration minister about her case. But Saliu and her daughters were deported to Nigeria in June 2014. In 2015, she was struggling to build a new life in Nigeria with the help of British supporters. The Home Office explained that Saliu "was not considered to be in need of protection." Despite Britain's ratification of the UN Convention on the Rights of the Child, the government did not consider the best interests of her UK-born daughter. Perhaps the five decision makers who ruled on her appeals did not think her claim was credible.

Lack of credibility is a frequently stated reason for rejection of asylum claims. The culture of disbelief – which posits that every asylum seeker must be lying – often rules, especially during the initial phase of decision making. Research by Amnesty International and Still Human Still Here, a migrant advocacy group, found that "in 84 percent of a random sample of cases, a flawed credibility assessment is the primary reason why the UK Border Agency's initial decision to refuse an asylum claim is found to be incorrect by immigration judges" (House of Commons, House Affairs Committee 2013: 24). Even forensic evidence of torture, presented by expert witnesses, is often ignored.

The UN High Commissioner for Refugees found asylum decision making to be deficient in the United Kingdom because of caseworkers' failure to understand human rights law, misjudgment of applicants' credibility, frequent use of speculative arguments to undermine credibility, failure to apply correct methodology in credibility assessment, failure to consider relevant evidence, and imposition of an unreasonable burden on the applicant to provide supporting evidence (House of Commons, House Affairs Committee 2013: 13).

Credibility has become an important factor in asylum decisions in LGBT cases. Until 2010, asylum caseworkers and judges rejected LGBT claims in 90 percent of cases, saying that homosexuals could avoid persecution in their home countries by "living discreetly, pretending not to be gay." However, a UK Supreme Court decision that year stated that "it was unacceptable to expect asylum seekers to conceal their sexuality" (quoted by Taylor and Townsend 2014). After the court decision, the UK Border Agency started interrogating gay asylum seekers about their sexual practices, rather than focusing on their treatment as members of a particular social group (one of the criteria for asylum under the Refugee Convention). Some of the questions seemed prurient, ignorant, or biased to applicants and their advocates. In essence, applicants were being asked to prove that they really were homosexuals, as the caseworker or judge understood the meaning of that term. A legal scholar pointed out, "In countries where sexual minorities are subjected to persecutory actions or serious harm, many applicants from those countries who identify as gay, lesbian, bisexual or otherwise may not exhibit any identifying characteristics, as they may have spent their life before fleeing to conceal their sexual orientation and/or gender identity. . . . Western stereotypes, out-of-date country-of-origin information and biased immigration officials create undue difficulty for members of a sexual minority to prove that they are in fact a sexual minority *and* that they fear persecution on that basis" (Arnold 2013: 27–28).

In seventy-six countries, including thirty-eight African countries, homosexuality is a crime. Same-sex acts are punishable by death in Iran, Mauritania, Saudi Arabia, Sudan, and Yemen, as well as some regions of Nigeria and Somalia. In other countries, sexual minorities are socially persecuted or ostracized. So for the estimated 1,300 to 1,800 LGBT people who seek asylum in the United Kingdom each year, these decisions are matters of life and death. That is why it is important for immigration decision makers to follow the UNHCR's 2008 "Guidance Note on Refugee Claims Relating to Sexual Orientation and Gender Identity," which some Home Office caseworkers and judges seem to know nothing about. Even in 2014, a parliamentary inquiry found that it was still extraordinarily difficult for homosexuals to prove their identity to the Home Office. In case after case, the culture of disbelief seems to trump the law.

Living in Limbo

In the United Kingdom, 22 percent of detained asylum seekers are in fast-track proceedings, but most are stuck in limbo because of backlogs, denial of bail, or time-consuming appeals. Even refused asylum seekers who agree to return to their home countries may remain in detention for long periods, because they cannot obtain travel documents or it is unsafe for them to go back. They suffer while they wait. The annual cost to detain an asylum seeker in 2013 was £37,230 (about US$56,000 at the time), but as the Quaker Refugee Action Network pointed out in parliamentary testimony, "The human cost cannot be measured. Many people suffer long-term damage to their physical and mental health" (Quaker Asylum and Refugee Network 2014: 6).

Many asylum seekers have been released from detention, only to be refused asylum later. Some could not be returned to countries where the British government recognized they would face violence or torture, and so they remained in Britain without legal status, ineligible for most benefits and mired in destitution. I have not been able to find any authoritative statistics on destitute asylum seekers in the United Kingdom. Published figures are fragmentary and often out of date. Suffice it to say that some six hundred community organizations in London alone are trying to help people in the "destitution underground." They include not only refused asylum seekers but also overstayers, unauthorized immigrants, and foreign criminals slated for deportation after their prison term ends. Altogether they may number in the hundreds of thousands.

Asylum seekers who are not detained receive pathetically meager social welfare payments – £36.62 (about US$55) weekly for a single adult. They are not allowed to work legally for a year after they apply for asylum, so that may be their only income in a country with high prices and a 20 percent value-added tax. In 2014, almost five thousand refused asylum seekers received £35.39 on a payment card good only in certain shops for certain items (United Kingdom Home Office 2015; United Kingdom National Asylum Support Service 2014). They could not use the card to buy cleaning products, socks, orange juice, children's clothes, shoe repair, bus or train fares, or English-language lessons.[13]

A study of refused asylum seekers in Scotland found that "many interviewees were literally penniless with no legitimate means of income. . . . Almost half (49%) were homeless, including families with children, 26 people with mental health issues, four disabled people and five pregnant women and two new mothers. . . . Some interviewees had been in the asylum system for more than a decade" (Briggs 2012).

Gary Christie of the Scottish Refugee Council commented:

Every day our case workers deal with people who are in desperate situations. We see people who have been tortured in Iran yet have been refused protection; others fleeing for their lives from the violence of war in Somalia but who don't meet the terms of the refugee convention; or pregnant women whose cases have been turned down and don't qualify for any support until they reach 32 weeks. While families are supposed to receive support until they leave or are granted status, our research shows that, terrifyingly, some are falling through the gaps. The system is complex, difficult to understand and is not working. (quoted by Briggs 2012)

A UK Border Agency spokesperson replied: "Failed asylum seekers need not face destitution if they simply comply with the law and the decisions of our courts and go home. There are routes of return home for all the nationalities once their asylum claims have been refused and the courts have confirmed that they have no need for protection and no legal right to stay in the UK" (quoted in Briggs 2012).

In 2014, the chief executive of Refugee Action reported: "Half of asylum seekers surveyed couldn't buy enough food to feed themselves or their families. . . . [R]esearch also found that 43 percent of asylum seekers miss a meal because they can't afford to eat, while a shocking 88 percent don't have enough money to buy clothes" (quoted by Bowcott 2014). In March of that year, the high court ruled that the home secretary had "acted unlawfully in freezing [asylum seekers'] essential living needs payments," which had not increased since 2011. The high court required the home secretary to review the support payments, and she decided that they were still adequate. So destitute asylum seekers faced one of the coldest winters in memory under Dickensian conditions.[14]

Even people who obtain asylum may find themselves in destitution. Once they gain refugee status, they have twenty-eight days to leave government-provided accommodation. To receive welfare benefits that would help them pay rent and buy necessities, they must have a national insurance number, which can take up to twenty-eight weeks to be processed. In an era of austerity and high under- and unemployment, they may have a hard time finding any kind of work, or they may take exploitative, subminimum-wage odd jobs or become prostitutes. Even refugees with professional qualifications may find themselves in minimum-wage jobs because they lack British work experience or encounter discrimination.

A University of Birmingham study found that asylum seekers' and refugees' "common experiences . . . include being unable to plan for the future and living each day as it comes, dependency on others and breakdown in family, friendships or other support networks" (Allsopp et al. 2014). Other features of destitution include hunger, homelessness, mental illness, and social isolation. No wonder the Birmingham study concluded that "the UK asylum system in and of itself emerges as a poverty producing machine."

The government's mean-spirited asylum policies have severe consequences for vulnerable people. Meltem Avcil, a Kurd, left Turkey with her parents at age four because of ethnic persecution. After being refused asylum in Germany, the family went to Britain. Meltem's parents split up, and she stayed with her mother. One morning in 2007, when Meltem was thirteen, security guards raided their house at 6 a.m. and took them in a "caged van" to Yarl's Wood detention center. The two spent three months there. Seven years later, she told a reporter, "I saw what my mother went through when she was in detention, and I worry that many women like her are still being locked up. If a woman has already experienced rape, torture, imprisonment in her home country, then it is really hard for her to be locked up here. Women become depressed and suicidal in detention" (Cochrane 2014).

Avcil's mother endured a failed deportation attempt that left her "so devastated she wouldn't talk, eat, sleep, walk, nothing." Eventually they were granted indefinite leave to remain in the United Kingdom, and Avcil is now a mechanical engineering student. Because of her experiences, she started a campaign to end women's detention and close Yarl's Wood. Novelist Zadie Smith and many women's groups joined the campaign, but in 2016 Yarl's Wood was still operating.

The government's obdurate insistence on continuing to implement inhumanly harsh policies, despite high court decisions and years of advocacy on behalf of asylum seekers by community organizations and NGOs, has driven many campaigners to despair. One told me in 2009 that she had long since given up hope of persuading the government to treat asylum seekers humanely, but she kept working on the issue out of a deep sense of obligation to denounce the human rights violations she was witnessing. Four years later, after thirty years' involvement in refugee issues, she had changed her strategy and was trying to work with the Home Office to improve detention conditions and decision making. Nevertheless, she called her regular meetings with government officials "horrendous."

When I visited Bail for Immigration Detainees' London office in early 2013, I asked the director if she felt asylum was endangered in the United Kingdom. She replied, "It's not so much asylum that's under threat, it's human rights," which sounded even more ominous than I had expected. She somberly added, "We don't know if we're going to be around next year."

About eighteen months later, when I returned to give a talk at Bail for Immigration Detainees about detention conditions in the United States, the office mood was vibrant. Packed into the small meeting space, volunteers and staff piled lunch food on the table, ate as I talked, but paid attention and asked probing questions. They were – and are – continuing their work despite all the obstacles the government erects.

9 Asylum Now in Europe and Beyond

> History teaches us that when human beings feel
> impelled to migrate, there is little that states can do
> to prevent it.
>
> — Dallal Stevens, *UK Asylum Law and Policy*

Asylum claims rose sharply in many countries from the 1980s on. The increase became acute at the end of the Cold War. France, Britain, Belgium, and the Netherlands became major destinations of African and Asian asylum seekers, many of whom were from those nations' former colonies. Germany, Austria, and Switzerland received asylum seekers from eastern Europe, especially when the Balkans exploded in war in the late 1980s and early 1990s. Because of its liberal asylum policies, put in place after World War II, West Germany received more asylum seekers than any other western European country. Its Basic Law of 1947 gave persecuted persons the right to *gain* asylum, unlike in other countries, where the state reserved the right to *grant* asylum. Other factors encouraging asylum seekers to pick certain countries included proximity or accessibility; economic, political, cultural, and linguistic links from colonial history; well-established migration routes; ethnic and labor networks; and family reunification possibilities (Bade 2003: 264).

As early as 1974, however, western European countries had stopped recruiting migrant workers and redefined themselves as "zero immigration countries." Would-be immigrants now had to apply for asylum to gain entry (Borjas and Crisp 2005: 41). Even at that time, it was assumed that migrants were seeking refuge under false pretenses and their true motives were economic and social rather than political (Bade 2003: 270). In 1980, some 150,000 people sought asylum in Europe; by 1992, the figure had jumped to 690,000. As the number of asylum applications increased, the percentage granted decreased.

Even West Germany became less generous in giving asylum. Because the West German government did not recognize torture as a form of political persecution, it did not constitute sufficient grounds for asylum (Bade 2003: 271). Even so, almost two-thirds of all asylum petitions filed in Europe in 1980 were in West Germany. As asylum seekers became increasingly unwelcome in that country, they went to France, Switzerland, the Netherlands, and Belgium. After the end of the Cold War, those countries passed restrictive laws and signed international agreements to limit entry of asylum seekers. As a result of the restrictive Schengen Agreement of 1985 and the Dublin Convention of 1990, asylum seekers became "refugees in orbit." And the more asylum seekers were excluded, the more illegal immigration and human smuggling increased.

Avoiding Asylum Commitments

Meanwhile, war, ethnic conflict, and genocide created millions of refugees and internally displaced people in Somalia, Sudan, Sierra Leone, Angola, Bosnia, Iraq, Afghanistan, Colombia, and other countries during the last decade of the twentieth century and the first decades of the twenty-first. In response, European Union states and other receiving countries traded strategies for avoiding their obligations under international law and preventing asylum seekers from arriving and gaining refuge. Since 1985, members of the Intergovernmental Consultations on Asylum, Refugee and Migration Policies in Europe, North America and Australia, known as the IGC, have met periodically, in secret, to exchange information and policy ideas (Tazreiter 2004: 185). Their publicly expressed goal is to "harmonize" asylum policies. Economist T. J. Hatton comments, "Some observers believed that the process of harmonization would produce a set of policies that would be more generous to refugees, at least for the countries with the toughest pre-existing policies. These hopes seem to have been dashed as those countries have exerted pressure to bring what were initially more generous proposals for harmonized policies more in line with their own" (2005: 110).

The UN High Commissioner for Refugees observed in 2014, "There is a European asylum policy, but it's still very dysfunctional and still very different from country to country in the way it's applied" (quoted by Sherwood 2014). Repeated calls for a "common European asylum policy" bode ill for asylum seekers, as more and more governments adopt restrictive or punitive measures borrowed from their neighbors.

Governments usually say they are driven by the force of public opinion to limit all kinds of immigration, including asylum. Opinion polls often find that most voters do not support increased immigration. Individuals who fear labor-market competition from immigrants or are likely to bear the financial costs tend to oppose it. Another factor is concealed or overt racism toward nonwhite immigrants. The larger the proportion of immigrants in the population, the more negative public attitudes toward immigrants are likely to be (Hatton 2005: 113).

In many receiving countries, including Britain, Ireland, Italy, Holland, and Spain, the foreign-born constitute 15 percent or less (in Italy and Greece, less than 10 percent) of the national population. However, foreigners are often numerous in large cities and conspicuous in small towns or rural areas (where asylum seekers and unauthorized migrants may be detained in prison-like establishments). Most people are unaware of the distinctions in status among legal immigrants, undocumented migrants, refugees, asylum seekers, and asylees, tending to conflate all foreigners (especially people of color) as unwanted, illegal intruders.

In the 1990s, for example, newly reunified Germany seethed with xenophobia, evidenced by the scapegoating of and violence against foreigners. Neo-Nazi groups were on the rise, especially in the east, where fire bombings of immigrant hostels resulted in dozens of deaths and hundreds of serious injuries. In Germany and across western Europe, both asylum seekers with genuine claims for protection and others classified as economic migrants were stereotyped as a drain on state resources and considered likely to engage in criminal activities (Tazreiter 2004: 106–7).

Politicians have long used negative attitudes toward foreigners to get elected and push anti-immigrant laws through Parliament or provincial legislatures. In Italy, for example, laws passed since the 1990s have made life increasingly difficult for asylum seekers and other migrants. The Bossi-Fini Law of 2002 authorized deportation of immigrants apprehended in international waters, a violation of the Refugee Convention. The Security Set Law of 2009 made unauthorized entry into Italy a crime with a prison sentence of six months or more. Helping an illegal immigrant enter Italy or providing housing to an illegal immigrant could be punished by up to three years in prison. A 2011 law allowed unauthorized migrants to be detained for eighteen months.

Asylum seekers and other migrants were detained in eleven privately run centers throughout Italy. Human rights groups, such as LasciateCIEntrare, Doctors for Human Rights, and the General Confederation of Labor's Immigration Department, called the centers "inhumane, ineffective and costly" (Povoledo 2013). Detention conditions were poor; mental illness, self-harm, and riots resulted. Detention does not deter unauthorized entry, however, and 440,000 "irregular immigrants" are said to live in Italy. Negative public attitudes toward them have led to hate crimes, violent attacks, and the growth of anti-immigrant political movements. Despite paying lip service to "harmonization," the European Union looked the other way. When Syrian and other refugees began arriving en masse in Europe after 2011, the European Union was unable to develop an efficient and humane asylum policy. The Dublin and Schengen Agreements seemed on the verge of collapse in 2016, as European governments re-erected barriers to free migration that had not existed for decades.

Meanwhile the EU's response to mass migration has become increasingly militarized. In 2004, Frontex, the European Agency for the Management of Operational Cooperation at the External Borders of the Member States of the European Union, was established. According to its website, among its main tasks are to "coordinate operational cooperation between Member States as regards the management of external borders; help Member States train their national border guards; assist member States in circumstances requiring increased technical and operational assistance at external borders; provide Member States with the necessary support in organising joint return operations; deploy Rapid Border Intervention Teams to Member States under urgent and exceptional pressure due to, for example, a massive influx of illegal immigrants" (Frontex 2015). Frontex operates along and beyond the EU's land and sea borders, plucking migrants from the Mediterranean – saving them from drowning, but also preventing them from seeking asylum in member states. Its officials describe their mission as humanitarian and life-saving, but a researcher described Frontex as a "thin blue line of police guarding the frontier of inequality" (Franko 2014).

In late 2014, Frontex took over an Italian operation to rescue Syrian and other migrants crammed onto rickety boats crossing the Mediterranean from the Mideast or North Africa. Smugglers were abandoning the boats far from shore, in the certainty that Frontex would pick up the migrants and deliver them to Italian ports. Over the next year, as the numbers of smuggled refugees swelled to the hundreds of thousands, they overwhelmed Frontex and national agencies in countries from Greece to Sweden. Migration to Europe became chaotic, part of the worst refugee crisis on the continent since 1945–48. In early 2016, NATO announced that it would patrol the Mediterranean to stop people smugglers, but it was unclear what would happen to the refugees the smugglers were transporting.

A reporter observed, "While all refugees are migrants, not all migrants are refugees. An increasing number are fleeing poverty rather than persecution." An official of the International Organization of Migration pointed out, "There are no other ways to enter. There's no common European policy on labour migration. The only way you have to migrate is to request asylum. . . . Legal travel from most of these countries is impossible. Many can't get the visas or documents, or even reach an airport. Asylum seekers can't apply for safe haven from within their own country – and economic refugees won't be able to obtain the required paperwork. So they turn to smugglers – at rates of $1,500–$3,500 per person" (quoted by Simmie 2014).

During 2014–15, more than one million migrants tried to cross the Mediterranean to enter Europe through Italy, Spain, and Greece.

A scholar sums up the problem: "There's no coordinated European system for managing the dispersal of migrants. So the migrants take dispersal into their own hands" (Witte 2014).

Some of the migrants fleeing Syria, Eritrea, and other countries engulfed in civil conflict made their way to the northern French city of Calais. Apparently they saw it as the gateway to Britain, just across the channel. At the end of 2015, about six thousand migrants were camping in squalid sites, called jungles, in and around the city; their numbers had multiplied six times since the beginning of 2014. The local authorities tried to discourage them by providing no services, water, sanitation facilities, food, or housing, but the desperate migrants, including parents with young children, kept arriving. Volunteers served them one meal a day near new camps that appeared as soon as the authorities closed the old ones.

Smugglers offered to take the desperate migrants to Britain for $1,200 to $4,000. Those without money tried to hitch rides on the undercarriages of trucks or buses or on ferries or trains. An unknown number of migrants died in transit across the channel during 2014–15. In early 2016, French authorities tried to tear down most of the tents in the Calais jungle and persuade their inhabitants to move into nearby containers, which the migrants saw as makeshift prisons. Meanwhile some three thousand Syrians, Afghans, and Iraqis had arrived at another camp, in Dunkirk, where the conditions were even worse. French and British officials traded accusations about which country was responsible for the situation, but nobody came up with a solution beyond making life for the migrants "as uncomfortable as possible" (Witte 2014). And so they waited for their opportunity to sneak into Britain, which had little or nothing to offer them during an era of self-imposed austerity.

Receiving countries usually have an underground of undocumented migrants and refused asylum seekers. In Britain, Germany, and France, it is said to consist of two hundred thousand to four hundred thousand people. In countries associated with the Organization for Economic Co-operation and Development, between 50 and 70 percent of asylum seekers receive no protected status but remain anyway, often with limited or no access to social services (Borjas and Crisp 2005: 74).

Since the late 1990s, asylum seekers in EU countries have been prevented from working for pay for varying periods while awaiting a decision on their claim, and refused asylum seekers can only work illegally. Unlike the United States, EU member states do give asylum seekers social and economic support and provide government-funded lawyers to help them make their claim (Frelick and Jacek 2013). Even so, migrants, who face pervasive discrimination, are often integrated into the labor market in dead-end, usually temporary, jobs, and are paid substandard wages for dangerous, unskilled, or soul-destroying work.

Borjas and Crisp point out that legal, moral, and practical constraints ensure that only a few refused asylum seekers are returned to their home country. Expanding deportation of unsuccessful claimants does not make asylum systems more effective (71). But the system does function in a perverse fashion: States consistently respond to increased numbers of asylum seekers through draconian strategies of prevention, deterrence, restriction, and management. They try to prevent asylum seekers from entering their territory in the first place; to deter them from claiming asylum by making procedures complicated, time consuming, and expensive; to limit their stay through restrictions and deportation; and to manage their movement inside the national territory through dispersal, detention, or registration. Abuse and neglect could be added to this list. These strategies may have limited the number of applications for asylum, but they have not reduced the number of people fleeing persecution. They keep arriving and staying, with or without authorization, because the conditions that led them to flee persist or worsen.

"While it may be in the short-term interests of Western governments to reduce the number of asylum seekers they receive, their actions can have hidden costs both for other actors and, in the long term, for themselves. . . . [P]olicies that deflect or contain refugees can generate regional instability or corrode international norms on refugee protection by creating great inequalities in the burdens between states," Borjas and Crisp observe (87). Their opinion was confirmed by the gigantic refugee crisis of 2015, when European governments struggled to agree on how to share the burden. Furthermore, repressive policies do not work: They do not produce the desired outcome of asylum seekers returning in short order to their own countries. Instead, the system consumes financial resources that could be used for more constructive purposes and contributes to the perpetuation of a destitute underclass in the host country.

Asylum Laws in France and Germany

Asylum seekers who manage to arrive in Britain, France, other European countries, or the United States often receive a cold welcome. Detention and deportation are important features of asylum policy and practice in all the major receiving countries. In France, for example, a 1945 law limited detention of foreigners to the time necessary to arrange for their departure: forty-eight hours, renewable for five days and renewable again for urgent reasons. This law may have been part of a reaction to the notorious internment and transit camps of the World War II Vichy regime, through which hundreds of thousands of Jews and other enemies of the Nazis were funneled on their way to Auschwitz. Over time and under the pressure of thousands of refugee arrivals, the time allowed for detention in France has increased to forty-five days, the period thought to be necessary to issue travel documents for expulsion. Under the law, if expulsion is impossible, detainees must be released unless they have resisted deportation.

French detention centers offer a paradoxical combination of repression and protection. Independent lawyers from five human rights organizations provide legal advice inside the centers. They see thirty-five to forty clients per day. Private maintenance contractors, medical doctors, and social workers are also on site. According to a French researcher, 60 percent of detainees are released, and many deportation orders are never carried out. But some destitute refused asylum seekers, without identification or other documents, are repeatedly arrested and may go in and out of detention indefinitely (Fischer 2014).

The German asylum system and, more generally, its immigration policies are complex, because by law migration is predominantly a state, not a national, matter. As a result detention, assistance, employment, and adjudication policies vary considerably across the country. In addition, German and EU courts have ruled against some state policies, putting the overall system in flux at a time when hundreds of thousands of migrants seek refuge in Germany each year.

The overall trend since 2008 has been to detain fewer migrants. "In 2013," the Global Detention Project reported, "Germany placed 4,812 people in immigration detention, roughly half the number detained in 2008." They were kept in state prisons as well as dedicated detention centers, although recent court rulings said that prisons were not appropriate places to hold them. According to the director of the German National Agency for the Prevention of Torture, "There are important discussions going on right now in Germany about whether we should be detaining immigrants at all" (quoted by Global Detention Project 2014). It remains to be seen if Germany is pioneering a new, more humane trend in treatment of migrants, or if it will reverse its policies under xenophobic political pressures, as Australia, Canada, and other receiving countries have done in recent years. As Germany struggled to cope with the arrival of almost one million refugees in 2015, it was unclear what direction the country would take.

Attempts at Reform

At least one European government recognized the wastefulness and ineffectuality of punitive asylum policies. In 2007, the Netherlands proclaimed an amnesty for more than 25,000 asylum seekers who had applied for refuge before April 2001 and had stayed in the country while awaiting a decision or after being rejected. Under the previous government, 11,000 asylum seekers had been rejected or deported, and 4,200 had been expelled by force. New arrivals had been kept in "departure centers" while their applications were considered, under the obvious assumption that they would be denied (Associated Press 2007). The change "marked an easing of policy in a country which has imposed some of Europe's toughest migration and integration laws" (*Sydney Morning Herald* 2007: 1).

Seven years later, however, the Dutch government still was making life difficult for unauthorized migrants, including refused asylum seekers. The latter were given twenty-eight days to leave the country with help from the International Organization of Migration. In 2014, the central government announced that it would detain and deport rejected asylum seekers who refused to leave "voluntarily." Those who were not detained would be denied the social services that make the Netherlands a good place to live. A 2014 report by the commissioner for human rights of the Council of Europe noted that "an unidentified number of irregular migrants end up in destitution on the streets or in camps, as they do not manage to access existing emergency shelters" (Muižnieks 2014: 4). He pointed out that everyone, whether in the country legally or not, has the right to a decent standard of living.

Mayors of major Dutch cities protested the government's policy change, saying they did not want homeless, destitute people wandering their streets. The mayor of Amsterdam spoke out in favor of giving them asylum. Volunteers tried to help them by providing temporary shelter, food, and medical attention. In Amsterdam, for example, a Catholic Worker house sheltered twenty to twenty-eight refused asylum seekers who could not or would not leave Holland for various reasons, from chronic or terminal illness to fear of torture or persecution in their home country.

Detention was still routine in 2014 for asylum-seeking families with children who arrived at Schiphol Airport in Amsterdam or were scheduled to be deported.[1] Seventy unaccompanied minors and 352 children in families were detained at Schiphol for up to fourteen days in 2012. A report by the No Child in Detention Coalition said that even short-term detention causes lasting trauma in children and violates the Convention on the Rights of the Child. Schiphol Application Center and Rotterdam Detention Center, the two main places where children were held, were prison-like facilities that the coalition considered unsuitable for children. A thirteen-year-old boy, who had spent seven days in detention with his mother and younger sister nine months earlier, described his experience: "As I passed through the first door, more appeared. There were so many doors. We were not allowed to leave. All we could do was sit there. I had to think a lot. It was a completely closed-off situation. The police had to check everything, even our clothes. They have examined every inch of my body. . . . I was devastated. What have I done? This is terrible. All those doors made me very angry. I wanted to destroy them" (Goeman and van Os 2014: 13).

The Netherlands' asylum system looks relatively humane on paper. Asylum seekers are provided with accommodation in more than fifty reception centers, and they receive legal advice, medical care, and modest financial assistance while they wait for their cases to be decided. The reception center I visited in 2014 was spartan but clean. Residents may leave the premises to work part-time for six months. The Council of Europe's human rights commissioner noted that some refused asylum seekers who could not be deported because of factors beyond their control had been given residence permits, including a so-called Children's Pardon; conditions for such permits were "very restrictive," however (Muižnieks 2014).

Migrants' advocates say that adjudicators make many mistakes, rushing asylum seekers through the initial decision-making procedure and denying asylum to people who deserve it. Although immigration detention is supposed to be limited, in practice it may be indefinite, the advocates claim. Among the problems for detainees are isolation, lack of programmed activities, and limited access to health care. A project manager from the social-service group Kerk in Actie explained in a report to the Protestant Church of the Netherlands:

> The Dutch government does not give support, with the exception of emergency medical care, to certain categories of asylum seekers staying legally in the Netherlands. As a result, large numbers of asylum seekers have to survive in the street without receiving any financial or social assistance from the government. Elderly people and people who are seriously ill are, unfortunately, not excluded from these extremely harsh policies. The three most important categories of asylum seekers that have become the victims of these policies are asylum seekers who are rejected in a reception center through an accelerated asylum procedure, asylum seekers who make a repeated request for asylum and those who have made an application for a residence permit on medical grounds. (Werkman 2013)

On a visit to the Netherlands in late 2014, I met asylum seekers who
had been waiting for years for decisions, prevented from working by
changing policies, or unable to find work and pay their bills. Some
were traumatized by torture and persecution in their home countries
and could not integrate into Dutch society.

An asylee from Sierra Leone, an articulate and intelligent man
apparently fluent in Dutch, said he had just moved from Amsterdam
to a town in southern Holland and had no money to pay rent. Waiting for four weeks to receive government assistance, he had looked
for work without success. He had studied for a diploma in welding
but was forced to stop his training because of a change in the asylum laws. Alone in the Netherlands for thirteen years, he did not
feel he had a future there and was thinking of leaving the country,
but he could not return to Sierra Leone. It was unclear where else
he could go legally.

When he arrived in the Netherlands, he said, every city was obliged
to help asylum seekers for one year. That assistance had long since run
out for him. A volunteer social worker at the Dutch Refugee Council
suggested that he go to a food bank. He wondered if it would help
if he changed his name, so that when he applied for jobs by e-mail,
the employer would not be able to tell that he was foreign. The social
worker was sympathetic but could not give him financial help, only
referrals to other agencies. He left even more disheartened than when
he arrived. Like some other asylees and asylum seekers I met in the
Netherlands, he seemed lost, one of a hundred thousand in the destitution underground.

Yet a Dutch government official I interviewed resignedly commented that an amnesty for refused asylum seekers and undocumented migrants is inevitable about once a decade. The Netherlands,
like other receiving countries, needs an inflow of cheap, disposable
labor to do its undesirable jobs and take care of its aging population.

The stakes for refused asylum seekers are very high: poverty and
discrimination in the receiving country versus persecution, torture,
and death at home. In 2014 Amnesty International said the Dutch
government was violating the principle of non-refoulement by forcibly returning refused Somali asylum seekers to parts of Somalia

under the control of al-Shabaab, a terror organization linked to al Qaeda. Amnesty added that the United Kingdom, Denmark, Norway, and Sweden had tried to do the same thing (Amnesty International 2014b).

Some observers consider Sweden to have the most enlightened asylum system in Europe. The government generally takes "a social service approach" to the treatment of asylum seekers, keeping them for a strictly limited time in administrative detention or reception centers that are not prisons or placing them under supervision without incarceration (Global Detention Project 2009). Red Cross volunteers visit the detention centers weekly. "Sweden received a favorable review of its detention infrastructure, which has led to its characterization as a European role model. . . . There were no allegations of abuse and . . . detention center staff were sufficient in number and skills. . . . Material conditions . . . were of a very high standard," the European Committee for the Prevention of Torture and Inhuman or Degrading Treatment or Punishment reported in 2009 (Global Detention Project 2009).

Nevertheless, researchers reported that even in Sweden, with only 235 migrants in detention for a maximum of twelve months, detainees felt unable to get attention to their practical needs and resolve their legal cases (Puthoopparambil et al. 2013). Confinement led inexorably to depression. Detainees claimed that they had no access to mental health care. They called detention "a prison with extra flavors," worse than prison because they had no idea how long they would remain inside or what the outcome of their case would be.

Yet tens of thousands of Syrians, Iraqis, Somalis, Serbians, and others have gained asylum in Sweden in recent years. In 2014, more than 28,000 asylum claims were granted out of 48,983 applications, a very high approval rate of 59 percent.[2] Even so, since 2014 a far-right, anti-immigrant political party has been putting pressure on the government to cut immigration into the country. Although the government admitted more than 160,000 Syrian and other refugees in 2015, it eventually decided to make their entry more difficult. Local communities tried to help the refugees, but strains increased on Sweden's social welfare system and its culture of hospitality.

Ironically, in view of the European obsession with limiting entry, none of the top ten refugee destinations in 2015 was in Europe. The major receiving countries, several of which had not signed the Refugee Convention, were Turkey, Pakistan, Lebanon, Iran, Ethiopia, Jordan, Kenya, Chad, Uganda, and China. They were hosting, willingly or not, the victims of brutal civil conflicts, from Syria to Somalia and beyond.

During the Iraq War, which started in 2003, millions of Iraqis fled, but most went to neighboring or nearby countries such as Jordan, Syria, and Egypt; relatively few – tens of thousands – managed to arrive in Western countries with the help of the UN High Commissioner for Refugees. Iraqis who tried to enter the European Union via Greece or Turkey found themselves stuck in a revolving door. According to a 2008 Human Rights Watch report, Iraqis who entered Greece "can't move onward because EU asylum law . . . normally requires asylum seekers to lodge their claims for protection in the first EU country in which they set foot and they also can't move back home because of fear of war and persecution" (Human Rights Watch 2008).

Greece unwillingly received and detained migrants while its economy foundered. In a series of hunger strikes from 2008 to 2011, asylum seekers from Afghanistan and Iran demanded recognition of their claims. Sometimes they sewed their lips shut as part of their protest. An Iranian asylum seeker explained the reasons for such extreme actions in "a nightmarish description of how, as he had waited for his asylum claim to be examined, Greece became a 'prison' shaped by bureaucracy, in which he had no services, no rights and no dignity." He felt "overwhelming helplessness and frustration" (Cabot 2014: 197).

The European Court of Human Rights ruled in 2011 that Belgium had violated the European Convention on Human Rights by sending asylum seekers to Greece, where they were in danger of inhuman or degrading treatment. Two years later, Italy still returned asylum seekers to Greece without reviewing their claims (Washington College of Law 2013: 63). In a 2014 report on Greek detention conditions, the Council of Europe's Committee for the Prevention of Torture and Inhuman or Degrading Treatment or Punishment (CPT) described "totally unacceptable conditions in which irregular migrants are held in police establishments all over the country for prolonged periods. . . . For example, in one [police] station, two or more women were held for months in a dark, mouldy and dilapidated basement cell of a mere 5m² with no access to outdoor exercise or hygiene products" (Council of Europe 2014).

In February 2015, the newly elected Greek government promised to close immigration detention centers and replace them with "open reception centers with better facilities" (Reuters 2015). But with the influx of hundreds of thousands of Syrian and other refugees during 2015, the Greek government's capacity to receive and care for them was overwhelmed.

The Syrian Refugee Crisis Explodes

In 2011, a huge crisis erupted in Syria.[3] By 2014, the vicious civil war had led to the flight of 9–10 million Syrians – almost half the country's population – from their homes. Some 6 million were internally displaced, while more than 3 million fled to the neighboring countries of Turkey, Lebanon, Jordan, and Iraq, which were ill equipped to help them. Almost one million Syrians were seeking asylum in the European Union by the end of 2015. EU member states pledged to resettle tens of thousands but could not agree on a quota system to share the burden. Together Germany and Sweden accepted about two-thirds of the Syrian asylum seekers in Europe in 2015.

The UN High Commissioner for Refugees (UNHCR) called the European response to his call for 130,000 resettlement spots "tepid," pointing to the "enormous challenge" taken on by Syria's neighbors, some of which had not signed the Refugee Convention (quoted by Migration Policy Centre 2014). Lebanon was overwhelmed by more than a million Syrians, constituting more than 25 percent of the country's entire population. The UNHCR was hard pressed to serve the 4,200 refugees arriving in Lebanon *each day*. The Turkish government also struggled to cope with more than one million Syrians, especially Kurds who fled to Turkey during Islamic State assaults on border towns and villages in late 2014. Jordan, Iraq, and Egypt took in hundreds of thousands of Syrians as well.

In Canada, the government had accepted two hundred Syrians by the end of 2014, in stark contrast to the thousands of refugees it had welcomed in the past. Australia offered to take five hundred Syrian refugees, but it was reported in March 2014 that the Department of Immigration had tried to persuade two out of five Syrians detained on the island of Manus to return to Syria, despite the International Organization of Migration's refusal to repatriate any Syrians (Laughland 2014a). The director of Human Rights Watch Australia remarked, "If Australia is putting pressure on Syrian citizens to return, this is in violation of international law and the principle of nonrefoulement" (quoted by Laughland 2014a).

The United States accepted only 350 Syrian refugees for resettlement in 2014, but by the end of the year it was considering nine thousand applications for admission. Anne Richard, the assistant secretary of state for population, refugees, and migration, told an interviewer that her office had received ten thousand requests from Syrians for resettlement via the UNHCR as of December 15, 2014, and they were coming in at the rate of 1,000 to 1,500 per month (Slavin 2014). During past refugee crises, the United States and other major receiving countries had followed a similar pattern of accepting very few refugees until public pressure forced them to open their doors a little wider.

The United States is relatively generous in accepting refugees, with an annual admission ceiling of 70,000 in recent years – as many as the other major receiving countries put together. In 2015 President Obama announced that he would raise the ceiling to 85,000, so that 15,000 Syrian and other refugees could enter. It would probably take eighteen months to two years for the Syrians to go through the government's rigorous vetting procedure, however.

The United Kingdom routinely accepts about 750 refugees under its Gateway Protection Programme each year. The deputy prime minister proudly told Parliament in January 2014 that Britain had accepted 1,500 Syrian refugees (out of more than two million) during 2013. In 2015, after an international outcry pressured the United States, Canada, and several other receiving countries to promise to take in tens of thousands of Syrians, Britain announced that it would accept 20,000 from Middle Eastern camps by 2020, a small fraction of the number already admitted by Germany and Sweden (Mason 2015). Under continuing pressure from international public opinion, the United Kingdom and other receiving countries took small steps to admit more refugees, especially children, but progress toward comprehensive immigration policy reform was glacially slow.

The Roma: Eternal Refugees

Although Syrian refugees attracted increasing attention from 2011 on, other groups were also continuing to seek refuge from persecution. Western countries had difficulty dealing with the reality of racist violence and discrimination against Romani who had lived in their societies for centuries.[4] According to Amnesty International, 10–12 million Roma live in Europe, from France to the Czech Republic and Greece. Ninety percent live in poverty, and governments do little or nothing to help them (Amnesty International 2014a).

In recent years, Amnesty International has reported a "marked rise in the frequency of anti-Roma violence in Europe. . . . Law enforcement agencies are failing to prevent attacks and ensure that hate motives are properly investigated" (Amnesty International 2014a: 30). Racism among the police, who are supposed to protect the Roma, goes unaddressed. The Roma are often blamed for the persecution they suffer; many locals describe them as antisocial, thieves, and unwelcome. As a result, thousands have fled their longtime homes in eastern Europe, only to encounter persecution, eviction, and discrimination in Western countries. The likelihood of their gaining asylum is almost nonexistent, because the countries they fled are considered "free" and "safe."

In 2012, Amnesty International reported that 130,000 to 170,000 Roma (0.2 percent of the national population) were living in Italy. Some had fled violence in Romania and the former Yugoslavia, while about 50 percent were Italian citizens. Most lived in squalid camps on the outskirts of urban areas until the land became desirable and they were evicted (Amnesty International 2012b: 5). Human rights violations against Roma in Italy and elsewhere included violent attacks and discrimination in housing, education, health care, and employment.

After Bulgaria and Romania were admitted to the EU in 2007, European and British politicians and the tabloid media reacted by stoking fears of a gypsy "invasion," citing their alleged involvement in human trafficking and organized crime. In 2008, the Italian government invoked "Nomad Emergency" measures. Municipal prefects were given special powers, and a state of emergency was declared. Although the government denied that these measures were aimed at Roma, their camps were invaded, their freedom of movement abridged, and their right to work violated. The regulations allowed officials to summarily evict Roma from their camps without providing alternative housing. Belongings were often destroyed. Children had to find new schools, and adults lost their jobs. Evictions took place without warning, but the Roma had no legal recourse. They were transferred to other camps, where they had to sign a statement in which they agreed to follow special restrictive rules. The Italian Council of State rescinded the emergency regulations in 2011. Amnesty International commented, "Although the Nomad Emergency . . . has been annulled . . . most of its legal and practical consequences persist" (2012b: 9).

The German government and politicians have shown increasing reluctance to give asylum to Roma arriving from Serbia, Macedonia, and Bosnia-Herzegovina. One-quarter of asylum requests in 2013 came from those three countries, which Germany, France, Belgium, Luxembourg, Austria, and Switzerland consider safe. Only 142 of 22,000 Western Balkan asylum seekers gained refuge in Germany (Grassler 2014).

During the presidency of Nicolas Sarkozy (2007–12), the French government carried on an intensive campaign to evict and expel Roma, both foreigners and citizens. It is estimated that about twenty thousand Roma who fled from Bulgaria and Romania now live in France, most in camps (Willsher 2014). In 2009, France deported nearly ten thousand Roma. Thirteen Roma who had been living there for a decade sought sanctuary in a Catholic church in 2010 but were ejected on the order of a priest. Roma had to go all the way to Canada to find refuge, and even there authorities seemed reluctant to admit them.

Beyond Europe

Countries outside Europe have imitated the EU's exclusionary policies. In 2012 Israel's prime minister said "illegal infiltrators" were "flooding the country" and "threatened the security and identity of the Jewish state" (quoted by Kay and Kain 2014). A commentator remarked, "Following years of systematic incitement against refugees by Israel government officials, the Israeli public now largely sees refugees as illegal migrants, undeserving of sympathy" (Tsurkov 2012).

Israel's Parliament then passed a draconian amendment to the 1954 Prevention of Infiltration Law, authorizing detention of asylum seekers for up to three years without trial. The law originally had aimed at preventing entry of armed Arab attackers, but the new provisions designated African asylum seekers as infiltrators. Other antimigrant measures included construction of a high-tech fence to keep asylum seekers from crossing the Egyptian border, at a cost of $360 million; construction of a large open-air detention facility for thousands of asylum seekers, at a cost of about $300 million; and enforcement of rules prohibiting employers from hiring asylum seekers. All government ministries would have their budgets cut by 2 percent to pay for these measures.

In September 2013, the Israeli Supreme Court ruled that the 2012 law was unconstitutional and violated Israel's commitments under international law.[5] Parliament passed a new law mandating detention of infiltrators for one year in an "open" facility in the desert that would hold 3,300 undocumented migrants. The establishment was surrounded by razor-wire fencing and locked at night. Detainees were not allowed to work. This law was also challenged in court.

In 2011, more than seventeen thousand asylum seekers, predominantly Muslims and Christians from Eritrea and Sudan, had crossed the Egyptian border into Israel. After the construction of the border fence, only thirty-six Africans managed to get through. The problem for the Israeli government was how to get rid of sixty thousand unauthorized African migrants already living in the country. Some had resided there for years, setting up small businesses or completing school. The vast majority had not applied for refugee status because almost nobody could obtain it. Out of some four thousand applications, only three had been processed and approved in recent years (Fein 2013). The government did defer deportation in a few cases, but that left migrants in a precarious position, lacking work permits, health care, and welfare benefits.

In September 2014, the Israeli Supreme Court ruled that the Holot Detention Center in the Negev Desert had to close within ninety days. Sudanese and Eritreans had been detained there indefinitely, until they would agree to leave Israel "voluntarily." It was unclear where they would go, since they were in danger of imprisonment or disappearance if they returned to their home country. The *Washington Post* reported:

> Adda Ahmed, who runs a computer repair shop, wondered why Africans are treated so differently from the legal foreign workers in Israel – the Filipinos who care for the elderly, the Thais who pick citrus, the Chinese who erect skyscrapers. "Africans do all the jobs that the Israelis don't want to do," Ahmed said. "Why not let us stay, at least for a while longer?" But the non-African immigrants come with legal work permits and employment contracts. They stay in Israel for a set period of time and then go home. Ahmed has no home to return to. A picture of his village in Darfur hangs on the wall of his shop. But no one lives there anymore. It was one of the more than 3,000 villages damaged or destroyed in fighting between government forces and rebel groups. (Booth and Eglash 2013)

For a few years, South Africa became the world's number one receiving country, as Zimbabweans and others fled repressive regimes on the continent. Like Israel, South Africa has framed migration as a security threat, creating the impression that detainees' legal claims lack legitimacy and encouraging immigration officials to deny detainees their rights to appeal and review (Amit 2013: 33). Requests for asylum are often ignored, and asylum seekers are detained as "illegal" foreigners, contravening South Africa's Refugees Act. Hundreds of asylum seekers may be held indefinitely, in defiance of a 120-day

limit on detention. Illegal deportation and refoulement are also taking place.

Halfway across the world, in Indonesia, the law allows up to
ten years' immigration detention without judicial review, and the
Indonesian government denies migrant children and their families
opportunities to obtain legal status or asylum (Farmer 2013: 15).
Like seventeen other Asian countries, Indonesia has not signed the
Refugee Convention or the 1966 Protocol, although 30 percent of the
global refugee population is in Asia. Human smugglers and traffickers use Indonesia and other nonsignatory countries as way stations.
The region is generally deficient in coherent migration policies (Abass
and Ippolito 2014).

The Bangkok Declaration on Irregular Migration of 1999 did not
mention refugees, human rights, or non-refoulement; security and
management were its main concerns. The Association of Southeast
Asian Nations (ASEAN) Human Rights Declaration of 2007 did not
include refugees and displaced persons in its list of vulnerable and
marginalized people. Nor did it mention refoulement. The ASEAN
Charter of 2008 did not mention a regional strategy to share responsibility for asylum seekers and ongoing refugee situations (Abass and
Ippolito 2014: 327).

Migrant workers, who are seen as cheap, exploitable labor, are
criminalized, and large numbers of "irregular migrants" in Asia are
actually refugees from civil conflicts in Afghanistan, Iran, Sri Lanka,
and other countries. Even countries that have an asylum system do
little to accommodate asylum seekers. For example, in 2012 South
Korea recognized 299 asylees out of 4,748 asylum seekers. Humanitarian leave to remain was granted to a further 151 individuals. Asylum
seekers awaiting decisions were not allowed to work.

Hundreds of thousands of Asian refugees languish in camps,
sometimes for decades, waiting for the conflict at home to end, never
becoming citizens or even legal residents of the receiving country. A
few lawyers' associations and advocacy groups try to help refugees
and work for immigration reform, but for most refugees in Asia the
outlook is grim.

Concentrated in the poorest nations, most people who flee persecution are internally displaced, never leaving their own country (Human Rights Watch 2008: 42). That is as far as they can afford to go. Only asylum seekers with sufficient resources to pay thousands of dollars in smuggling fees or plane fares manage to reach Europe, Britain, the United States, or Australia. First World nightmares of desperate millions invading from Bangladesh as it sinks under the waves or from North Africa as the desert encroaches are politically potent but unlikely. The UNHCR estimated 38.2 million internally displaced people in the world at the end of 2014 – almost twice the number of refugees (United Nations High Commissioner for Refugees 2015). Antonio Guterres, the High Commissioner for Refugees, pointed out: "We need to put things in perspective. Eighty-six percent of the world's refugees live in the developing world, and this is the highest percentage since the beginning of this century. . . . [W]e see a growing trend for refugees to stay in the developing world. To say that Europe is under overwhelming pressure is an exaggeration" (quoted by Sherwood 2014).

It is true that millions of desperate people, including economic refugees, political refugees, and asylum seekers, set out for richer countries every year, smuggled or stowed away in boats or trucks or on foot. They are usually intercepted, although an unknown number eventually arrive or die in the attempt to escape untenable situations at home. Many are detained for short or long periods and then deported. Only a relative few apply for asylum. According to the UNHCR, 1.66 million applications for asylum were received in 157 countries in 2014, a 54 percent increase over 2013. More than half of all refugees were children. Asylum seekers' and refugees' top countries of origin were Syria, Afghanistan, and Somalia; they accounted for 53 percent of all refugees. Sudan, South Sudan, and Democratic Republic of Congo followed. These numbers reflected the continuing high level of civil conflict in many developing countries.

Under these circumstances, desperate migrants look beyond Europe, to Australia, Canada, the United Kingdom, or the United States, the self-described "nation of immigrants," for refuge. If they manage to arrive at the golden door of Emma Lazarus's poem, what they find there might or might not be what they had hoped for.

10 The Golden Door Ajar

US Asylum Policy

Give me your tired, your poor, / Your huddled
masses yearning to breathe free

— Emma Lazarus, "The New Colossus," 1883

The DRO strategic plan sets in motion a cohesive
enforcement program with a ten-year time horizon
that will build the capacity to "remove all removable
aliens," eliminate the backlog of unexecuted final
order removal cases, and realize its vision.

— US Bureau of Immigration and Customs Enforcement,
"Endgame: Office of Detention and Removal Strategic Plan,
2003–2012"

Like Canada and Australia, the United States has used immigration policy to build the nation. Like the United Kingdom and
European countries, the United States also has sought to manage the
kinds and numbers of people who could enter the country. For most
of the nineteenth century, local jurisdictions regulated entry into the
United States. Most immigrants arrived at major ports, and port com-
missioners decided how to handle them (Dow 2004: 6). Only at the
end of that century did the federal government create administrative
structures to carry out immigration policies.

Ellis Island, the government's reception center in New York for
immigrants from Europe, opened in 1892, and its detention facilities
were notoriously bad. Between 1892 and 1930, some three thousand
detainees committed suicide there. From 1930 until it closed in 1954,
it became what its official history calls "a grim detention center."
In 1953 a Supreme Court justice described it as an "island prison"

197

(quoted by Dow 2004: 6). After Ellis Island closed, the Immigration and Naturalization Service abandoned detention in most cases until the 1980s. During that period, undocumented immigrants, including asylum seekers, were usually paroled pending administrative proceedings.

Since the 1880s, US immigration laws have included quotas and prohibitions to prevent certain kinds of people, whether Chinese or Mexicans, from entering or staying in the United States. Like other receiving countries, the United States increasingly resorted to detaining asylum seekers and unauthorized migrants after the end of the Cold War. The Illegal Immigration Reform and Immigrant Responsibility Act (IIRIRA) of 1996 made it even more difficult to gain asylum in the United States. "Congress barred asylum for most persons who did not apply for it within a year of entering the United States. It also created a new system of 'expedited removal,' under which airport immigration inspectors (and, later, land border officials) could summarily deport, without hearings, many foreign nationals who arrived in the United States without valid passports or visas" (Kenney and Schrag 2008: 3). Under the 1996 law, an asylum seeker placed in expedited removal may gain "relief from removal" if he or she establishes a credible fear of persecution in the home country. But around 60 percent of asylum seekers in the United States never gain asylum (United States Department of Justice 2014).[1]

The Horrors of Detention

Asylum seekers face the prospect of arrest and detention as soon as they set foot in the United States. Threatened by gangs in the Haitian slum where he had his church, eighty-one-year-old Rev. Joseph Dantica fled to the United States in October 2004, while United Nations forces were occupying Haiti (Danticat 2007). Although he had a valid multiple-entry visa and passport, Rev. Dantica asked for asylum at Miami Airport. He was immediately arrested, detained, and placed in expedited removal proceedings. Author Edwidge Danticat tried to gain access to her uncle at the airport, but officials told her she could not see him. Apparently the reason for Rev. Dantica's detention was an administrative mix-up, but it took his niece many months to find that out, and by then it was too late.

After an uncomfortable night on a cement bed at the airport, Rev. Dantica was taken to Krome along with his son, who was handcuffed. The elderly, chronically ill man spent the weekend in detention without his medications, which officials had taken from him. During an immigration interview at Krome the following Monday, Rev. Dantica had a seizure and started vomiting violently. He was taken to the clinic at Krome, and the immigration interview was canceled. Sometime later he was transferred, in shackles, to a hospital.

Rev. Dantica did not see a doctor until twenty-four hours after his arrival at the hospital emergency room. He died in the hospital after two days' acute illness. The authorities at Krome denied Edwidge Danticat access to her uncle there, even after he died. An autopsy determined that he had suffered from acute and chronic pancreatitis, "for which he was never screened, tested, diagnosed or treated while he was at Jackson Memorial Hospital," his niece later wrote.

At least 140 other stories could be told about immigration detainees, including asylum seekers like Rev. Dantica, who have died in custody since 2003 (United States Department of Homeland Security 2014). This one may not be the worst. Surely Jason Ng's months-long ordeal, recounted in chapter 1, was more atrocious, because the abuse, neglect, and cruelty he suffered and the pain he endured went on so much longer.

These horror stories highlight the punitive nature of immigration detention in the United States for asylum seekers and other migrants. Detention centers, jails, and prisons are built and run according to a correctional model, in defiance of the Refugee Convention. It could be said that immigration detainees are treated even worse than criminals, since many have not been charged with a crime, do not understand why they are detained, and have no idea how long they will be held or what will happen to them after detention ends. Frequent transfers to facilities far from families or lawyers, lack of medical attention or treatment for chronic or serious conditions, isolation from fellow lan-

guage speakers, and lack of recreation or organized activities make
detention a hellish experience, especially for traumatized survivors
of torture, war, or civil conflict.

It is easy to conclude that the purposes of detention include coerc-
ing asylum seekers into abandoning their claim and returning to their
home country, as well as sending a warning to anyone thinking of seeking asylum in the United States. As long ago as 1981, attorney general
William French Smith said, "Detention of aliens seeking asylum was
necessary to discourage people like the Haitians from setting sail in
the first place" (quoted by Dow 2004: 7). In mid-2014, the president
and the secretary of homeland security announced that they would
deport children and families back to Central America as quickly as
possible, without considering any asylum claims, to deter thousands
more from fleeing to the United States (Hylton 2015).

Especially since the September 11, 2001, attacks, the United States
has vastly expanded detention and deportation for more and more
migrants. By law, up to 34,000 migrants may be detained every day
in some 250 facilities, many run by private corporations, around
the country. The yearly number of detainees now surpasses 300,000,
the vast majority of whom are undocumented migrants, overstayers,
and foreign-born criminals who have served their sentences and are
awaiting deportation. In 2012, 68,795 people applied for asylum,
of whom 24,505 were detained (Hamilton 2014). The federal budget for detention and deportation has reached $2.8 billion per year.
Although much cheaper alternatives, including electronic monitoring,
are available, the federal government pays public and private jails and
prisons an average of $160 per head per day to hold migrants while
their cases are being decided. Migrants may be detained for months
or even years because of huge court backlogs. As of December 2015,
more than 400,000 cases were pending in immigration courts, with
an average wait time of 659 days (Transactional Records Access Clearinghouse 2015).

Private prison corporations and localities benefit financially from
immigration detention. York County, Pennsylvania, was able to reduce
its local property tax as a result of receiving federal payments for
detaining undocumented migrants and asylum seekers. A county

jail superintendent in New Hampshire explained, "I simply have an opportunity to make use of available beds that exist within my facility to reduce the burden on my local taxpayers by creating a revenue to offset the operating expenses" (quoted by Dow 2004: 229). In addition, the "prison industrial complex" of private prisons and detention centers, which hold both domestic and foreign inmates, has become a major industry in the United States. Between 2005 and 2008, six large privately run immigration detention centers were constructed, and ICE contracted private companies to build or expand at least ten detention facilities after 2009 (Rubinstein 2012: 80).

Part of the federal border security budget (which totaled almost $18 billion in 2013, and almost $187 billion since 1986) went to construct, repurpose, or expand immigration detention facilities (Meissner et al. 2013). For example, the South Texas Detention Facility, a complex of giant tent-like, windowless structures resembling a postmodern concentration camp, was built in 2005 in a remote part of Texas. Run by the private GEO Group, it holds almost two thousand detainees, including asylum seekers. Most of the inmates there are detained because of immigration offenses, such as unauthorized reentry.

Many immigration offenses, such as being in the United States without a visa or valid passport, are not classified as crimes under federal law.[2] ACLU researchers point out that detained immigrants and asylum seekers are "civil detainees held pursuant to civil immigration laws," and hence are covered by the Fifth Amendment to the Constitution, which protects any person in US custody "from conditions that amount to punishment without due process of law" (Patel and Jawetz 2007: 2). For these reasons, those accused of such offenses, as well as those in expedited removal proceedings, should be detained apart from criminals.

However, by calling imprisonment "administrative detention," the government denies immigration detainees basic constitutional protections, such as free legal representation (Alaya et al. 2007: 11).[3] Thus administrative detention has become part of a parallel apparatus outside the bounds of the criminal justice system. Although ICE has promulgated immigration detention standards for jails, prisons, and private facilities, these guidelines are not mandatory and do not have the force of law. As a result, abuses are common and take place with impunity.

Numerous reports by advocacy organizations have told stories of asylum seekers – including children, torture survivors, disabled and elderly people, such as Rev. Dantica, who had chronic health problems – housed with convicted felons or in overcrowded conditions, denied emergency medical treatment, deprived of medication, abused physically and psychologically by guards, placed in isolation for prolonged periods, punished for calling attention to abuses, transferred in the middle of the night without notice, and incarcerated after being granted asylum – in violation of federal court decisions, federal statutes and regulations, and international law.

Many stories highlight the problems plaguing the US asylum system:

> Twenty-eight-year-old Rosa and her seven-year-old daughter, Ana, fled Honduras in July 2014 after gangs violently threatened the family with kidnapping, the destruction of their home, and death. Rosa and Ana were detained at Artesia [detention center] shortly after entering the United States, and are seeking asylum. Ana, who had been traumatized by the violence in Honduras, suffered severe emotional distress from being in confinement and was unable to keep down any food. She lost over ten pounds as Rosa desperately tried to get her daughter to eat. Her weight loss was so extreme that facility medical staff told Rosa that if she did not force Ana to eat and gain weight, the facility would force feed her daughter through a catheter. Out of despair, Rosa asked for bottles with milk to be provided instead. Because Ana could still not keep any other food down, Rosa had to hold her seven-year-old daughter in her arms like a baby at meal times to feed her by bottle. Finally, after over three months in detention, Rosa and Ana were able to be released on bond with the help of an attorney and are now staying with relatives. Since being released, Ana has begun to attend school and is finally beginning to gain weight again. (Brané et al 2014: 7)

In its "Expose and Close" reports on the ten worst detention centers in the United States, the Detention Watch Network gave numerous examples of abuses:

Roberto Medina-Martinez, a 39-year-old immigrant, died at Stewart Detention Center in Georgia in March 2009 of a treatable heart infection. An investigation conducted following his death revealed that the nursing staff failed to refer Mr. Medina for timely medical treatment and the facility physician failed to follow internal oversight procedures.

At Hudson County Jail in New Jersey, an HIV-positive woman was not receiving any medication until a local NGO intervened.

Irwin County Detention Center in Georgia is more than three hours from Atlanta, making family and legal visits essentially impossible.

At Pinal County Jail in Arizona complaints regarding sanitation include receiving food on dirty trays, worms found in food, bugs and worms found in the faucets, receiving dirty laundry, and being overcrowded with ten other men in one cell and only one toilet. (Detention Watch Network 2013: 2)

Mentally ill or traumatized detainees have especially difficult experiences. If they are suicidal, have an anxiety attack, or break down, they may be considered unmanageable rather than ill, and be segregated in solitary confinement cells instead of receiving treatment. A report by the Justice Department's inspector general said that four of five audited detention facilities did not comply with suicide watch standards. As a result, a number of detainees, such as Tiombe Carlos, whose story was told in chapter 1, have committed suicide.

The Special Problems of Children

Despite the clearly stated position of the UN High Commissioner for Refugees against detention of immigrant children, many children are kept in prison-like facilities for short or long periods. The inappropriately named T. Don Hutto Residential Center in Texas received considerable attention in 2007 after an advocacy organization, the Women's Refugee Commission, published a highly critical report about abuses there, and the American Civil Liberties Union sued ICE over conditions at the facility. The government was paying $2.8 million a month to the Corrections Corporation of America to manage the former medium-security prison, which housed immigrant families in cells, kept them under twenty-four-hour surveillance, forced even children and babies to wear uniforms, threatened children with separation from parents if they did not behave, and failed to provide adequate schooling, recreation, or medical care. As a result of the lawsuit, conditions improved somewhat at Hutto, but the Women's Refugee Commission continued to campaign for an end to detention of children. In August 2009, ICE announced that families would no longer be kept at Hutto, which then became a detention facility for women. Migrant children and families were to be housed in facilities that did not resemble a prison.

But after the 2014 "humanitarian crisis" of Central American children and families entering the United States in large numbers, the Department of Homeland Security placed hundreds of them in the Artesia (New Mexico) and Karnes County (Texas) detention centers. After protests about conditions at Artesia, Homeland Security announced that all the inmates there would be transferred to a new family facility in Dilley, Texas, which would eventually become the largest and most expensive immigration detention center in the country, holding up to 2,400 children and families at a cost of more than $300 per person per day. The Corrections Corporation of America (which had been responsible for Hutto) would run the new facility, a converted oilfield workers' camp, from Eloy detention center, nine hundred miles away in Arizona. The arrangement was made without competitive bidding, public comment, or an environmental impact assessment.

The secretary of homeland security traveled to Dilley to open the facility in December 2014. The *New York Times* reported that he "tried to leave no doubt that the administration was committed to detaining families. 'I believe this is an effective deterrent. . . . Frankly, we want to send a message that our border is not open to illegal migration, and if you come here, you should not expect to simply be released,' Mr. Johnson said" (Preston 2014). Advocacy organizations had beseeched the US government in vain not to reinstitute indefinite detention of families and children, citing UNHCR guidelines that call such detention inherently inhumane and abusive.

It has become increasingly hard to gain release from detention. During and after the surge of Central American children and families, the government argued against releasing any of the detainees at Artesia on national security grounds. One family detained there was told they would need to pay an unaffordable $25,000 bond to be released. Since many detainees are destitute, they have remained in detention for months or even years, making a mockery of the term *expedited removal*. Restrictive regulations, often promulgated in the name of efficiency or to reduce backlogs and caseloads, have abridged asylum seekers' human rights to an alarming degree. Probably in reaction to the 9/11 attacks, in 2002 attorney general John Ashcroft ordered the Board of Immigration Appeals to stop writing opinions and issue summary judgments. He ordered the board to dispose of 55,000 cases within 180 days (Martin and Schoenholtz 2006: 169–70). Similarly, in 2014 authorities instituted a "rocket docket" at Artesia, in an attempt to rush detained children and families through deportation proceedings and deny them the opportunity to present asylum claims. Squads of pro bono attorneys from the American Immigration Lawyers Association arrived to provide legal representation. With their help, fourteen out of some five hundred detainees obtained asylum before Artesia closed in December 2014.

Asylum seekers who are not detained may be allowed to work or receive welfare benefits only at the discretion of the attorney general during the entire appeals process, even if it takes years. Detained or not, they must pay for legal representation, find pro bono assistance, or defend themselves. The US government does not provide lawyers for indigent asylum applicants who face possible deportation, and Congress has prohibited federally supported neighborhood law offices sponsored by the Legal Services Corporation from representing asylum applicants (Kenney and Schrag 2008: 315).

Some asylum seekers who do not gain asylum are granted "withholding of removal," which is "something like asylum, because the respondent who wins it is not deported. However, it is not as good as asylum, because the person whose removal is withheld may not become a permanent resident or a citizen. If conditions ever change for the better in the respondent's country, even decades later, after the person has established a new life in the United States, he or she can be deported at that time" (Kenney and Schrag 2008: 105).

Studies of immigration judges' decisions have found that more than two hundred immigration judges in the United States grant asylum at widely differing rates, even to applicants from the same country (Kenney and Schrag 2008: 307). For example, law professor Philip Schrag discovered that judges' asylum approval rates for Kenyans in Arlington, Virginia, ranged from 0 to 67 percent. The judge who rejected the asylum petition of David Kenney, who was Schrag's client, granted the lowest number of positive asylum decisions in the entire district – 17 percent, in contrast to more than 30 percent by other judges.

Nondetained asylum seekers who have legal representation in immigration proceedings are almost three times more likely to win asylum compared with those without representation; detained asylum seekers with legal representation are six times more likely to win (Kenney and Schrag 2008: 315). At least a third of asylum seekers are not represented, however, and do not have knowledge of complex immigration law or access to law books so they can represent themselves effectively.

The adjudication system is hobbled by an enormous caseload: about 250 asylum officers at any one time interview an average of 28,000 asylum seekers (Schoenholtz et al. 2014: 2). They often have only an hour to read hundreds of pages of documents before each interview. Criteria for asylum are ambiguous and ever-changing. Asylum seekers often do not fit into the neat and outdated categories specified in the 1951 Refugee Convention or the 1966 Protocol. One officer stated that "the higher your education, the more likely you are to be involved in politics at least at a level that would make you susceptible to persecution" (quoted by Schoenholtz et al. 2014: 128). This presupposition, which does not reflect evolving definitions of "social groups," would exclude a traumatized child fleeing gangs in Guatemala, a threatened transsexual from Uganda, or Fauziya Kassindja, who fled Togo to avoid genital mutilation.

Asylum officers and immigration judges are often suspicious of the testimony or documentation of people from certain countries (86). They also find women applicants more believable than men. Unacknowledged racial, ethnic, and national-origin discrimination is rife. Even the part of the country where the asylum seeker applies affects the decision: Somalis in the Midwest received asylum 34 percent of the time, while Somalis in the Pacific Northwest gained asylum 89 percent of the time (204). Thus asylum has become a lottery, known as "refugee roulette," seemingly designed to make sanctuary least available to the vulnerable people who need it most.[4]

Some asylum seekers get lost in the system for months, years, or even decades. Tam Tran, a twenty-four-year-old graduate student at UCLA, and her family were arrested and detained by ICE in October 2007, five months after she testified before the US House of Representatives' Immigration Subcommittee about the plight of undocumented immigrant students.[5] The subcommittee's ranking member, Representative Zoe Lofgren, called the arrests intimidation, but ICE claimed they had not known about Tran's congressional testimony when they stormed the family's home in a predawn raid. The family members were arrested because they had lost their asylum appeal in 2001 and received a deportation order at that time. The Trans were lucky, however, because after only one night in custody they were released with electronic monitoring devices.

The family had been in transit since 1980, when they fled Vietnam and went to Germany, where their application to resettle in the United States as refugees was denied. Tam was born in Germany during their six-year stay in that country. In 1989 they arrived in the United States and applied for asylum. At the time it was easy for asylum seekers to obtain work permits, so they were able to establish themselves as taxpaying, law-abiding residents. Every year they renewed their work permits as required. Nobody appeared to deport them until after Tam Tran became visible by testifying publicly.

In 2001 the Board of Immigration Appeals rejected their asylum claim despite their legitimate fear of persecution in Vietnam. The court ruled that the family should be deported to Germany, a "safe third country" under international agreements, but Germany refused to accept them because they had been absent from that country for more than six months. US officials insisted they would keep seeking travel documents for the Trans to return to Germany, or perhaps even to Vietnam. However, at that time Vietnam had no repatriation agreement with the United States. So the Trans waited in legal limbo for resolution of their case. Meanwhile Tam graduated cum laude from UCLA and went to work part-time to pay for graduate studies in American civilization at Brown University.

What would be the point of deporting this hardworking, upstanding family? Did the government merely want to show that it could? Perhaps the answer may be found in US authorities' tendency to see asylum seekers as potential terrorists ever since the organizer of the 1993 World Trade Center bombing entered the United States legally and sought asylum (which he did not gain). The inclusion of expedited removal and mandatory detention of certain categories of asylum seekers in the 1996 immigration law may be attributable to that one unsuccessful attempt to subvert the asylum system.

In 2010 Tam Tran, then twenty-seven, and a close friend, Cinthya Felix Perez, were killed in a car accident. Both women were pro-immigration activists, campaigning for the DREAM Act, which would provide undocumented migrants brought to the United States as children with legal status. "She was happiest, family and friends said, when she had her hand on a camera, filming undocumented immigrants, whose stories she felt were important to chronicle. The films she shot were, her brother Thien said, 'also a way to express herself. She used it as a tool to tell about the plight about undocumented students'" (Stickgold 2010).

Tam Tran died without gaining asylum or legal status. "The family received a 'withholding of deportation' exemption, but their status does not lead to legal residency or US citizenship. Tam was Vietnamese, but she had never been to Vietnam and was not a Vietnamese citizen. She was born in Germany, but Germany does not grant citizenship based on birthright. And although Tam subsequently spent more than twenty years in the United States, the American government refused to give her legal status. So she was not only undocumented but stateless, trapped in a disgraceful immigration morass" (Wong and Ramos 2011).

The System Tightens Its Grip

Anti-immigrant suspicions have worsened since 2001, as the immigration system has become increasingly militarized and politicized. Among the federal measures instituted after 9/11 were the Absconder Apprehension Initiative, in which the government arrested and detained thousands of Arabs and Muslims during immigration enforcement investigations, and Operation Liberty Shield, in which the government detained and interrogated asylum seekers from thirty-four countries designated as hosts of terrorists (Barry 2009: 1). Dow (2004) points out that these initiatives "did not come out of nowhere," but rather were offshoots of the mandatory detention system established for undocumented migrants and asylum seekers in expedited removal under the 1996 immigration law.

Asylum seekers, most of whom had committed no crime, were swept into the post-9/11 maelstrom along with undocumented migrants and other detainees. In 2003 the ICE Office of Detention and Removal created a ten-year plan called Endgame, to "build the capacity to remove all removable aliens" from the United States by 2012 (United States Department of Homeland Security 2002). These "removable aliens" included people like Mary and Jason Ng, the asylum seekers whose stories were told in chapter 1. Mary was subject to a deportation order she knew nothing about, issued because she did not attend a hearing her lawyer did not tell her about. Jason never received an immigration hearing notice sent to the wrong address.

Estimating that 500,000 people were "ignoring" such orders, ICE tried to deport them all as quickly as possible. It could not accomplish Endgame's overall goal in the allotted time but made plenty of mistakes in the process – arresting and even deporting US citizens for nonexistent immigration violations, breaking up families with US-citizen children, sedating deportees with powerful and inappropriate drugs, and breaking international laws and agreements against refoulement (American Civil Liberties Union 2014a; Rabben 2014).

The new Obama administration promised to introduce immigration reform legislation in 2009, and early that year the secretary of homeland security appointed a special adviser to review immigration enforcement measures. However, that year the US government deported almost four hundred thousand undocumented people, more than ever before. The administration kept up the pace and magnitude of its punitive policies, deporting some two million undocumented people, including asylum seekers, between 2009 and 2014, more than any previous administration. Meanwhile several immigration reform bills failed in Congress, leaving millions of migrants, including asylum seekers, in legal limbo.

Thousands of Iraqi and Afghan interpreters and others, who risked their lives to assist US forces and international agencies in their countries, found themselves in a Kafkaesque situation when they tried to enter the United States under the Refugee Crisis in Iraq Act of 2008 and the Afghan Allies Protection Act of 2009. Armed with glowing recommendations from their American commanders or associates, they found their way blocked by the Departments of State and Homeland Security.

An Afghan interpreter who had worked for US forces for two years applied for a special visa under the 2009 law. He received a letter from the State Department denying his application because he "might be a terrorist or have provided material support to a terrorist organization" (quoted by Sieff 2013). The State Department did not explain what this material support might have been. Nevertheless the US military continued to employ him in Afghanistan. Another Afghan, who had gained asylum in the United States in 1988, was denied permanent residence in 2008 because he had carried supplies for a US-backed militia in the 1980s. The 2001 Patriot Act listed the militia, which no longer existed, as an "undesignated terrorist group" (Sieff 2013).

The most disturbing story came from Becca Heller, director of the Iraqi Refugee Assistance Project (IRAP), and involved an Iraqi human rights activist whose work was funded by the US Agency for International Development. Homeland Security denied her application for a special visa so she could join her US citizen parents in the United

States. Sixteen years earlier, she had been convicted during the Saddam Hussein regime "for the crime of being raped" (Heller 2014).

To summarize a long and convoluted story, DHS officials decided she was therefore a felon and ineligible for the visa. Her lawyers were not allowed to attend her interviews, and DHS was not obliged to reconsider its decision. But after two years' advocacy work by IRAP, with help from Congress members and concerned members of the public, DHS agreed to reverse its negative decision. The story did not end there, however. In early 2015, she was still in exile in a neighboring country, which had become dangerous as a result of civil conflict in the region, waiting for multiple US government agencies to conduct their own security reviews. A year later, more than five years after her initial application for refugee status, the human rights worker was living safely in the United States.

Special visa applicants often waited years for decisions, their cases "stuck in redundant background-check processes" (Heller 2014). Meanwhile many went into hiding or fled to neighboring countries where they had no assurance of refuge. The special visa program was due to expire at the end of 2014, leaving some six thousand applicants in the lurch. Finally, after intense lobbying by US military officials, NGOs, and several Congress members, Congress passed an extension and expansion of the program in mid-December 2014. However, in 2016 several Afghans and Iraqis who had applied years before for visas under the program were still waiting for admission to the United States.

Numerous community and nonprofit advocacy groups have been pressuring the government for years to reform the immigration system. In the mid-1990s, a coalition of advocacy organizations started meeting regularly with federal officials, trying to persuade the INS (later ICE) to make detention standards legally binding on the hundreds of jails, prisons, and private facilities that were holding hundreds of thousands of undocumented migrants and asylum seekers. As of 2016 and after publishing dozens of critical reports about detention center abuses, the groups still had not succeeded in this effort.

In February 2014, the Department of Homeland Security's asylum office issued a new policy with the Orwellian nickname "the Lesson Plan," in response to increasing numbers of asylum seekers coming across the US border with Mexico. Its intention was to reduce the backlog of asylum cases by eliminating migrants from consideration at an early stage of the asylum process: the credible fear interview. This nonadversarial proceeding is supposed to determine if a migrant in expedited removal proceedings may bring an asylum claim before an immigration judge. The standard of proof is low, in accordance with the US Supreme Court decision *Cardoza v. Fonseca*. Not by coincidence, the new policy materialized soon after a congressional hearing chaired by Representative Robert Goodlatte (R-Va.), who claimed that up to 70 percent of asylum applications were fraudulent. (Asylum advocates thought he had plucked this figure out of the air.)

In previous years, asylum officers had passed the vast majority of applicants along to the next phase of the asylum process, a hearing before an immigration judge. The new directive instructed asylum officers "to approve only those immigrants who demonstrate a 'significant possibility of success'" in immigration court. An immigration attorney practicing in San Diego, California, wrote that "the denial rate for our clients for credible fear is actually higher than the average denial rates for regular asylum cases, both at the asylum office and in immigration court" (Khonsari 2014).

A group of advocacy organizations protested that "the 2014 Lesson Plan risks leading to an increase in erroneous determinations that will prevent the most vulnerable asylum seekers from ever having an opportunity for safety and protection. . . . [It] is misleading because its organization, formulation and tone suggest a higher standard for making a positive credible fear determination than appropriate under applicable law" ("Call for Integrity" 2014). Khonsari charged, "It appears that the new guidelines were formulated by DHS with no public input, transparency or oversight." The result, a legal expert believed, would be more deportations of migrants with potentially strong asylum claims, especially LGBTQ people and victims of domestic violence (Khonsari 2014; M. Chen 2014). Above all, the policy did not address the reasons for the large increase of asylum applications from Guatemalans, Hondurans, Salvadorans, and Mexicans, whose claims of persecution the US government did not want to recognize or address – and not for the first time.

The humanitarian crisis or surge of 2014 was not a unique occurrence. Over the previous three years, the number of unaccompanied minors and families crossing the southern border from Mexico, Guatemala, Honduras, and El Salvador had doubled each year. Indeed, the pattern went much further back. Over the past two decades increasing numbers of young people have fled their homes in Mexico and Central America and tried to reach the US border alone. They seek to escape violence, gangs, or domestic abuse, or they make a desperate attempt to reunite with parents who left them to work in the United States (Chomsky 2014: 154). This phenomenon may be traced all the way back to the 1980s, when hundreds of thousands of desperate adults and children fled civil wars in El Salvador, Honduras, and Guatemala. The US government's refusal to recognize their asylum claims, and its determination to deport them to the places they had fled, triggered the Sanctuary Movement described in chapter 7.

A series of federal court decisions from 1985 to 1997 forced the Immigration and Naturalization Service to develop special policies for detained minors. They were to be released to a sponsor if possible or placed in the least restrictive setting, and the INS was to implement appropriate standards for their treatment. Slowly the government improved its programs for child migrants. After 2002, responsibility for them was transferred to the Department of Health and Human Services and the Office of Refugee Resettlement (ORR). In 2003, ORR created the Division of Unaccompanied Children's Services to care for them. Although conditions for child migrants improved for a while, they were still caught in a "disjointed, labyrinthine system" (Chomsky 2014: 156).

In 2008, Congress passed the William Wilberforce Trafficking Victims Protection and Reauthorization Act, named for one of the great British abolitionists. Under the provisions of this law, Central American and other unaccompanied minors were to receive special attention, but Mexican children could (and would) be quickly deported. Apparently agreements made with the Mexican government to deter unauthorized migration and asylum claims overrode any humanitarian concerns for Mexican minors fleeing the same human rights abuses that were sending Central American children north. "Central

America's political and economic crises – exacerbated by US military involvement and trade policies – virtually guarantee that children will continue to try to escape," Chomsky wrote (2014: 157), and experts on the region agreed (Stinchcomb and Hershberg 2014). Meanwhile the Mexican government was busy detaining Central American children and families as they tried to make their way to the United States. Attacks and abductions by bandits, drug gangs, and human traffickers made the journey horrific.

Inside the United States, increasing numbers of children were losing parents to deportation. In 1998, 8 percent of removals were parents of US citizens; in 2011 the number had shot up to 22 percent (Chomsky 2014: 159). Human Rights Watch (2014) found that 50,000 parents of US citizen children were deported annually in 2011 and 2012. Forty percent had been deported previously; apparently they kept trying to return to their families in the United States. Some five thousand US citizen children were placed in foster care because their parents had been detained or deported (Chomsky 2014: 159). This is the context in which parents paid smugglers to deliver their children to the United States, minors set off alone to join their families in El Norte, and mothers or other relatives accompanied children as they fled the onslaughts of gangs, traffickers, other criminals, police, military, or abusive relatives from whom the state would not or could not protect them.

The Elusiveness of Integration

Salvadorans in the United States, who had been granted temporary protected status (TPS) in the 1990s, were in a particularly difficult position. Many had gone north during the civil conflict that devastated their country in the 1980s; others arrived later. In 2004, 290,000 Salvadorans had TPS, under which they had no path to citizenship and no legal way to bring their families to the United States (Mountz 2010). They risked losing TPS if they left the United States to fetch their children, who could not gain legal status through them. Their chances of obtaining asylum were no better than those of other asylum seekers. Stuck in long-term immigration limbo, they tried to remain invisible to the government. Some of their children may have been among the tens of thousands trying to enter the United States in recent years, as conditions deteriorated in El Salvador and neighboring countries.

The State Department addressed their plight by instituting the Central American Minors (CAM) Refugee/Parole Program in December 2014. The program made it possible for permanent residents, TPS and Deferred Enforced Departure holders, immigration parolees, deferred action recipients, and withholding of removal grantees to request refugee status for their children in El Salvador, Guatemala, and Honduras. Its purpose was to provide "a safe, legal and orderly alternative to the dangerous journey that some children are currently undertaking to the United States" (Chishti et al. 2015). Since the program does not guarantee that applicants will receive favorable consideration, it remains to be seen whether CAM will make it easier or harder for children to gain asylum in the United States.

Partly as a result of the Central American humanitarian crisis of mid-2014, the administration delayed reforms promised months earlier until after the midterm elections. Implicitly acknowledging failure to reach Endgame's goal or advance comprehensive immigration reform, President Obama announced temporary administrative actions in November 2014 to benefit about 5 million undocumented people (fewer than half the estimated total of 11.5 million). These measures specifically excluded recent Central American arrivals from the list of beneficiaries.[6] Obama's opponents in Congress immediately announced that they would quash the new policies by defunding the government agencies responsible for their implementation and taking the administration to court. A federal judge in Texas halted implementation of the president's administrative measures in mid-February 2015. In 2016 the case was on its way to the Supreme Court. Comprehensive immigration reform seemed further away than ever.

At that point it was still unclear if ICE and the border patrol would continue their Endgame-inspired rush to detain and deport millions of undocumented migrants who were ineligible for the president's administrative relief. The ACLU and other legal advocacy groups had already filed suits challenging detention and expedited deportation proceedings for Central American children and families. On February 20, 2015, a federal judge in Washington, DC, granted a preliminary injunction that halted the Obama administration's policy of detaining asylum-seeking mothers and children to deter others from coming to the United States (American Civil Liberties Union 2015; Boasberg 2015).

Meanwhile the Immigrant Legal Resource Center claimed that one program, Secure Communities, whose termination the president had announced in November 2014, would continue under a new name, Priority Enforcement Program, or PEP-Comm (Immigrant Legal Resource Center 2014). The immigration enforcement juggernaut kept rolling.[7]

Meanwhile nine voluntary agencies, or VOLAGs, were managing resettlement of thousands of refugees across the United States with federal funding from the Office of Refugee Resettlement, based in the Department of Health and Human Services.[8] The VOLAGs helped refugees and asylees (but not asylum seekers, who were ineligible for such government support) to find housing, schooling, employment, training, medical care, and very modest financial assistance for a maximum of eight months.

Some of these agencies had advocacy offices that produced or endorsed campaigns, reports, letters, and statements supporting the human rights of asylum seekers and calling for the improvement of detention conditions, enforcement of nonbinding detention standards, or the end of detention of children, asylum seekers, and other vulnerable people. But like the Australian refugee assistance organizations discussed in chapter 8, their effectiveness as advocates was limited by their close relationship with the government whose punitive immigration policies they were seeking to change. Their limited budgets, which the government had failed to increase or sometimes had even cut, made resettlement work chronically difficult.

The United States has resettled more than two million refugees since passage of the Refugee Act of 1980. "Nevertheless, almost as soon as it was established, federal backing for the domestic resettlement program began to erode, placing the program under increasing stress," explain immigration experts Anastasia Brown and Todd Scribner of the National Conference of Catholic Bishops. As a result, "the United States has not fully lived up to its obligations under the law" (Brown and Scribner 2014).

The focus of resettlement shifted from social integration to economic "self-sufficiency," which the Office of Refugee Resettlement crudely defined as full-time employment sufficient to support a family. The period of federal financial support to state refugee programs decreased from eighteen months in 1982 to eight months in 1991; in some states, refugees received assistance for only three months. Budget cuts reduced the period of federal contributions to state Medicaid, AFDC, and SSI payments from thirty-one months in 1986 to zero months in 1990. Health care and mental health care became difficult to obtain at a time when up to 75 percent of Iraqi refugees suffered from some sort of mental illness (Brown and Scribner 2014: 114).

In many states English language instruction and job training programs for refugees were terminated for lack of funding. Since the economic downturn of 2008, several states have tried to stop refugee resettlement entirely because of its cost. Resettlement agencies closed in nine cities, from Fresno to Atlantic City, after the federal government passed on increased costs of refugee programs to the VOLAGs.

Even so, the VOLAGs were in the forefront of efforts not only to shelter but also to integrate persecuted outsiders into US society. Asylum and sanctuary may be conditional and temporary according to law and custom, but integration is an enduring form of welcome and acceptance, the greatest hope of those with no place to go back to and nowhere else to go.

11 Contemporary Sanctuary Movements

> We are not in hiding. We have come out into the daylight.
>
> – Sans-Papiers Manifesto, 1997

The history of sanctuary and asylum shows that the two institutions are not identical. Since the seventeenth century, when the British Parliament formally abolished it as a legal institution, sanctuary has remained a morally and religiously based obligation that often takes place outside or against the law. By contrast, asylum has become a formal category in international and national law, distinguishing the treatment and status of one kind of person (the asylum seeker) from other kinds (the refugee, the immigrant, and the undocumented migrant). The word has been used to exclude and discriminate as much as to include and welcome. As a legal institution, asylum is often provisional, temporary, and grudging, hedged by rules and restrictions, while sanctuary is a temporary or permanent act of hospitality, generosity, and compassion. Like that of mercy, to which it is closely related, the quality of sanctuary is not strained: "It droppeth as the gentle rain from heaven / Upon the earth beneath." As a form of reciprocal altruism, sanctuary "is twice blessed / It blesseth him that gives and him that takes."[1]

Those who seek and give sanctuary operate in a separate realm, far from the hearing room where asylum is granted or denied (usually denied, in most places). And even when the authorities grant asylum, real, enduring sanctuary – in the form of integration into the host society – may be difficult or impossible to obtain. For every ballet dancer who lept over the Iron Curtain to freedom and acclaim, thousands of unknown refugees have struggled, sometimes unsuccessfully, to establish themselves in the new country or to re-create the kind of life they left behind when they fled their native land. Sanctuary can compensate for but cannot reconstitute what has been lost. True integration often has to wait until the next generation, and sometimes it does not come even then.

Those who seek sanctuary or asylum suffer from what sociologist Erving Goffman called spoiled identity; they are stigmatized by their flight and their outsider status. Reconstructing their dignity can take decades. In the meantime they may be treated as nonpersons, herded into "pig pen" enclosures in front of Lunar House, detained for months in windowless tents in Texas, shackled on their way to the hospital, disbelieved when they tell their story in court. And yet they sometimes manage to transcend and defeat the stigma.

France: Refugees Rescue Themselves

In the mid-1990s, a group of undocumented migrants and refused asylum seekers calling themselves the Sans-Papiers ("Without Papers") created an independent radical movement in Paris and other French cities. They became visible in March 1996, when 324 African migrants occupied the Church of Saint Ambrose in Paris. Evicted after a few days, they moved on, starting hunger strikes in Paris, Lille, and Versailles and setting up twenty-five collectives around the country. In August 1996, "300 undocumented African women, children and men were violently evicted by police from the St. Bernard Church in Paris, where they had taken sanctuary for several months. The Sans-Papiers of St. Bernard have organized several occupations, gone on hunger strikes and toured France in a caravan to mobilize support against deportations. They demand papers for all, an end to detention and deportation, the return of all deportees, and the repeal of all immigration laws" (Cissé 1997: 1).

After the incident at Saint Bernard, twenty thousand protesters marched in solidarity with the Sans-Papiers in Paris. In 1998, Sans-Papiers occupied Notre Dame de la Gare and Saint Jean de Montmartre churches in Paris in response to passage of repressive anti-immigrant

laws. The following year, the Sans-Papiers National Coordinating
Committee convened a large demonstration in Paris to call for reg-
ularization of all undocumented migrants in Europe. One of their
leaflets called for a new vision of the world: "To accept the Europe
as conceived by states and governments, both of the right and of
the left, means to accept the vision of a world where inequality and
misery reign while a minority which monopolizes all wealth protects
itself by every means possible. . . . To tolerate this situation means
to tolerate apartheid on a world scale" (quoted by Hayter 2004: 146).

The Sans-Papiers's first visible leader was the outspoken Madjiguene Cissé, an undocumented worker from Senegal. In a booklet
published in the United Kingdom, Cissé wrote:

> There were organizations which came to support us and which were
> used to helping immigrants in struggle. They were also used to acting
> as the relay between immigrants . . . and the authorities, and therefore
> more or less to manage the struggle. They would tell us, "Right, we
> the organizations have made an appointment to explain this or that";
> and we had to say, "But we can explain it very well ourselves." If we
> had not taken our autonomy, we would not be here today. (quoted by
> Hayter 2004: 146)

According to Helene Trauner, women and families stood out in
the movement, resisting the police, staging sit-ins and strikes, or
occupying public spaces (2005: 232). Women constituted more than
30 percent of participating adults in the Sans-Papiers movement.

Over time, the Paris group split over disagreements about tactics
and alliances with political parties. But they were back in the head-
lines in April 2008, when, with the help of the General Confederation of Labor (CGT), about a thousand Sans-Papiers launched strikes
and occupations in the cleaning, construction, retail, security, and
catering industries where they worked. The government responded
by offering to legalize a thousand undocumented workers out of the
estimated four hundred thousand in France.

In May 2008 the Sans-Papiers occupied CGT headquarters in Paris
after the CGT would not allow them to submit their own applications

for legal residency to the local government. One member of the group declared, "The CGT has taken the Sans-Papiers movement hostage. We are taking the union hall hostage" (quoted by Ira and Lerougetel 2008: 1). They were still occupying the building a month later.

Yiribou, an Ivoirian who had lived in France for nine years before being "regularized," described his plight:

> The worst thing about not having papers was always being afraid, hiding from the cops, knowing that at any moment they could come and say, 'You, show me your papers.' But all the same you had to go out every day and work to feed your family, in spite of the risk. . . . To get your papers, you've got to go and make your request in a big, big group. If you go alone, they mess with you. . . . If you go in a large group, they know you can't be fooled, and it's harder for them to arrest you. But you have to fight for your papers. You can't just go and make the request, because the government is against you. You have to fight. (Maltby 2008: 3)

In the venerable style of French labor militancy, the Sans-Papiers do not request; they demand. They seek not only sanctuary but visibility, and they act unhesitatingly, sometimes at great risk, to secure it for themselves. Their classically French discourse expresses their claim to membership in French society:

> We came to France with the intention of working here and because we had been told that France was the "homeland of the Rights of Man"; we could no longer bear the poverty and the oppression which was rife in our countries, we wanted our children to have full stomachs, and we dreamed of freedom. . . . The prime minister of France had promised that families would not be separated: we demand that this promise finally be kept and that the principles of humanity often proclaimed by the government be implemented. We demand that the European and international conventions, to which the French Republic has subscribed, are respected. (quoted by Hayter 2004: 143)

The Sans-Papiers defy the identity imposed on them as nonpersons by standing up to defend their interests. In acting politically, they reconstruct their dignity. As Brazilian educator Paulo Freire would put it, they become the subjects, not the objects, of their own history. During the twenty-first century's first two decades, Sans-Papiers movements were active in France, Belgium, and Switzerland.

Campaign and advocacy organizations such as SOS Racisme, Droits Devant, Comité des Sans Logis, and the Ligue des Droits de l'Homme continued to act in solidarity with the Sans-Papiers, despite the ambivalence of the general population, which saw political refugees as frauds and an unacceptable burden on taxpayers (Patsias and Williams 2013: 185). Meanwhile refugees and migrants became major protagonists in political struggles as they actively engaged in creating new forms of citizenship (Millner 2013: 62). The powerful, secular French state saw religious sanctuary as a threat to its sovereignty and control. Thus sanctuary in France became politicized, reflecting "erosion of the state" and "resistance to authority," while migrants took action outside institutions and power structures (Patsias and Williams 2013: 186).

Increasing numbers of migrants traveled through Europe from the south and the east, seeking opportunity and refuge. Thousands arrived at a Red Cross camp called Sangatte in the port city of Calais in northern France. In 2002, the Sarkozy government shut down Sangatte, but squalid squatter camps replaced it. Like the Sans-Papiers, the squatters and their supporters formed solidarity groups. Thus refugees and migrants emerged as political actors under the harshest conditions (Millner 2013: 62). Even so, Calais became a focal point of despair and destitution for migrants desperate to reach Britain, where they imagined they would find a promised land.

German Sanctuary Evolves

In Germany opposition to restrictive asylum policies has taken a different form. A church sanctuary movement began in 1983, when a Protestant church in Berlin took in three Palestinian families facing deportation to Lebanon. As a result, the families were permitted to remain in Germany. The following year, a church in Hamburg gave shelter to the wife of a Filipino sailor and her two children. They were violently evicted by sixty police and deported the same night. After a public outcry, the police stopped invading churches to remove sanctuary seekers.

Over the following decade, church sanctuary networks grew on the local and regional levels. In 1994 a national church sanctuary conference with 150 participants founded the German Ecumenical Committee on Church Asylum (GECCA). In 2010 GECCA organized a Berlin conference on the new sanctuary movement in Europe, which produced a charter for action. Accordingly, GECCA provided temporary protection for asylum seekers in physical danger or facing deportation that would cause unacceptable hardship. Thus the church would interpose itself between asylum seekers and the authorities to gain time for negotiations and legal action. Churches allowed the authorities to enter their premises and used the media to bring public attention to the situation of asylum seekers. In several cases, clergy and congregants were prosecuted for "supporting the illegal stay of foreigners" (Just 2013: 141). A few were fined, but most were acquitted. Apparently the German high court did not find church sanctuary to be illegal.

The contemporary sanctuary movement sees itself as the defender of the values enshrined in the German Constitution, including freedom of conscience and religion. "In the case of deportation where people's dignity and human rights are at risk and their person, life, freedom and security are threatened, it is the churches' position that such people are constitutionally entitled to protection. If the state fails to offer such protection, others must step in to help," wrote theologian and sanctuarian Wolf-Dieter Just (2013: 141). Rotating groups composed of a few volunteers care for refused asylum seekers in church sanctuary by providing food, mattresses, donations, legal advice, and medical care. They see the state as violating local traditions of hospitality, which has become marginalized in the modern world, and they are willing to go outside the law to preserve what international law scholar Hiroshi Oda calls sanctuary's "old and universal culture" (quoted in Just 2013: 160).

Sanctuary cases in Germany are numerically insignificant, Just insists; only 299 instances were documented from 2000 to 2007, while thousands of asylum seekers and undocumented migrants were deported. Yet the symbolic value of church sanctuary is high, stimulating public debate and reconsideration of some cases. "As long as German and European asylum policies continue to be insufficient to protect asylum seekers from unacceptable social hardship, torture or even death, there will be congregations in Germany that grant sanctuary," he concludes (144).

Other German organizations doing sanctuary and refugee work have included the Red Cross, the Trade Union Federation, and religious charities such as Diakonie and Caritas. In general, Tazreiter writes (2004), German NGOs work on individual cases, understanding that narrowly framed definitions of refugees exclude some who need humanitarian protection. The Jesuit Refugee Service, an international organization operating in Germany and other receiving countries, has gone somewhat further by helping undocumented migrants afraid to return home.

From time to time, however, egregious cases have resulted in public protests and campaigns. In 2012 an Iranian asylum seeker killed himself after seven months in an immigration reception center. Nationwide protests, hunger strikes, and a refugee bus tour ignited a year-long campaign in German cities to document the plight of asylum seekers living on the fringes of society. In March 2013 thousands gathered in Berlin to demand changes to Germany's asylum practices, which aimed to discourage asylum seekers from pursuing their claims (Chai 2013: 29).

The best-known NGO working on behalf of asylum seekers in Germany is Pro Asyl, founded in 1986 to do public education and lobbying. Major political parties called it "radical and extremist" in the mid-1990s, because it strongly criticized government policies. Pro Asyl still works on individual cases, providing legal advice to asylum seekers, as well as campaigning in Europe for more humane asylum policies.

Organizations such as Pro Asyl confront powerful anti-immigrant sentiment in Germany and beyond. In 2014 the populist Pegida movement (Patriotic Europeans against the Islamization of the West) spread from Germany to Sweden, Austria, and Switzerland. Thousands of protesters in cities across Germany called for the immediate deportation of Muslim migrants. Their banners read, "Send the criminal asylum seekers packing" (Connolly 2015).

And yet, thousands of Germans stepped forward to help asylum seekers during the refugee crisis of 2015. A German sociologist commented, "We're seeing a growing emotional willingness among people in Germany to help others who are in need. . . . The decisive question being asked by many right now is, do we just want to stubbornly focus on our own interests or, as the richest, perhaps also most powerful, society in Europe, are we willing to be generous towards others and to offer them help?" (quoted by Connolly 2015).

The Netherlands: Asylum Seekers Find Allies

In the Netherlands, draconian policies imposed on municipalities by the central government have resulted in refused asylum seekers and other migrants struggling to find food, shelter, and medical care. Churches have responded by providing shelter to asylum seekers whom the government sought to make homeless (Werkman 2013: 2). The Protestant Church of the Netherlands, with 1,800 affiliated churches, set up the International Network of Local Initiatives with Asylum Seekers (INLIA) to oversee emergency accommodation centers for several thousand migrants around the country. By contributing to the INLIA initiative, local authorities bypassed government orders not to help the migrants.

As in France, migrants in the Netherlands have taken matters into their own hands. In 2012, Iraqi migrants in The Hague set up a tent camp to protest their treatment by the government, which sought to send them back to Iraq. After being evicted, about thirty migrants occupied a disused church. In Amsterdam, migrants evicted from a tent camp occupied an abandoned church that became known as the Vluchtkerk (Refugee Church). On an outside wall, they tacked up a bedsheet with the legend (in English): "The greatness of a nation will be judged by the way its refugees are treated. – Gandhi" (Boer 2013). Some 130 migrants spent a cold winter in the cavernous building before being evicted. Then they moved to an unoccupied office building, which they called the Vluchtflat. The migrants set up an organization called We Are Here, to bring attention to their plight as they moved from one abandoned building to another. Eventually they took over another empty building, the Vluchtgarage. More than a hundred volunteers helped them.

Also in Amsterdam, Somalis, Iraqis, and Sudanese were denied asylum but not forced to leave the Netherlands because their home countries were too dangerous to return to. They set up tent camps to draw attention to their precarious situation without social benefits. INLIA mediated with the government, and the Somalis were given accommodation. In other Dutch cities, local groups gave various types of help. In Rotterdam, for example, the church-funded Omzo Foundation provided counseling to about 160 people a month and set up medical visits for 820 people. In 2012, Omzo housed seventy people. No government funds subsidized this effort.

Churches also helped Roma who arrived in the Netherlands without identification papers. Some were stateless, but in other cases embassies refused to help them, "probably because they are Roma" (Werkman 2013: 9).

Scandinavian Sanctuary Traditions

Sanctuary has a long history in Scandinavia, going back to the twelfth century CE. As a formal legal institution, it ended in 1537, during the Reformation. Even so, sanctuary continued as a common practice based on ancient customs (Loga et al. 2013: 121). Sanctuary in Scandinavia usually takes place in Lutheran churches, where congregants and employees care for asylum seekers with the support of national church leaders, refugee support groups, women's associations, human rights organizations, social service organizations, and political activists.

In Finland, migrants are sheltered quietly in homes or hiding places. However, highly publicized incidents do take place. In 1996 a Bangladeshi asylum seeker was deported after a priest offered him sanctuary in Helsinki Cathedral. Nonetheless, about one-third of sanctuary incidents resulted in cancellation of deportation. The practice became well established, with the Finnish Ecumenical Council publishing a guide, "Church as Sanctuary," in 2007. Supporters often cite their obligation to give hospitality in a sacred place, help their neighbors, and address concerns about migrants' suffering. Two thousand Finnish citizens expressed their solidarity with migrants by demonstrating in Helsinki to protest deportations in 2010. The Finnish authorities may not formally recognize the validity of sanctuary, but they collaborate with church agencies, and the advisory board of the Finnish Immigration Service has external members from the Ecumenical Council, the Lutheran Church, and civic organizations.

From 1996 to 2010, dozens of asylum seekers stayed in Norwegian churches every year, and some families spent several years in sanctuary. One Iranian lived in a Pentecostal church for seven years, finally obtaining leave to remain in Norway in 2007. Overall, however, Norwegian attitudes toward sanctuary seem enduringly ambivalent, with many people apparently unable to decide if the state church should take such a political action.

Sweden is less ambivalent about sanctuary. Alsike Monastery, a Lutheran convent near Uppsala, has sheltered refused asylum seekers since 1978. A sign at the entrance says it is a "sanctuary for refugees in danger" (Loga et al. 2013: 129). In 1993 police arrested thirty-six asylum seekers there. Thirteen were deported, but the rest were allowed to return to the convent and granted residency later. A refugee-hider movement emerged in the early 1990s, when individuals and church congregations spontaneously sheltered asylum seekers. It is difficult to estimate how many were hidden. After a petition campaign in 2005, a temporary measure gave thirty thousand "hidden refugees" an opportunity to reapply for asylum. Seven major sanctuary incidents, lasting weeks or months, took place in Swedish churches from 1990 to 2011.

The British Grassroots Tradition

A long-lived organization exemplifies the tradition and practice of sanctuary in modern Britain. CARA, the Council for Assisting Refu-

gee Academics, began as the Academic Assistance Council in 1933.[2]
Headed by prominent scientists, it helped eminent German and Austrian scholars escape from the Nazis and find safety in Britain. It continued during the Cold War, helping Hungarian, Czech, Greek, Polish,
South African, and East German academics, artists, and intellectuals.
However, its "support of displaced academics was modest during the
upheavals associated with the last part of the Cold War; and with
dictatorships, military juntas and authoritarian regimes in much of
Central and South America, Africa and Asia, its resources could not
possibly answer the demand" (Seabrook 2009: 106). It did manage to
bring about a thousand Chileans to the United Kingdom in the 1970s
and provide more than nine hundred scholarships for them.

After the end of the Cold War, CARA's beneficiaries arrived in Britain from a new set of developing countries, bringing new challenges.
Instead of being prominent, internationally known researchers, many
were students whose education had been interrupted by civil conflict.
Because of changes in immigration and asylum policies, they were
not welcomed in Britain.

Joseph Ndalou was tortured in prison in Cameroon because of his
political activities while a student during the 1990s. He paid a smuggler to take him to Britain in 2004. "At my first interview I was told
I should have claimed asylum within 72 hours of arrival," he told Jeremy Seabrook. "I was handcuffed. I left the office with my hands tied.
I stayed three days at the police station but couldn't leave the cell.
There was no window, just a grill. There was a plastic bed. I couldn't
use the toilet. I pleaded for fresh air. Nothing. Just morning tea and
breakfast. I wasn't physically beaten, but it was a psychological beat-
ing" (Seabrook 2009: 211). After that, he was briefly detained in an
immigration center, then denied asylum but released. When Ndalou's
wife and children arrived a year later, she told authorities she was
single. She gained asylum. "It is ironic; they believed her story, but
not mine, although I was the one telling the truth," he commented.

Years later, when he still had not received asylum, the Refugee
Council of Wales helped Ndalou contact CARA, which gave him and
his wife grants for study. He was working on a master's degree in
public health when Seabrook interviewed him. "Before I knew about

CARA I felt trapped. I intend now to work with refugees, and others who need help – minority groups, black ethnic groups. . . . I can't find praise high enough for CARA. It has been my savior" (220). Seabrook observes, "A heartening tradition of British life is that no oppression, atrocity or injustice happens in the world which does not call forth some group, however small, dedicated to righting the wrong. . . . What is often ridiculed at first later becomes a matter of common decency" (25).

One small British group dedicated to righting wrongs is Medical Justice, founded in 2005. Six paid workers and dozens of volunteer physicians, lawyers, campaigners, and ex-detainees "use medical evidence to expose and challenge medical mistreatment of detainees and document the toxic effect of indefinite detention. We hold the government to account and campaign for lasting change through policy work, strategic litigation, public and parliamentary awareness raising and mobilising medical professionals" (Medical Justice 2014: 2). Fifty volunteer physicians investigate one thousand cases each year, visiting eleven detention centers to document detainees' medical status and mistreatment. They do not treat the detainees, but reports and legal actions by Medical Justice bring the realities of immigration detention to public attention.

Another small but effective organization is Bail for Immigration Detainees (BID), which has thirteen paid staff and dozens of volunteers in London. In 2014 BID's pro bono attorneys and others assisted 3,071 individuals by providing information via a telephone helpline, workshops, and legal clinics in detention centers; preparing and presenting bail applications; conducting research for advocacy purposes; informing policy makers and the media; and preparing legal cases to challenge detention practices it considered unlawful (Bail for Immigration Detainees 2014). BID also carries out "strategic litigation." In a case before the European Court of Human Rights, BID argued that indefinite immigration detention, combined with the lack of automatic and independent judicial oversight, amounts to a violation of immigration detainees' human rights (8).

Many nongovernmental organizations, including the Campaign against Racial Discrimination, the Joint Council for the Welfare of

Immigrants, the Institute of Race Relations, the British Refugee Council, Asylum Aid, and the Churches' Commission for Racial Justice, have organized and participated in campaigns or published reports exposing the plight of asylum seekers in Britain.

The national Still Human Still Here campaign started in late 2006 with the backing of nongovernmental and religious groups. A few months later, a large march through central London streets and a rally at Trafalgar Square expressed the campaign's concerns. Dozens of organizations, from Amnesty International UK to the Welsh Refugee Council, supported allied initiatives to end destitution in the asylum system and allow asylum seekers to work. After eight years, Still Human Still Here continues to campaign and publish reports.

Historians Tony Kushner and Katharine Knox have pointed out that "governments and their state apparatus have often been too eager to satisfy negative sentiment and too willing to dismiss alternative voices calling for more generous refugee policies. . . . [A]nti-asylum and anti-immigration laws have only legitimized and increased hostile sentiment" (1999: 402). Nonetheless, they emphasize that ordinary people have played a crucial role, caring for refugees locally and campaigning on their behalf nationally and internationally. The Still Human Still Here campaign may not have attained its objectives, but it bears witness to the plight of hundreds of thousands of destitute migrants, and its cosponsors persist in speaking out and working on their behalf.

Because women are not mentioned in the Refugee Convention, women's groups have made special efforts to bring them to public attention on the local and national level. In addition to Women for Refugee Women (London), groups such as Women Asylum Seekers Together (London and Manchester), Women Seeking Sanctuary Advocacy Group (Wales), Bradford Refugee and Asylum Seeker Stories, and Refugee Women's Strategy Group (Glasgow) coordinate self-help projects organized by women asylum seekers and migrants.

Twenty groups affiliated with the Association of Visitors to Immigration Detainees (AVID) visited about two thousand detainees in 2013. A national network started in 1994 and funded by foundations, trusts, churches, fundraising events, sales, and training fees, AVID runs on a shoestring, taking in about £78,000 per year and spending £72,000 (about US$105,000). It cooperates with twenty-five organizations, including BID, Medical Justice, and the Independent Inspectorate of UK Borders and Immigration.

Religious denominations help asylum seekers in various ways. A Quaker activist described their work: "Quakers in various places around the country offer people who are destitute somewhere to stay, sometimes in a night shelter, sometimes in a scheme whereby they stay with a family. Other times in a house that has been bought specifically for that purpose." The Quaker Asylum and Refugee Network advocates inside and outside the Religious Society of Friends for more-humane immigration laws and policies, collaborates with the Still Human Still Here coalition, and makes submissions on asylum issues to parliamentary committees. Likewise, the Church of England, in a submission to a parliamentary inquiry in late 2014, called for ending indefinite detention, in removal centers, because of the stress it places on detainees and their families (Doward 2014b). Soon after, the Anglican bishop of Croydon, where Lunar House is located, joined a campaign to end indefinite detention, organized by Citizens UK, the country's largest coalition of civil society organizations.

Participants in the campaign condemned indefinite detention. The director of Detention Action cogently expressed his disapproval: "Most long-term detained migrants return to their communities in the UK, bearing the scars of indefinite detention. It is quite simply a dysfunctional practice that wastes taxpayers' money and human lives." An official of the Refugee Council added, "It's utterly abhorrent that at the stroke of a pen a Government official can deprive someone of their freedom indefinitely, without them having been charged with or convicted of any crime" (quoted by Owen 2015). Ex-detainees told grim stories of their time in custody. Campaigners tried to gain public attention before the national election in May 2015 but had little success. Asked if she believed that moral pressure from religious authorities and advocacy groups could make a difference, BID's director shook her head no. Political change and media work were more likely to lead to policy changes. Pro-immigrant forces had to take the offensive and challenge the right wing, she said.

Another approach to reform involves sanctuary cities. In 2005 the first City of Sanctuary group organized in Sheffield, and in 2007 Sheffield became the first official City of Sanctuary in the United Kingdom, with the endorsement of the city council and numerous local organizations. Since then, fifty-seven other British cities have joined the movement, and twenty-one more were in the process of becoming cities of sanctuary in 2016. City of Sanctuary describes itself on its website as "a movement to build a culture of hospitality for people seeking sanctuary in the UK . . . to create a network of towns and cities throughout the country which are proud to be places of safety, and which include people seeking sanctuary fully in the life of their communities."

City of Sanctuary sponsors a great variety of events, campaigns, and services. In 2014 its Sanctuary Summit in Swansea attracted four hundred participants, and in 2015 a national conference titled "Ending Asylum Destitution" took place in Bristol. In Leeds, which I visited in 2013, local teachers set up "Schools of Sanctuary" to promote multiculturalism and a "Theatre of Sanctuary" to introduce newly arrived migrants to the city. Several Catholic organizations managed Saint Monica's Housing, which provided accommodation to destitute asylum seekers.

In Wakefield, a Yorkshire city of 80,000 that I also visited, initiatives ranged from a Welcome Café to a winter clothing drive for residents of a shabby and depressing migrants' accommodation center located next to a medium-security prison. The Quakers offered help after the city council withdrew its funding for immigrant integration efforts. A "Drop-In for Asylum Seekers and Refugees" took place in a Quaker meeting house, where volunteers provided health advice and referrals to social service agencies.[3] An ecumenical group called Churches Together worked with the city council to provide services to migrants. The Wakefield Baptist Church provided English classes and a night shelter. The Community Awareness Project, which had long helped homeless people in Wakefield, provided assistance to six destitute asylum seekers. In addition, an asylee from Iran founded a local group called Refugee and Asylum Seeker Advocacy.

A Struggle for Integration in Glasgow

In Leeds I heard about a group called "the Glasgow Girls." Their story, later made into a musical and produced in London, started in 2005, when fourteen security guards raided a public housing estate in Glasgow at dawn and forced a migrant family into a van that took them more than four hundred miles to a removal center outside London. A fifteen-year-old friend of the family, an asylee herself, told her teacher, "I don't understand why a child is being treated like a criminal. She's done nothing wrong" (BBC 2014). She and her friends decided they had to do something. They organized a petition drive on social media, talked to BBC reporters, and visited the Scottish Parliament, becoming known as the Glasgow Girls.

Thanks to her friends' efforts, at least one of the students scheduled for deportation in 2005 was still in Britain in 2014. She told the audience at the Sanctuary Summit, "It was horrible, horrible, horrible. . . . If you've done nothing wrong, don't let them snatch you away." Another of the girls laughed as she described keeping watch at dawn for Home Office vans coming to their housing estate to take asylum-seeker families away. When they saw where the security personnel were going, they would phone the families, who escaped down the back stairs. Supported by the local media, politicians, the community and their teachers, "seven schoolgirls took on the Home Office and won," a Glasgow newspaper reported (Civic Leicester 2014). One of the Glasgow Girls, now a BBC reporter, told the Sanctuary Summit that a humane asylum system is possible in Britain: "We are getting there slowly but surely. . . . One day we will have justice" (Civic Leicester 2014).

In 2000 the Home Office dispersed hundreds of asylum seekers to various cities far from London, including Glasgow. A survey by Shelter, a nongovernmental organization focused on housing, found that 26 percent of dwellings set aside for asylum seekers were unfit for human habitation, and 86 percent were unfit for the number of occupants housed; more than 80 percent posed a fire hazard.

Ahlam Souidi, an Algerian asylum seeker, told me in 2008 how shocked she had been by the house she was sent to in Glasgow. Classified as unfit for habitation, with no heating, it had stood empty for decades. The next-door neighbor harassed her and her family from their first night in the house, but authorities did nothing to stop the harassment. One of her children contracted chronic eczema from the dampness. They stayed for four years before the house was demolished and they were resettled in better accommodations.

Ahlam told me that she had started to hate Glasgow and Glaswegians and became severely depressed. Her health suffered, and she found it difficult to learn English. She and her family worried constantly about being deported. They watched as Iraqi neighbors were taken away in handcuffs during dawn raids and children were separated from their parents. On one occasion, immigration police broke down the apartment door of a Kurdish asylum-seeker family. The father threatened to jump from a twentieth-floor window, and his wife had a heart attack. Protesters gathered for four hours until the father surrendered and was taken to jail. On another occasion, authorities stopped the raid only when a father threatened to throw his child out the window.

At first, Ahlam's petition for asylum was denied, and the family could see no future but detention. "But we are lucky to have local people and organizations to support us. We are very grateful to them," she said. She was convinced that such pressure resulted in her family's finally receiving indefinite leave to remain after about seven years of waiting. The local people who helped said they did not want to see asylum seekers treated unfairly in Scotland. They told her they were ashamed of government actions such as dawn raids.

Eventually Ahlam took English classes at the YMCA and began to feel better. She was the first member of the Framework for Dialogue, a committee that liaised with local officials, and she became active in the Scottish Refugee Council. Unable to work legally while she waited for her asylum case to be decided, she taught French as a volunteer at a local school. She joined the Scottish Refugee Policy Forum, a group of asylum seekers and refugees that met regularly with government agencies and policy makers. "We built a very strong bridge with the Home Office," she said. She also testified before a parliamentary human rights commission about the situation of asylum seekers in Glasgow.

Ahlam pointed out that Scotland's population was aging and its numbers declining; the country needed new workers. As more asylum seekers and refugees arrived, the economy improved, and so did local attitudes. The organizations she joined continue to campaign on behalf of asylum seekers, sponsoring visits to schools to talk about their situation and taking other actions to change public opinion.

Unable to return to Algeria, Ahlam told me she no longer felt like a foreigner in Glasgow. Her youngest child had been born in Scotland, and her oldest felt Scottish. Her life and the lives of her children were there. Still, she identified with new arrivals and was ready to help them. In 2015 Ahlam wrote me that she was working for Maryhill Integration Network,

> an organization that helps refugees and asylum seekers to integrate into Scottish life. My role in MIN is community engagement and advice worker. I help refugees and asylum seekers to be integrated into the community, move them on from the asylum system . . . and help them to be settled. I am also one of the founders of an organization which was established last year, Uniting Nations in Scotland. It helps refugees, asylum seekers and migrants living in Glasgow to come together to integrate; my role is coordinator. I am happy with life now, as I feel that I am more settled and part of this country, with all my experience from my involvement with refugee organizations and groups. . . . I am passing on the support that I received in the past. (Personal communication, February 21, 2015)

Through her activism, Ahlam became integrated in the local community and made it her own. She found – and achieved – enduring sanctuary.

Eveline Louden McNair is one of the Scots who helped people like Ahlam. A longtime resident of the Toryglen public housing estate in southern Glasgow, she began doing volunteer community organizing there in the early 1990s. Developed in the 1950s and 1960s, Toryglen is a rundown housing project located on barren marshland. Contractors found asbestos buried there when a "regeneration" project started in the mid-2000s. The site's former use as a dump might explain the high level of environmentally caused health problems from which residents suffered. When I visited in 2008, Eveline pointed to a high chain-link fence that circled the entire estate during the redevelopment project, saying it did not feel good to be surrounded in that way.

After the sudden arrival of hundreds of dispersed asylum seekers on the estate in 2000, Eveline became involved in efforts to help them. She ended up managing Integrating Toryglen Community, a project funded by the Glasgow government, at Toryglen Community Base, an outwardly shabby but inwardly tidy and lively oasis in a row of boarded-up shops. In conjunction with nearby Langside College, its Integration and Orientation Programme offered dozens of classes and workshops in everything from money management and home safety to health care and English as a Second Language. Eveline and other residents of Toryglen worked to improve the community by helping asylum seekers integrate into it.

As the regeneration project progressed, most of the old houses were demolished, new ones were built, and the high-rise apartment buildings were scheduled to be razed. Eveline's project closed. In early 2015 she wrote:

> Sadly we have no asylum seekers left in the area, and nearly all of the families who were granted refugee status moved to other areas of the city. . . . They have built new friendships and new lives. . . . I always said that when people moved on, my work was done, and I have done my job. Don't get me wrong; it was sad at the time, as I loved my job and all the people I had met over the years. I always wanted to travel the world, but I was fortunate enough that I didn't need to, as the world came to Toryglen. I still see many of the women when I am out and about shopping; it's a fantastic feeling knowing that they don't forget [me] as I don't forget them. (Personal communication, February 2015)

Activists in Glasgow were the only advocates I encountered in Britain who expressed optimism about the prospects of asylum seekers. They phrased their opinions in practical and pragmatic terms. One suggested that the British government was unlikely to change its punitive immigration policies until it acknowledged that it would be impracticable to deport all the undocumented people, so adequate provision would have to be made for those in destitution. She and others pointed out that Britain would need to admit millions of young immigrants in the coming years to care for its aging population and replace older workers as they retired.

Why are things better for asylum seekers in Glasgow? The reasons are mainly political. Scottish asylum advocates told me that nationalists had gained ground after the British government devolved authority for local lawmaking to Scottish, Welsh, and Northern Irish Parliaments in 1997. In 2007 the Scottish National Party, which seeks independence for Scotland, won control of the Scottish Executive. Since then it has jousted with London for greater control over immigration policies, protesting dawn deportation raids, detention of immigrant families, denial of some social welfare benefits to asylum seekers, and especially measures that negatively affect the children of asylum seekers. The Scottish government also pressed London to grant amnesty in so-called legacy cases involving asylum seekers, such as Ahlam Souidi, who had been waiting years for decisions on their claims. It made life easier for them by furnishing services and benefits that London refused to provide, including access to higher education.

The Scottish Executive proposed to address refugees' housing, health, justice, employment and training, community development, and children's welfare. It organized a "One Scotland" campaign, encouraging schools to use advocacy organizations' materials containing accurate information on refugees and asylum seekers. It sponsored the "Framework for Dialogue" with the Scottish Refugee Council, the Glasgow City Council, and ten refugee organizations. In addition, the Scottish Executive and local authorities allocated funding to grassroots projects and initiatives to help asylum seekers. Reform of the immigration system was one of the main issues in the Scottish independence referendum that took place in September 2014. Although asylum policy was not at the top of the list, Scotland's Refugee Council took the opportunity in 2013 to publish a report that recommended asylum policy changes whether or not the referendum passed.

It is easier for asylum advocates to make and keep in contact with authorities at the local and regional level in Scotland, a smaller political arena than England. Since most asylum seekers in Scotland live

in Glasgow, community activists have one place in which to focus
their efforts and enlist thousands of potential activists. For all these
reasons, Scotland could provide a model for successful integration
of asylum seekers, refugees, and immigrants throughout Britain – if
the government and lawmakers could move beyond a punitive system
based on fear and exclusion. Even if the government cannot bring
itself to reform the asylum system, citizens and asylum seekers have
shown that they can join together to challenge the system constructively and effectively.

Canada's Sanctuary Tradition Continues

The Canadian government stepped back from its commitment to
give refuge to political exiles as the Cold War waned. In response,
the General Council of the Church of Canada declared in 1992 that
congregations had "the moral right and responsibility . . . to provide
sanctuary to legitimate refugee claimants who have been denied refugee status" (quoted by Cunningham 2013: 166). Canada's Catholic
bishops followed suit in 1993, saying, "The decision in conscience
to offer sanctuary, which is a decision of last resort, is part of every
major faith tradition" (166). Various churches and faith-based organizations started giving sanctuary. Romero House in Toronto hid two
families, the Auto Workers Union paid their living expenses, and doctors and local hospitals volunteered medical services. In 1993 Romero
House and other groups formed the Ontario Sanctuary Coalition,
which still helps asylum seekers and refugees around Canada as the
Sanctuary Network.

Mary Jo Leddy, the founder of Romero House, a shelter for refugees in Toronto, explains their strategy: "We decided that . . . placing
refugees publicly within a church building [was not appropriate]. . . .
We opted more for the World War II model in which Christians hid
those refugees whose lives were in danger. We began to offer Sanctuary without announcing what we were doing" (171). The coalition
feared that officials would walk into churches and take asylum seekers
away, so they did not tell anybody where the refugees were hidden.
The coalition also advocated publicly for changes in the immigration

laws that would make it easier for asylum seekers to gain refuge. In this initiative, they did not succeed. As the years passed, and especially after 9/11, Canada's immigration laws became increasingly restrictive.

In 2004 alone, 250 people took refuge in Canadian churches. That year "Sanctuary Week" was commemorated across the country after police raided a church to seize an Algerian who claimed to fear torture in his home country. In his book on Canadian sanctuary, Randy Lippert (2005) writes that the government tried to make a secret agreement with churches to speed consideration of immigration cases, but the churches insisted on their right to give sanctuary. Lippert does not see sanctuary in Canada as similar to the institution in the United States, where the division between church and state is more clear cut: "Sanctuary in Canada was . . . a collection of local incidents that were disconnected socially and geographically from one another, temporally limited, and surprisingly, often not primarily religious in orientation" (13). Nonetheless, incidents keep happening in which churches proclaim publicly that they will shelter migrants. Local groups have taken it upon themselves to hide migrants from police, but according to Lippert, these actions do not constitute a coordinated movement.

Asylum seekers have tended to stay in churches for about five months, but some have remained for more than a year. The longest recorded incident that Lippert found lasted 630 days. There were three usual outcomes: the asylum seeker gained legal status, went underground, or surrendered for deportation. Sometimes lawyers, politicians, television talk-show hosts, or even police officers suggested that migrants take shelter in a church; at other times, the migrants themselves came up with the idea. In twenty-seven of thirty-six incidents that Lippert investigated, the churches themselves did not initiate sanctuary; rather, they responded to urgent pleas. Decisions to give sanctuary were ad hoc, with no coordination among congregations.

Sanctuary providers were predominantly middle-class, middle-aged, white Canadians. Women cared for migrants in sanctuary, while men handled media relations and other publicity efforts. Clergy were seldom heavily involved. Community members visited migrants in sanctuary, provided food and furniture, organized fund-raising events, participated in protests, marches, and vigils, and met with immigration officials to discuss alternatives to deportation. Public reaction to church sanctuary was overwhelmingly supportive, and usually the local press covered the incident sympathetically (32–34).

More than 260 migrants gained sanctuary in the thirty-six incidents that Lippert recorded. These incidents involved both individuals and families, including children. Asylum seekers came from twenty-eight countries. All had tried to gain legal status via official procedures but had been denied humanitarian waivers. They sought sanctuary when all other means had been exhausted. As in medieval times, church sanctuary gave time for the authorities to reconsider their decision, the community to raise support, and lawyers and officials to negotiate. In most cases, the migrants gained legal status or permission to remain in Canada (40).[4] In addition, the government responded to public outcry by staying the deportation orders of some two thousand asylum seekers from Guatemala, Turkey, and Algeria.

Perhaps these incidents were the means by which the public civilly protested or appealed the restrictive immigration policies the government had introduced in the 1980s and '90s. It was clear that the authorities wanted to avoid deporting massive numbers of migrants and the political embarrassment such outcomes might bring. Canada wanted to keep its international reputation as a compassionate shelter for persecuted people (and a welcoming haven for hard workers) while responding to US pressure to keep out dangerous strangers. After 9/11, this balancing act became more difficult.

Pressure on sanctuary providers increased after 9/11, too. Tax authorities told church administrators that their tax exemption could be taken away for the "political activity" of sheltering asylum seekers. Some sanctuary workers made sure the church was always unlocked, so the police would not have any excuse to break in to apprehend migrants. One worker commented, "If Immigration's decided that they wanted to come pick her up, they [can] just tell us. We'll hold the door. . . . We aren't going to stand in the way of an actual apprehension, but we are also going to grant her sanctuary" (quoted by Lippert 2005: 146). For Lippert, the ritual of sanctuary provides a means for citizens to resist governmental power and readjust the government's relationship with them. In the process, the refugee is redefined as a potential citizen with a face, a story, and a self. In Canada, sanctuary is a last resort in exceptional cases, when the government oversteps its moral, if not its legal, boundaries.

As a result of drastic policy changes over a relatively short period, refused asylum seekers and others in danger of deportation are again finding refuge in Canadian churches. A Roma family fled death threats in Hungary in 2009, as a result of the father's public political activities. They went to Canada, where the government rejected their asylum application. In 2012 an Anglican church in Toronto agreed to hide them, thereby risking its tax exemption. Their lawyer filed a petition asking the government for humanitarian leave to remain in Canada but received no answer. Nor did the police go to the church to arrest them. "There are clear errors in our system and an error in a refugee determination is a life and death error," the lawyer argued. "The church in this case is stepping in to ensure the protection of life. They don't do it to operate above the law. They do it to hold Canadian law to its highest legal obligation and it's tragic that it's come to this" (quoted by Westhead 2012).

In April 2014, a Salvadoran asylum seeker was reportedly "holed up in a Vancouver church to avoid being marched out of the country by border officials" because he had supported rebel forces in El Salvador in the 1980s and was thereby classified forever as a terrorist under an obscure provision of Canadian immigration law (Ross 2014). Against mounting odds and with the support of local communities, asylum seekers still struggle to find refuge in Canada.

Australia's Sanctuary Movement without a Name

Australian community organizations, including the Refugee Council of Australia, A Just Australia, Justice for Asylum Seekers, Rural Australians for Refugees, and Chilout (Children Out of Detention), have advocated on behalf of asylum seekers for decades. For years residents of outback towns near a desert detention center visited detainees weekly. In the late 1990s, the Refugee Action Collective, a grassroots group, and Australians for a Fair Australia, which included prominent public figures and ordinary citizens, conducted information campaigns and convened university study groups on behalf of asylum seekers. In 2001–2, a network of activists gave sanctuary to asylum seekers who had escaped from detention facilities, risking a ten-year prison sentence for "acts against the state" (Tazreiter 2004: 183).

The Professional Alliance for the Health of Asylum Seekers and Their Children, composed of fifty thousand physicians and health workers, the largest group ever to work on a single social issue in Australia history, issued reports documenting cases of post-traumatic stress disorder among detained children (Moorehead 2005: 119). The Australian Catholic Social Justice Council called detainees' treatment torture, the World Council of Churches protested against detention practices, and the president of the Australian Medical Association spoke out on public radio about the damaging effects of detention on asylum seekers. During the Howard government, a network called Justice for Asylum Seekers, based in Melbourne and including large church and welfare organizations, successfully lobbied for the release of children from detention into the care of welfare agencies (Grant Mitchell, personal communication, 2015). After the government reintroduced the Pacific Solution, opposition to government policies grew, although opinion polls indicated broad support for them. The Refugee Advocacy Network listed thirty-four pro-immigrant organizations in the state of Victoria alone, from the Australian Green Party to the Melbourne Catholic Migrant and Refugee Office.

A Sri Lankan refugee started Rise: Refugee Survivors and Ex-Detainees, the first pro-asylum organization in Australia run by ex-detainees and people of color. Its founder had spent months in detention on Christmas Island and the Australian mainland. Resolutely independent, Rise refuses to accept funding from the central government. It offers social services to 1,600 members and conducts campaigns against government asylum policies. Also in Victoria, the Asylum Seekers Resource Center feeds lunch to 150 asylum seekers every day, provides other social services, and carries on advocacy activities. Its main funding source is private donations, with only 5 percent of its budget coming from the state government. Both groups feel freer to criticize government policies than the bigger immigration organizations, which rely on central government funding. Many Australian organizations, both religious and secular, protest loudly against government policies that they abhor. In early 2016 public protests erupted when the Supreme Court declared that the government could legally deport 267 asylum seekers, including thirty-seven children born in Australia, to Nauru. Ten churches in six cities offered them sanctuary. The Anglican dean of Brisbane said he was prepared to be prosecuted for trying to prevent federal authorities from entering cathedral grounds. "We offer this refuge because there is irrefutable evidence from health and legal experts that the circumstances asylum seekers, especially children, would face if sent back to Nauru are tantamount to state-sanctioned abuse," he announced (Farrell 2016). And so advocates for asylum seekers continue to resist the immense power of the state, in Australia as elsewhere.

As harsh government policies threaten asylum, sanctuary endures, taking many forms. The stories of sanctuary movements in this chapter show that the practice is well established, global, often effective, and strongly but not exclusively rooted in religious convictions and customs. As conditions change, traditional sanctuarians develop new tactics. The Sans-Papiers who occupied French churches and the Iraqi refugees who took over abandoned buildings in Amsterdam overcame their powerlessness by recasting sanctuary's ancient traditions. The examples of the ex-detainee in Australia, the Glasgow Girls, and asylum seekers who started self-help organizations in many countries send a heartening message to the next generation of sanctuary seekers and givers: with the help of willing strangers, it is possible to come out of hiding and into the daylight.

12 The News from Tucson

> We don't call it the New Sanctuary Movement; it's
> the Sanctuary Movement.
>
> – Rev. Alison Harrington, Southside Presbyterian Church, Tucson

As I started doing research on sanctuary in 2006, hundreds of thousands of demonstrators, including undocumented migrants, were marching in cities across the United States to support comprehensive immigration reform. But an immigration bill failed to get through Congress, and the government kept detaining and deporting migrants. Beginning in 2007, something called the New Sanctuary Movement (NSM) began receiving media coverage. Within a year it was said to stretch "from Massachusetts to Washington state, with 35 different networks in at least 10 states. The Associated Press estimated earlier this year [2008] that there are at least 13 undocumented immigrants currently receiving physical sanctuary at congregations around the country. Thousands more immigrants – illegal and legal – have been aided by the movement with clothing, food, money and legal counseling. Among the movement's main goals is a more compassionate US immigration policy" (Religionlink 2008).

The new movement did not focus on providing church sanctuary or challenging US law, however: "The New Sanctuary Movement . . . has been less about physical sanctuary than about providing a new means of telling the story of the human costs of current US deportation policy. . . . Participating churches believe that providing humanitarian assistance does not violate the law as long as it is done openly and they do not hide illegal immigrants" (Caminero-Santangelo 2013: 92). NSM activists argued that they were not breaking the law; instead, the law itself was broken. This rhetoric echoed Jim Corbett's conception of sanctuary as civil initiative – holding the government to account for its violations of domestic and international law – rather than civil disobedience (Corbett 1986).

In 2008 I went to Tucson, Arizona, to find out more about the 1980s Sanctuary Movement, which had started there. As far as I knew, the movement had ended around 1990, after a federal court gave Central Americans the opportunity to have their rejected asylum cases readjudicated and Congress passed a law giving temporary protected status to Salvadorans and other migrants in the United States.[1] But I wondered if the New Sanctuary Movement was operating in Arizona. Were activists again giving undocumented migrants and asylum seekers refuge in churches and homes, as they had twenty-five years before?

What I found there in 2008 was different. A number of groups had been providing humanitarian aid since around 2000 to undocumented migrants crossing the Sonoran Desert. They were responding to the grim fact that the number of migrant deaths in the desert had been climbing, since the border patrol had made it impossible for migrants to cross the border in more accessible areas in the mid-1990s. Tucson's *Daily Star* kept publishing reports of migrant deaths that moved both veterans of the Sanctuary Movement and younger activists to take water, food, and clothing to places in the desert where border crossers were known to rest.

In March 2001 a new group, Humane Borders, placed sixty-five-gallon water barrels on public and private land near Tucson, and dozens of volunteers started to drive trucks out to the desert every week to refill the barrels. Pennants with the group's logo waved above the water stations. The logo consisted of the North Star and the Big Dipper pouring water, reminiscent of the code signals used by the Underground Railroad in ferrying slaves to the North (Cook 2007: 5). Humane Borders sought permission from local, state, and federal agencies to maintain the barrels and insisted that the group had no intention of violating any laws. They even obtained an annual grant of $25,000 from the Pima County Board of Supervisors, which reasoned that the initiative would save some of the $300,000 spent annually to recover, identify, autopsy, store, and bury bodies found in the desert (12).

Other groups undertook humanitarian efforts in the desert. The Samaritans formed in 2002 to send out patrols along known migrant paths in the desert, looking for people who needed water, food, or medical attention (5). They went beyond Humane Borders' approach by not asking permission to carry out rescue missions. No More Deaths (NMD) formed in 2004, setting up camps in the desert and patrols that searched for migrants in distress. It attracted volunteers and donors from around the country. Both groups deliberately operated in the "grey area of legality" (5).

Other Tucson organizations focusing on border issues, many with overlapping membership lists, included Derechos Humanos, the Border Action Network, BorderLinks, the American Friends Service Committee of Arizona, and the American Civil Liberties Union. They carried out community organizing, public education campaigns, lobbying, and monitoring of Border Patrol operations. Most of these groups were faith based. Religion provided the framework and justification for direct action. In 2014, when I visited Tucson again, Rev. John Fife, Fr. Ricardo Elford, Margo Cowan, and other cofounders of the 1980s Sanctuary Movement still were intensely involved in border issues. (Jim Corbett had died in 2001, but his spirit hovered over southern Arizona.)

Although the government and numerous immigration opponents insisted that the migrants came to the United States for economic rather than political reasons, the new sanctuary groups drew parallels with the situation in the 1980s, when "the United States was complicit in the torture, disappearances and killings of tens of thousands of people in the region, and responsible for the welfare of those fleeing the violence and repression" (7). Over time, old and new sanctuary movement participants adjusted their perspective to justify supporting economic migrants as well as asylum seekers. They contended that they had a moral obligation to help the innocent victims of the North American Free Trade Agreement and globalization.

In mid-2005, Border Patrol agents arrested two young NMD volunteers who had driven three migrants from the desert to a Tucson clinic, for "transportation in furtherance of an illegal presence in the United States" and conspiracy – felonies with maximum sentences of fifteen years (18). A vocal campaign erupted in southern Arizona on the volunteers' behalf with the slogan "Humanitarian Aid Is Never a Crime." At about that time, NMD made an agreement with the state of Sonora, Mexico, to operate a shelter there for returning migrants. From mid-2006 to mid-2007, NMD helped 136,000 migrants at two stations in Mexico.

In September 2006, the government dropped the charges against the volunteers. However, in 2009 the federal government charged eighteen NMD members with littering after they left bottles of drinking water on migrant trails inside the Buenos Aires National Wildlife Refuge near the Arizona-Mexico border. Charges against sixteen members were dropped, but two of the activists were convicted. One of them, Dan Millis, appealed. In September 2010, the Ninth Circuit Court of Appeals overturned his conviction. The court found that clean bottles of drinking water left on known migrant trails could not be considered garbage because their purpose was to prevent death by exposure (No More Deaths 2010). Subsequently, the government decided it was not worth the time and expense to prosecute NMD activists for littering.

Claiming to obey a higher moral law, advocacy groups engaged in a struggle with officials over the legality of humanitarian assistance (Cook 2007: 21). For a time, an uneasy collaboration developed between the humanitarians and some government officials in the name of saving lives. John Fife told a *New York Times* reporter about a conversation he had had with the Border Patrol chief in southern Arizona. Fife told the chief, "You know I'm not going to turn over anyone I find to Border Patrol for deportation." The chief responded, "If I find you reverting to your old ways, I'm going to put the cuffs on you myself" (Goodstein 2001). Fife continued his involvement with the new movement and was not arrested. Meanwhile, in 2005 Representative James Sensenbrenner sponsored legislation that would have criminalized both migrants and any organizations or individuals that helped them, but his bill failed after an outcry by nonprofit – especially faith-based – groups.

Desert deaths continued to rise as migrant smugglers took ever more remote routes in the continuing effort to evade capture. Border Patrol workplace raids increased, and eventually the numbers of migrants crossing the southern border fell as economic conditions in the United States became less attractive to undocumented workers. Even so, Humane Borders, No More Deaths, Samaritans, and other groups continued providing humanitarian assistance to migrants in the desert.

In 2008, I drove with Humane Borders volunteers from one water station to the next in the unforgiving April heat. Migrants' personal effects lay recently abandoned on the trails. The *Daily Star* continued to print stories of their deaths in the desert. Along the highway, I glimpsed a migrant weeping as she sat on the ground next to the Border Patrol bus that would deport her and dozens of others to Mexico. Twenty-five miles from the border, the Border Patrol stopped every vehicle at a checkpoint, demanding identification. The ceaseless war against the undocumented continued, fortified by increasing congressional appropriations, no matter how much water and medical assistance the volunteers provided. I left Tucson for El Paso and Albuquerque, where I found more signs of continuing sanctuary activity by veterans of the 1980s and a new generation of activists.

El Paso is located across the Rio Grande from Ciudad Juárez, one of the most violent cities in Mexico. Since 2006, when "hyperviolence" exploded in that country, hundreds of thousands of people have fled Juárez and other cities. Thousands of Mexican journalists, human rights activists, former police, business owners, and others – including witnesses to crimes, domestic violence victims, and children persecuted by gangs – have sought asylum in the United States. Very few have gained it. About fifteen Mexican journalists have obtained asylum, according to Carlos Spector, an immigration lawyer in El Paso who represents hundreds of asylum seekers. Spector and human rights activist Cipriana Jurado founded a nonprofit organization, Mexicanos en Exilio (Mexenex), which publicizes the dire situation in their home country (Levy 2014).

El Paso's flagship advocacy organization is Annunciation House, which shelters released, indigent asylum seekers, helping them find legal representation and apply for work permits. Annunciation House has been in existence since 1978 and was active in the 1980s Sanctuary Movement. The Border Network for Human Rights, the El Paso Press Club, and Las Americas Immigrant Advocacy Center are among the organizations in El Paso that work on behalf of asylum seekers and other migrants. In nearby Las Cruces, New Mexico, the Southwest Asylum and Migration Institute, Alianza for Political Asylum Seekers, and Catholic Charities also assist Mexicans fleeing persecution.

In 2009 the New Sanctuary Movement's website was blank and the domain name was up for sale, but in 2010 several websites sprang up, recording the activities of local sanctuary groups from Oregon to Pennsylvania. Public attention had shifted elsewhere, however, and the New Sanctuary Movement remained in obscurity until 2014. Typically, asylum seekers receive only sporadic attention, and the media tend to focus on so-called illegal aliens who are thought to enter the country for economic reasons. But asylum seekers are often detained in substandard conditions along with undocumented workers and criminals awaiting deportation. Migrants who might have presented strong asylum claims if they had adequate legal representation are deported. As a result, advocacy groups that try to inform the public about asylum issues find themselves challenging the entire immigration enforcement system.

Religious and Other Advocacy after 9/11

During the first decade of the twenty-first century, many local groups sprang up to help immigration detainees known in their communities. The Interfaith Coalition for the Rights of Immigration Detainees and Their Families, a New Jersey grouping of about twenty organizations, sponsored vigils at the Bergen County Jail. One of the participating groups, Families for Freedom, came into existence in September 2002 to fight secret detention and deportation of undocumented migrants, deportable criminal aliens, and unsuccessful asylum seekers, after thousands of foreign males were arrested in the wake of the 9/11 attacks. Other groups included venerable faith-based organizations such as the American Friends Service Committee, ethnic community groups, and prominent advocacy organizations such as the American Civil Liberties Union Prison Project, Human Rights Watch, and Human Rights First. These organizations did not distinguish between detained or deported asylum seekers and undocumented migrants.

One initiative that harked back to the 1980s Sanctuary Movement was the struggle against local implementation of two programs, Secure Communities and provision 287(g) of the 1996 immigration law, which authorized police departments to apprehend and hand over undocumented or criminal aliens to ICE. Many towns and cities signed on to these federal programs. But activists in more than thirty localities, which had passed sanctuary laws or resolutions to protect Central American asylum seekers in the 1980s, tried to prevent city councils from allowing local police to enforce federal immigration laws in the 2000s.

For example, in 2007 the city council of Takoma Park, Maryland, just outside Washington, DC, held a public hearing at which the police chief asked for permission to participate in 287(g), which violated the town's sanctuary law, passed in 1985. The chief described meeting with representatives of a local advocacy group founded by Central American exiles, who objected to the alleged unreliability of the federal crime database and stressed the importance of not damaging the immigrant community's trust in the police (*Washington Post* 2007: B1). The city council unanimously voted to uphold the local sanctuary law.

In several states, including Arizona, Georgia, and Pennsylvania, as well as in the US Congress, bills were introduced to prohibit cities from providing sanctuary and to criminalize anyone who aided and abetted an illegal alien for any purpose. Some of these bills passed but were overturned by state and federal courts before they could be implemented. In 2014, Takoma Park's police chief reaffirmed that the town was still a sanctuary city: "We do not enforce immigration warrants from ICE. . . . The Takoma Park Police does not make inquiries regarding the immigration status of individuals that are contacted or arrested. . . . We do not and did not participate in ICE cases based only on immigration status" (Alan Goldberg, personal communication, December 2014).

Also in 2014, President Obama announced plans to end the Secure Communities program. Sanctuary City resolutions not only expressed community sentiment; they may have prevented some local authorities from cooperating with ICE and hastened the end of Secure Communities.[2]

Local churches have quietly offered sanctuary to refused asylum seekers for years. The pastor of the Highland Park, New Jersey, Reformed Church, Seth Kaper-Dale, tried to help Indonesian Christians for more than a decade. They had fled predominantly Muslim Indonesia in the late 1990s and early 2000s, when churches were being burned and Christians persecuted. Knowing nothing about asylum, they arrived in the United States with tourist or student visas and stayed on.

Kaper-Dale encouraged them to report for the post-9/11 National Security Entry-Exit Registration System (NSEERS) inspection, which targeted males from predominantly Muslim countries, in 2003. However, their registration in the program brought them to ICE's attention. Their applications for asylum were rejected because they had failed to apply within a year of arrival, as required by the 1996 immigration law. In 2009 an Indonesian church elder was detained for eighty days. Kaper-Dale worked out a deal with ICE, and 203 Indonesians reported to ICE offices in New Jersey, New Hampshire, and New York. By that time, several thousand Indonesian Christians and their US citizen children were living in the United States and waiting nervously for immigration decisions.

In June 2011, ICE's director issued the "prosecutorial discretion" memo, in which he said immigration prosecutors could decide not to proceed against asylum seekers and undocumented migrants if they had "longstanding ties to the community, U.S.-citizen family members, or other characteristics that merit a favorable exercise of discretion," such as lack of a criminal record (Immigration Policy Center 2011). Such cases could be considered low priority and removed from the immigration court docket.

Kaper-Dale mistakenly believed the Indonesian Christians – who had no criminal record, had US citizen children, and were working legally and paying taxes – would be safe, thanks to prosecutorial discretion. But late in 2011 the local ICE office placed Indonesian Christians in deportation proceedings, even though their cases were still unresolved. Dozens were deported.

In March 2012 Kaper-Dale's church gave sanctuary to nine Indonesians. For almost a year the congregation waged a campaign to stop
their deportation, because, they said, the Indonesians were still vulnerable to persecution in their home country. Sympathetic members
of Congress introduced legislation, the Indonesian Refugee Family
Protection Act, on their behalf. Almost a year later, in February 2013,
Kaper-Dale managed to strike another deal with ICE. The nine sanctuary seekers were placed on "orders of supervision," whereby they
would report regularly to ICE but would not be detained or deported
as long as their cases were under consideration. The Indonesians left
the church and returned home to their families, still waiting for comprehensive immigration reform to resolve their precarious situation.
Until such a reform was passed, they had to return to ICE each year
to request extension of the stays of deportation.

Highland Park Reformed Church did not identify itself as part
of the New Sanctuary Movement, but other churches did. The New
Sanctuary Movement of Philadelphia (NSMP) started in 2008 as "an
interfaith coalition of immigrants, congregations and individuals
dedicated to taking a public stand for immigrant rights" and "part
of the National New Sanctuary movement based in congregations
around the United States which are connected to immigrant families
who are facing the possibility of separation through deportation," as
described on its website (www.sanctuaryphiladelphia.org).

Eighteen religious congregations participated in NSMP. The organization's office, in a working-class neighborhood in North Philadelphia, was staffed by three young people, including a former Catholic
Worker and a former volunteer at Southside Presbyterian Church in
Tucson. The group visited immigration detainees, assisted families
of detainees, attended deportation hearings, did outreach to community groups and congregations, conducted "Immigration 101"
educational workshops at congregations, and conducted "Know Your
Rights" training workshops for migrants.

In September 2014, NSMP joined church groups in more than a
dozen cities to announce that it would defy government deportation
orders by providing refuge for immigrants facing imminent expulsion
from the United States (Matza 2014). A letter to President Obama,

Secretary of Homeland Security Johnson, and ICE Director Muñoz announced that fifteen congregations around the country were making the sanctuary offer.[3] Churches in Tucson, Phoenix, and Chicago had already taken in undocumented migrants. A few weeks later, on November 18, 2014, West Kensington Ministry in Philadelphia gave sanctuary to Angela Navarro, a Honduran woman at risk of deportation. Navarro is the wife and mother of US citizens, a restaurant worker who quit her job to enter sanctuary. She explained, "I have lived in fear for 10 years and I can't continue living this way" (Matza 2014).

Navarro told a journalist that her parents had been allowed to enter the United States legally after Hurricane Mitch, but she "was caught at the border soon afterward, trying to join them. She's been dodging a deportation order ever since – getting married and having two children along the way – but now she's hoping that by challenging the deportation order head-on, she can defeat it" (Hangley 2014). Early in 2015, Navarro got word that ICE had decided to exercise prosecutorial discretion in her case. She would receive two years' stay of deportation and a work permit. After fifty-eight days inside, she left church sanctuary on January 17, 2015.

None of the ten migrants originally featured on the Sanctuary Movement website (www.sanctuary2014.org) was a classic asylum seeker fleeing political persecution. One might have been able to make a case for asylum because he had fled criminal gangs in Guatemala, and one was eligible for a U-visa as the victim of a violent crime who had testified against her assailant in court. Several might have been eligible for relief under President Obama's administrative directive of November 2014. The others, like Navarro, had gotten entangled in the coils of the immigration bureaucracy. One had been stopped by local police and turned over to ICE only because his car was emitting too much exhaust.

As of January 2015, the New Sanctuary Movement website announced that six sanctuary cases had been "won," four were active, twelve cities had sanctuary congregations, twenty-four congregations were offering sanctuary, and twenty-three congregations were supporting sanctuary.[4] In early 2016 the website announced that ten sanctuary seekers were sheltered in churches around the country.

Most but not all of the 2014 sanctuary seekers were continuing to fight for asylum or other protected status, their deportation stayed. According to Noel Andersen of Church World Service, some forty congregations have offered sanctuary in fifteen states, and more than three hundred congregations around the United States have offered support to the sanctuary churches (personal communication, October 7, 2015; Burnett 2016). But only time—and the persistent efforts of thousands of sanctuarians—would tell whether their work might lead to a resolution allowing the sanctuary seekers to live in peace with their families in the United States.

Tucson in the Forefront Again

As in the 1980s, Tucson was in the vanguard of sanctuary efforts in 2014. In May, the Southside Presbyterian Church, where the 1980s sanctuary movement had been launched in 1982, gave sanctuary to Daniel Neyoy Ruiz. It was the first time in thirty years that the church had given refuge to a migrant. After twenty-eight days at the church, he received a stay of deportation and went home to his family.

In August, Southside gave sanctuary to Rosa Robles Loreto. Like Neyoy, she was eligible for prosecutorial discretion, had no criminal record, and had lived in the United States with her family for many years. But it turned out that she was ineligible for Obama's administrative relief because she had gone home to Mexico to have her two children. They would be eligible to remain temporarily in the United States under amended Deferred Action for Childhood Arrival (DACA) rules, but she could not obtain relief through her children because of provisions in the 1996 immigration law. Her husband was also in deportation proceedings but had not received a final deportation order. Why had the authorities decided they wanted to deport her but not her husband? Perhaps her husband had received better legal representation at an early phase of the process.

Rosa looked as if she were about to weep as she waited to speak at a press conference at Southside after Obama's announcement on November 20. She had been living for more than a hundred days in a little room in the church, where her husband and children visited her

every day. Her pro bono lawyer, Margo Cowan, one of the cofounders of the Sanctuary Movement, was still optimistic that she could
obtain a stay of deportation for Rosa. Across town, in sanctuary at
the Saint Francis in the Foothills United Methodist Church, Francisco
Perez Cordoba was celebrating after Obama's speech. He was eligible
for relief because his five children were US citizens. The reasons for
Francisco's joy and Rosa's sorrow seemed cruelly arbitrary. Finally,
on November 11, 2015, after more than a year at Southside, Rosa
left sanctuary, her deportation stayed, and returned to her family.

While Rosa was still waiting in sanctuary, I went to the desert
with three Samaritans who were checking on water bottles they had
left in a small canyon a few days before. They told me the story of
"Sheriff Arpaio's van," as they called it, in which we were riding.[5]
The notorious lawman's officers had pulled over and harassed two
Samaritans who happened to be lawyers. They had sued the Maricopa
County Police Department and won a large settlement. The lawyers
had decided to donate the money to charity, and the Samaritans had
used the funds to buy the van.

Unfortunately I did not have the opportunity to visit No More
Deaths' medical tent in the desert. NMD has affiliated with the American Red Cross to provide emergency medical assistance to migrants
there, but this did not stop twenty-five Border Patrol officers on
horseback from raiding the tent without warning and threatening
the volunteers with felony charges. Because they had no search warrant, they could not enter the tent, which was classified as a building
because volunteers had put a door on it.

Sanctuary groups coordinate many creative activities in the Tucson area. Hundreds of students from all over the country visit No
More Deaths, the Samaritans, Humane Borders, and other organizations to participate in their projects for weeks or months at a time.
Some stay for years. The intentional community Casa Mariposa was
packed with young volunteers when I went to a potluck supper there.
Its guiding spirit is John Heid, a former Catholic Worker who, with
support from local Quakers, created the house in 2009. When the
house had to move in 2012, one of its Quaker benefactors told Heid,
"I love the work the community does. I haven't seen anything like it

since the Sanctuary days. You find a house that meets your needs and I will purchase it. This is not charity!" (Heid, personal communication, February 3, 2015).

According to its mission statement, Casa Mariposa "seeks to live in right relationship with one another, the community, and the earth through hospitality, simple sustainable living, playful spirituality, and peaceful prophetic action." According to Heid, "Over time the community came to learn of the myriad needs among those caught up in the immigration web and began to offer hospitality accordingly. The 'bus station ministry' became one of these efforts." Around 2011 Heid started noticing that the Border Patrol was leaving increasing numbers of migrant families at the Tucson bus station; over one Labor Day weekend, eighty people were left there. Casa Mariposa gave shelter to scores of the migrants, until the house became overwhelmed. Eventually the Catholic Diocese and local social service agencies took over. Heid estimated that two hundred migrants had been housed in Tucson in October and another two hundred in November 2014.

My last conversation in Tucson was with John Fife, former pastor of Southside Presbyterian Church and one of the cofounders of the Sanctuary Movement. I asked him why he thought the New Sanctuary Movement had lain fallow for so long. He replied that advocacy groups worked on comprehensive immigration reform for three years, and the administration encouraged them to keep working. As long as they believed that Congress would pass reform legislation or the president would take administrative action at the end of summer 2014, as promised, they backed away from confrontation. But movement groups found no more reason to delay when the Republicans declared the legislation dead and the president postponed taking administrative action until after the midterm elections. They were painfully aware from pastoral experience that every day 1,100 migrants were being deported and thousands of families broken up.[6] They went ahead with plans to offer sanctuary to migrants at risk of imminent deportation. In Fife's words, it was past time to move from advocacy to resistance. And John Fife is an expert at resistance, with more than thirty years' experience. He embodies Rev. Alison

Harrington's affirmation, quoted above, of the long-term viability of the Sanctuary Movement, of which the New Sanctuary Movement is only the latest manifestation.

Some scholars have questioned the viability of sanctuary as a political strategy, however. Grace Yukich wrote that the New Sanctuary Movement "struggled to re-imagine sanctuary to meet the demands of a new political environment"; she believed that "sanctuary's powerful history is an obstacle to strategic adaptation" (2013: 108). The new movement, she argued, "lacks resources and networks to successfully disseminate a new understanding of sanctuary among potential recruits." She doubted that church sanctuary could be an effective tool to advance the legalization of undocumented migrants. What I saw in Tucson in late 2014 belied her skeptical conclusions, written before sanctuary's revival in mid-2014.

Although decentralized, the sanctuary movement is more powerful and enduring than some observers might imagine. As Rev. Alexia Salvatierra, executive director of Clergy and Laity United for Economic Justice, wrote in 2007, "Sanctuary is an act of compassion, an expression of mercy. It is, however, not mercy at the expense of justice. Participants in the New Sanctuary Movement believe that our current immigration system is profoundly unjust – so unjust that we believe that we are facing one of those unique moments throughout history when divine law and human law are in conflict, and God's justice demands that we stand with those who break unjust laws even at the risk of sharing their punishment" (quoted in Michels and Blaikie 2013: 35). In cities from Denver to Philadelphia, sanctuary coalitions continue to develop and work on new campaigns that support and extend church sanctuary in the local community.

Other Kinds of Sanctuary

Individuals as well as churches provide sanctuary. Henry Reese founded City of Asylum, a refuge for writers fleeing persecution, after hearing a talk by Salman Rushdie, who had spent many years in hiding after Ayatollah Khomeini of Iran issued a *fatwa* calling for his death. In a memoir, Rushdie wrote about the International Cities of Refuge Network, which included "three dozen cities from Ljubljana to Mexico City by way of Amsterdam, Barcelona and Las Vegas. Nations often had reasons not to give refuge to persecuted writers – foreign trouble might derail a trade deal – but at the urban level, mayors often saw this as an initiative with no downside. It didn't cost much to provide a threatened writer with a small apartment and a basic stipend for a couple of years" (Rushdie 2013: 419).

Inspired, Reese bought a former crack house in a rundown Pittsburgh neighborhood, renovated it, and invited threatened writers to live and work there. From 2004 to 2014, five writers, from China, Burma, Iran, El Salvador, and Venezuela, each received two years' support for themselves and their immediate families, housing, medical benefits, transportation to the United States, and legal services. Another eleven writers visited Pittsburgh with short-term fellowships. City of Asylum also helps its writers to find translators and publishers.

Reese told an interviewer, "Primarily it is just us saying, 'Who is the best writer and who has the most trouble?'" Started as a modest individual project, City of Asylum has become a lively arts center with thriving exchange programs, local events, and a $750,000 budget. Two other US cities, Las Vegas and Ithaca, NY, also give refuge to writers fleeing persecution. These programs help soothe the pain and privations of exile, which blunt the creativity of many talented people.

In Tucson, El Paso, and Albuquerque, I met people who had sheltered migrants in their homes before, during, and after the 1980s Sanctuary Movement. These kinds of activities still go on across the country. Most recently, one remarkable woman, Nora Sandigo, has taken it upon herself to help and care for the US-itizen and undocumented children of migrant parents threatened with deportation. In mid-2014 she was the legal guardian of 812 children, ranging from nine months to seventeen years old, in fourteen states. Sandigo, who lives in a Miami suburb, "does this as a volunteer and often at her own expense, not because she considers herself capable of providing a safety net for 812 children but because no one else does it" (Saslow 2014: A8).

Sandigo started helping deportees' children in 2009, when an undocumented Peruvian friend asked her to take in her two daughters. Every day she makes 120 lunches, delivers school supplies, seeks housing, and takes children to school, to the doctor, or to visit their detained parents. If one parent or both are deported, she arranges for relatives or friends to care for the children. Otherwise they would be placed in foster care. She observed that it is not hard to convince parents to trust her; they are desperate.

Twenty-five percent of deportees say they are parents of US citizens, "which means more than 100,000 American children lose a parent to deportation each year" (Saslow 2014). The federal government, Sandigo said, does not track what happens to the children of detainees and deportees. Likewise, no state or federal official monitors the activities of Sandigo and other guardians. She could be held liable if relatives with whom they live mistreat or neglect any of the children (Saslow 2014).

The Urban Institute found that 60 percent of migrants' children show adverse behavior changes after their parents are deported. They cannot concentrate in school and show symptoms of post-traumatic stress disorder. Under such difficult circumstances, Sandigo calls herself "a band-aid" and admits that "there is no way I can give 812 children the love and attention they need, but it has to be me. The system is broken. Nobody else is taking responsibility for them" (Saslow 2014).

Sandigo, who is from Nicaragua, gained asylum in the United States after arriving with a tourist visa in 1979. She charges that since the passage of the 1996 immigration law, "the US government has violated the civil rights of American children and caused them 'extreme, grave and irreparable hardship,'" in the words of a lawsuit she is preparing (Saslow 2014).

Immigration opponents often rhetorically ask immigrant advocates if they would be willing to take migrants into their own homes, feed, and care for them. Nora Sandigo's answer is yes. Despite her heroic efforts, however, individuals' inability to address the problems of 4.5 million mixed-status families in immigration limbo clearly shows the limits of private hospitality.

Responses to the Central American "Surge"

The New Sanctuary Movement revived at about the same time as the highly publicized surge of Central American children and families across the US-Mexican border in mid-2014. The NSM congregations decided to focus not on those recent arrivals but rather on undocumented migrants who had already been living for some time in the United States under threat of deportation. Meanwhile, a host of other organizations sprang into action to help the Central Americans. The following survey of a few of the advocacy, legal, and media activities by hundreds of groups shows the varied forms that support for asylum took during and after the surge.

Even before President Obama announced on June 2 that a humanitarian crisis was going on at the southern border, organizations were already calling attention to the dire situation in Central America. In congressional testimony in June, the president of the American Bar Association (ABA) called for Central American children to be treated humanely in detention and provided with legal representation. In mid-June the Border Patrol allowed reporters to visit holding facilities in Nogales and Brownsville, Texas. News services published photographs of children sleeping on mats in cages. The ACLU Border Litigation Project, Human Rights First, the Catholic Legal Immigration Network (CLINIC), and the Lutheran Immigration and Refugee Service published reports denouncing detention conditions.

In July the ABA issued a report demanding due process for the unaccompanied minors, so that they would have an opportunity to request asylum. The American Immigration Lawyers Association (AILA) sent squads of pro bono attorneys to the hastily refitted Artesia, New Mexico, detention center, where hundreds of unaccompanied minors and families were being held. AILA lawyers published or recorded individual accounts of their experiences at Artesia.

In August the American Civil Liberties Union and other legal organizations filed a motion for a preliminary injunction in US District Court in Seattle, to compel the federal government to provide legal representation at deportation hearings for children fleeing gangs in El Salvador. The ACLU later filed a national class-action lawsuit,

RILR v. Johnson, over the detention of Central American mothers and children after they had passed credible-fear interviews.[7] *Democracy Now!* and other broadcasters drew attention to the fact that five years to the day after the government had ended family detention, ICE transferred hundreds of Central American mothers and children from Border Patrol facilities to the Karnes County detention center.

Also in August, the Inter-American Court of Human Rights issued an advisory opinion, "Rights and Guarantees of Children in the Context of Migration and/or in Need of International Protection." The state of Maryland, one of the top five states receiving Central Americans, set up the Unaccompanied Alien Children Program to assist recently arrived children and families. Catholic Charities published a bulletin that listed volunteer opportunities at social service agencies and suggestions for advocacy efforts on behalf of detainees. Twenty-eight members of Congress sent a letter expressing concern about conditions for children at Artesia and Karnes County detention centers to the secretary of homeland security. The New York Bar Association issued a report about the children's due process rights, and the *New York Times* editorialized against the "rocket docket" at Artesia and other immigrant detention centers. The *Huffington Post* reported that at least five to ten children had been killed in the gang-controlled city of San Pedro Sula, Honduras, after deportation from the United States.

In September the government announced that a new family detention center would open in Dilley, Texas, in November. Some 160 organizations signed on to a letter to President Obama asking him to cancel plans to open Dilley. AILA called on the government to stop the mass detention and rapid deportation of Central American children and families. The National Immigration Forum published a report on conditions at Artesia. The Migration Policy Institute published a detailed report on *La Bestia*, the train that thousands of Central American migrants were taking through Mexico. Six advocacy organizations published a forty-three-page digest of media articles about the Central American surge. The Detention Watch Network published "Expose and Close: Artesia," one of a series of reports on inhumane conditions in immigration detention facilities.

In October AILA focused on the denial of bonds to the Central American detainees on national security grounds, under a post-9/11 directive left over from the Bush administration. The Inter-American Commission on Human Rights issued a report on its recent visit to the US-Mexico border. Its concerns included mandatory and arbitrary detention of families and children, bond denial, lack of legal representation, poor detention conditions, discrimination against Mexican unaccompanied minors, and lack of court-appointed guardians for children. Articles appeared in Texas newspapers about the agreement between the government and Corrections Corporation of America to run the Dilley detention center from CCA's detention facility in Eloy, Arizona, nine hundred miles away.

Also in October, lawyers at the University of Texas Law School's Civil Rights Clinic sent a nineteen-page letter, pointing out that no environmental impact assessment had been done at Dilley, to the Department of Homeland Security and the Environmental Protection Agency. Gulf Coast Jewish Family and Community Services published a report on conditions in El Salvador. Lutheran Immigration and Refugee Service and the Women's Refugee Commission published "Locking Up Family Values, Again," a thirty-one-page report on conditions in Artesia and Karnes – the sequel to a report they had published in 2007 on the Hutto family detention center. Human Rights Watch published "You Don't Have Rights Here: US Border Screening and Returns of Central Americans to Risk of Serious Harm."

In November the New York Bar Association and many other groups wrote to the president opposing the opening of Dilley, which was rescheduled for December. Newspapers and AILA reported that a few children and families were gaining asylum in hearings at Artesia or being released on bond.

Also in November, American University's Center for Latin American and Latino Studies published "Unaccompanied Migrant Children from Central America: Context, Causes and Responses." The report was intended to inform pro bono attorneys and other advocates about the violence faced by their child clients, to provide background information for expert affidavits and testimony in immigration court proceedings, and to help experts develop analyses to be used in judicial and administrative review processes (Stinchcomb and Hershberg 2014: 1).

On December 15, secretary of homeland security Jeh Johnson opened the euphemistically named South Texas Family Residential Center in Dilley, Texas. Bishop Eusebio Elizondo of Seattle, chair of the United States Conference of Catholic Bishops, commented: "It is inhumane to house young mothers with children in restrictive detention facilities as if they are criminals. Already traumatized from their journey, these families are very vulnerable and need care and support, not further emotional and psychological harm" (quoted by Preston 2014).

It was left to immigration lawyers such as Steven Manning, who led the AILA defense team at Artesia, to point out that many of the detainees might have strong claims for asylum—a word that neither President Obama nor Secretary Johnson had ever mentioned. AILA published summaries of twelve asylum cases its lawyers had won at Artesia.[8]

After six months of intense advocacy by hundreds of organizations and considerable media attention, the Central American surge story faded from view after Dilley opened. The numbers of Central American mothers and children entering the United States decreased markedly by the end of 2014. The unaccompanied minors who had joined family members in many states and the detainees in Texas were out of sight, out of mind. In January 2015 an AILA attorney told the *Huffington Post*, "Nearly all the women and children held at Dilley are asylum seekers, the vast majority of whom have legitimate asylum claims," but it was not clear if anybody was paying attention (Planas 2015).

Nonetheless, the lawyers continued to represent clients and publish reports, and the advocacy organizations kept campaigning. Churches and community groups offered assistance and refuge. Quietly, sanctuary efforts continued. At the Posada Providencia in San Benito, Texas, nuns were providing emergency shelter to homeless migrants and asylum seekers, as they had for twenty-five years. As ICE released mothers and children from detention centers to await court proceedings, its local office often called the Posada and asked them to take the migrants to the bus station or give them a bed for the night. The

Posada also provides long-term shelter, English as a second language classes, life skills training, legal and medical services, three meals a day, and a safe place to sleep for migrants who have nowhere else to go. The shelter has received eight thousand migrants from more than seventy countries over the past quarter century. In 2014 it served more people than ever before – some 1,400, including 631 minors and 555 women, many from Central America. A nun who works there with the migrants expressed the essence of sanctuary: "I'm not a doctor. I can't fix bodies. I'm not a lawyer. I can't represent them in court. But I can simply be with them" (4).

A Sea Change in Public Opinion

US public opinion is moving toward favoring the possibility of legal status for undocumented migrants, such as the people who pass through the Posada Providencia or who live invisibly in the United States for years.[9] Seventy percent of those surveyed by the Pew Center in December 2014 expressed sympathy for them. This marks a change from the previous decade, when anti-immigrant groups seeking to deny medical care, education, social services, driver's licenses, and housing to undocumented migrants achieved some success in state legislatures. These groups persistently called for the expulsion of more than 11 million undocumented migrants from the United States, the goal of Operation Endgame. Xenophobic commentators with millions of followers and some Republican presidential candidates kept up a drumbeat of dire warnings about outsiders who steal Americans' jobs, don't want to integrate into US society, refuse to learn English, consume scarce resources, spread disease, and plot terrorist attacks. They constitute a persistently vocal minority with the power to influence lawmakers and public discourse.

The immigration issue became more visible during the 2016 presidential campaign, as Democratic candidates tried to counter Republican candidates' negative statements about undocumented immigrants, refugees, and asylum seekers. Meanwhile, the Obama administration's attempts to deport hundreds of Central American mothers and children in early 2016 triggered loud protests from immigrant advocacy organizations, Congress members, and local communities. The government appealed federal court decisions overturning administration policies, sometimes all the way to the Supreme Court. The struggle for refuge continued with no end in sight.

Americans' conception of the United States as a nation of immigrants mixes uneasily with traditional strains of nativism, racism, and intolerance. On the one hand, the United States resettles tens of thousands of refugees every year; on the other hand, ICE oversees the detention of thousands of asylum seekers in harsh, prison-like conditions. The underlying reasons for these contradictory policies and attitudes are not only political, economic, and social but profoundly human. Under cover of national security, they express inescapable, overwhelming fears of the unknown other. Yet punitive laws and cruel government practices are countered by irrepressible acts of hospitality, as ordinary citizens protest and lobby on behalf of strangers and give them refuge. It seems inevitable that the might of government will prevail and expel the stranger. But in American society, as in so many others, sanctuary endures, perpetuated by people whose determination to welcome the stranger impels them to action.

Afterword

Does Asylum Have a Future?

> Nowhere it is written that the forces of humanity
> and tolerance will triumph; but that is scarcely a
> reason to cease the struggle.
>
> —Jeremy Seabrook, *The Refuge and the Fortress*

Everywhere capital encounters no obstacles, but the free movement of human beings is blocked. Even if they manage to cross deserts, oceans, and fortified borders, people fleeing persecution, poverty, and conflict can find no sure welcome or refuge. The structures of humanitarian protection have corroded and failed over time. The legal framework of asylum perversely serves to exclude, imprison, and segregate the stranger. Even in the era of globalization, borders undermine the sense of moral obligation and human dignity that the Universal Declaration of Human Rights and other instruments of international law accord to all members of our species. Their promise of shelter and safety has been broken, especially for the weak and vulnerable. In contrast, sanctuary opens an escape hatch that asylum fails to provide.

Underlying asylum is the principle of "a universal moral/legal order as the source of just norms" (Stastny 1987: 288). This principle emerged from religious beliefs and practices to become part of the secular political culture over the past four hundred years. However, for various political and economic reasons, governments have repeatedly found ways to undermine or overrule international agreements guaranteeing the availability of asylum. As government support for asylum has degenerated into lip service, public opinion has turned against the institution. In response, sanctuary movements have become the "self-appointed instrument striving to close the gap between the needs for a safe haven and the official grants of political asylum" (294).

Looking back to the development and decline of the institution of sanctuary from the seventh to the seventeenth century, we can see that it gradually became corrupted and discredited as the church lost its power and influence vis-à-vis the state. Meanwhile secular authorities came to use asylum as an instrument of foreign policy, giving the state, rather than the church, the sovereign right to grant asylum and deny extradition.

An early example of the political role of asylum is the case of Martin Luther. In 1521 the elector of Saxony gave Luther sanctuary in Wartburg Castle in defiance of the Holy Roman emperor Charles V, who had declared Luther an outlaw, made it a crime to give him food or shelter, and called for him to be killed because of his heretical activities. With the long-term support of the elector of Saxony and other secular political leaders, Luther survived and flourished – unlike Jan Hus, Giordano Bruno, and other religious dissidents, who lacked such protection.

Even at its height in the late Middle Ages, sanctuary was usually temporary and limited. Accused criminals could stay in British churches for only a few weeks, and then they had to decide whether to surrender to legal authorities or abjure the realm and go into exile. When it became possible for thieves and debtors to remain permanently in sanctuary, the institution lost its moral authority. It seemed wrong for the church to provide immunity from prosecution to those who ventured out to commit more crimes and then returned to their haven. Along with the state's increasingly effective claim to a monopoly over legal authority and coercive force, this unintended consequence fatally compromised church sanctuary.

In our time the pendulum has swung: asylum has become corrupted and discredited while sanctuary has regained its moral authority. For example, despite the lack of protection for sanctuary in US law, in recent years federal officials have made it known that they will not raid churches, schools, or hospitals to apprehend undocumented migrants. (They have arrested undocumented people as soon as they left the church or hospital or on their way to or from school, however.) When Representative James Sensenbrenner proposed criminalizing those who would give sanctuary or assistance to undocumented migrants in 2005, he had to back down in the face of outraged opposition by nonprofit and faith-based organizations. A similar congressional initiative against sanctuary cities in 2015 precipitated an indignant outcry. Police who raided Saint Bernard Church in Paris and brutally expelled Sans-Papiers occupiers in 1997 sparked mass public protests on behalf of undocumented workers and influenced Catholic bishops to support them. Although opinion polls suggest that the German public disapproves of immigrants and asylum seekers, churches and individuals shelter undocumented migrants. When Canadian or Scandinavian authorities seek to deport unsuccessful asylum seekers, again and again local communities give them sanctuary.

Perhaps it was inevitable that asylum would lose legitimacy over time. Every limitation of entry into receiving countries over the past twenty-five years by governments and international agreements has led to an increase in human smuggling, fraudulent asylum claims, overstaying, and the destitution underground. Whether for political or economic reasons, desperate people find ways to migrate, no matter what obstacles they encounter on the way. It is now impracticable for governments in the United States, Britain, and the European Union to remove all the undocumented migrants living in those countries. They have reacted by trying to prevent individuals from seeking asylum, but their methods have proven futile in stopping smuggling, fraud, overstaying, or destitution. On the contrary, these problems are likely to worsen with each turn of the screw. In the meantime, hundreds of thousands of vulnerable people, many with legitimate asylum claims, suffer harm at the hands of those who are supposed to give them refuge, simply because they present themselves to the authorities and are therefore the easiest to apprehend and deport.

Yet, despite their continuing attempts to make migration more difficult, governments have established and maintained formal resettlement programs for asylees and refugees. Thus they acknowledge their obligation to protect those fleeing persecution, as well as the possibility of providing permanent sanctuary in the form of integration into national society. These programs may be underfunded and inefficient, but at least they exist. With all their limitations, they embody the commitment nation-states have made to the principle of refuge.

In the United States, Britain, and other countries, NGOs and advocacy groups have made detailed recommendations for reform of the asylum system, with a view to making it adhere to the Refugee Convention, other international agreements, and national laws. However, these agreements and laws have serious shortcomings. Genuine reform is likely to be obstructed by the system's entrenched nature, the privatization of detention, and politicians' unwillingness to abandon the political advantages of scapegoating the powerless, alien other. And the treatment of asylum seekers is only a small part of a much larger immigration system, in which they get lost all too easily. Policy makers and lawmakers must consider what to do about asylum in the context of overriding concerns about national security, terrorism, economic crisis, and political gridlock.

The world may need a new refugee convention that reflects both post–Cold War realities and changing human aspirations. But even if a new convention were created, it would soon need an overhaul. Any law, regulation, or policy governing asylum is likely to fail sooner or later without serious reconsideration of the unintended consequences of reform and rededication to basic human rights.

In the meantime it makes sense to monitor and replicate asylum systems that combine legal efficiency and humanitarian treatment. Perhaps the relatively liberal Swedish system, with its social service approach, limited detention, and permission to work, could be a model, as it was for a few years in Australia.

In 2013 the Scottish Refugee Council proposed changes to the British asylum system that could provide a basis for reforms in other countries. Among its numerous recommendations were the following:

- improve training and guidance for asylum decision makers and address the culture of disbelief that pervades asylum procedures;
- establish an independent agency to deal with asylum applications;
- improve access to legal and other kinds of advice for asylum seekers and detainees;

- preserve the full range of appeal processes;
- improve initial asylum screening "to identify vulnerable applicants early and act on their needs";
- consider the best interests of children throughout the asylum process and develop guardianship for unaccompanied minors;
- abolish detention of asylum seekers "solely for the purpose of assessing their claim," detain them for the shortest possible time, and never detain vulnerable asylum seekers;
- permit the applicant to work after six months if no asylum decision has been reached during that period;
- introduce cash support throughout the asylum procedure, until the asylum seeker leaves the country or gains refugee status. Support should be equivalent to what citizens receive, based on "the need to ensure a dignified standard of living";
- develop reception and integration policies and practices that benefit all asylum seekers and host communities;
- provide full access to health care and language instruction;
- grant permanent residence to asylees;
- allow child refugees to be reunited with their families;
- increase the number of refugee resettlement places;
- grant legal status to refused asylum seekers and "stop forcing them into destitution";
- provide temporary residence permits to refused asylum seekers who cannot return to their home country;
- never detain refused asylum seekers in prisons. (Shisheva et al. 2013)

The American Friends Service Committee laid out principles for reform of the US immigration system in a 2013 proposal to the Congress and the president:

- develop humane international economic policies to reduce forced migration;
- protect the labor rights of all workers;
- develop a clear path to citizenship for undocumented migrants;
- respect the civil and human rights of immigrants;
- make family reunification a top priority;
- ensure that immigrants and refugees have access to services. (American Friends Service Committee 2013)

Like the Scottish Refugee Council's suggestions, these principles could be broadly applicable to other receiving countries' asylum systems.

A certain amount of political courage is necessary to reform punitive, inefficient, and inhumane policies that create more problems than they solve. If they are to abide by their legal obligations to refugees, political leaders must be ready to tell the public some inconvenient truths about the important contributions migrants make to the national economy, the difficulty and expense of removing undocumented workers, and the benefits of integrating strangers into national society. They must resist the temptation to scapegoat the most vulnerable outsiders for their own policy failures, and they must defend the human rights of noncitizens they have a legal and moral obligation to protect.

These are demanding tasks. If political leaders make an honest effort to carry them out, they will encounter strong opposition, not only from reactionary and racist elements, but also from progressive activists who worry about overpopulation, environmental degradation, crime, and other compelling problems that they associate with the unrestricted entry and long-term presence of migrants. Consequently, fostering public debate and education about immigration and asylum must be ongoing priorities for political, economic, and social leaders.

It is often said that the problems of immigration could be solved by advancing social, political, and economic justice in the countries from which people flee. Then, the argument goes, they would have fewer reasons to leave and more reasons to stay to improve their own societies. If progressive land reform were implemented in the Philippines, the daughters of small farmers would not have to leave home to become domestic servants or nurses overseas. If Mexican youths could farm in or near their own village or find jobs in the city, they would not feel compelled to cross the Sonoran Desert to mow lawns in Southern California. If minority-group members had freedom of speech or religion in Cameroon, Sudan, or Indonesia, they would not seek asylum in France, Britain, or Australia. If women had equal rights in Iran, they would not seek refuge with relatives in North Dakota.

To solve these and many other problems, significant, long-term social, economic, and political change is necessary in those coun-

tries. Generous and effective development assistance from First World
nations could help to a modest extent. Change is taking place, however precariously and incrementally. But people from all walks of
life still leave their homes for better, safer lives in other countries,
undeterred by border patrols, indefinite detention, entry quotas, or
any other bureaucratic obstacles. Recognition of these hard facts by
politicians and the public might make a difference in the conception
and implementation of asylum and immigration policies.

Are Borders and Sovereignty Unquestionable?

One doctrine that most politicians are reluctant to question or even
address is the unassailability of borders as the first line of defense
of countries and their populations against all manner of interlopers.
Borders and sovereignty are sacred categories in modern political discourse, the very foundations of nationalism, even though galloping
globalization threatens them. A few utopian theorists and critics have
questioned the viability of fortress states by pointing to the possibility
of opening borders in a world where the Internet links everybody and
everything almost instantaneously. Open Borders proponents "pose
a significant moral challenge. . . . [T]hey help us to think about the
central dilemma of the global world order, the role of the sovereign
state in an increasingly interconnected world," Gibney and Hansen
point out (2005: 2:459).

Open Borders theorists generally focus not on asylum, but rather
on immigration in general. They base their arguments on several
basic ideas:

- "Freedom of movement ought to be regarded as a fundamental
  individual right" for all, regardless of "arbitrary" criteria such as
  nationality.
- All human beings are free and equal and of equal moral worth.
- One's labor is one's private property, to be disposed of as one
  chooses.
- Inequality of wealth among nations should be redressed by the right
  of individuals to move where there is more opportunity.

- No one way of life or culture is superior to others; therefore people should be able to choose which society they live in. (Gibney and Hansen 2005: 2:457–58)

These ideas are attractive to libertarians, capitalists, and some human rights advocates, but other theorists point out that states also have the "right to exclude." For example, political philosopher Michael Walzer believes in the universal equality of human beings, who are all "culture-producing creatures" (quoted by Gibney and Hansen 2:458). He acknowledges that states must give aid to strangers when it is urgently needed, and the costs of providing it are low. But the obligation to help is not absolute, he insists.

For Gibney and Hansen, the broader underlying question raised by Walzer is "how to reconcile the moral obligations we owe to any individual human being, simply on the basis of our equal moral dignity, with the special duties we acquire toward particular people and groups on the basis of particular relationships and attachments" (2:458). Politicians are almost never elected with a mandate to protect all humankind; rather they are expected to advance the interests and rights of the people who elected them (and perhaps even people who did not vote for them – but not strangers in far-off countries who might need help).

Claudia Tazreiter quotes the philosopher Immanuel Kant to make an argument for open borders that is based on human rights and international law: "The peoples of the earth have . . . entered in varying degrees into a universal community, and it has developed to the point where a violation of laws in one part of the world is felt everywhere. The idea of a cosmopolitan law is therefore not fantastic and overstrained; it is a necessary complement to the unwritten code of political and international law, transforming it into a universal law of humanity" (Kant quoted in Tazreiter 2004: 23).

Tazreiter admits that "there are cogent arguments to defend the actions of a state in ensuring its sovereignty is not threatened, and the economic and social well-being of its citizens is safeguarded. This does not, however, relieve the state of obligations to noncitizens in their territories" (13). She raises but does not answer the question of how to balance local and universal needs and interests (15). Policy makers face these dilemmas when they try to craft asylum policies that uphold international commitments while protecting both citizens and strangers.

Teresa Hayter (2004) takes a more radical position in reacting to exclusionary immigration and asylum policies. She argues that immigration controls do not work, restrictions do not keep migrants from entering countries, and deportation en masse is not feasible. Economic migrants come to receiving countries because of intolerable conditions in their own country, and they come to work, not to sponge off the welfare system. Aging populations in receiving countries make it likely that young migrants will keep coming to fill job places and to care for the elderly in coming years. The current immigration system works for the benefit of employers who hire illegal workers. These workers drive down the cost of labor and can be fired with a telephone call to the police if they try to organize other workers. Detention and deportation are extremely expensive and not cost effective. For practical reasons, therefore, borders should be open, and workers should be able to come and go as they need to, Hayter insists.

Khalid Koser responds to Open Borders theorists in a sober and measured way, by pointing to the recalcitrant realities of migration in the post–Cold War world:

> It has become clear that control measures such as border fences, biometric testing and visas are in isolation unlikely to reduce irregular migration in the long term. They probably need to be combined with more proactive measures that address the causes of irregular migration, including achieving development targets to increase security and improve livelihoods in origin countries, as well as expanding opportunities to move legally. At the same time, it is unrealistic to expect states to dismantle controls altogether and open their borders, as is sometimes advocated. Most commentators now acknowledge that irregular migration will continue for the foreseeable future. (2007: 119)

Some writers stress morality in calling for generous and humane asylum policies. Hugo Gryn, an Auschwitz survivor who became a rabbi in London, told the British Refugee Council in 1996: "It is imperative that we proclaim that asylum issues are an index of our spiritual and moral civilization. . . . I believe that the line our society will take in this matter on how you are to people to whom you owe nothing is a signal. . . . I hope and pray it is a test we shall not fail" (quoted by Kushner 2006: 234). Yet Gryn follows Walzer's line of reasoning in saying that British people owe nothing to asylum seekers. In trying to characterize asylum as a test of virtue, he contradicts the universalistic values of reciprocal altruism and equality underlying both human rights law and Open Borders theory (not to mention many religious traditions, including his own).

A sanctuarian operates out of a broad sense of moral obligation to *anyone* who needs help, not only members of his or her family, clan, neighborhood, city, state, country, or religion. How else can one explain the actions of Sanctuary Movement activists, Holocaust rescuers, and Underground Railroad conductors, who saved the most stigmatized people in their society or outsiders with no apparent relation to themselves? They reinvented sanctuary in response to life-threatening realities, without taking time to theorize about systemic change. They did not challenge the idea of borders, but they transgressed them whenever they believed it necessary, in the name of a higher law.

In the twentieth century, people had to redefine and expand the meaning of sanctuary to respond to the realities of total war and its aftermath. Demilitarized zones, nuclear-free zones, weapons-free zones, humanitarian relief corridors, and refugee camps acquired the status of sanctuaries under international treaties and agreements. The organizations that maintained them struggled to keep them safe in the midst of violent conflict.

For example, Zones of Peace were first established in the Philippines in 1988, after the overthrow of Ferdinand Marcos by a people's revolution. A Zone of Peace is "a geographical area that community residents themselves declare to be off-limits to war and other forms of armed hostility" (Hancock and Mitchell 2004: 11). The Catholic Church was instrumental in setting up and maintaining these sanctuaries in the Philippines. In 2000, when the Filipino government was waging war on the Moro Islamic Liberation Front (MLF), officials tried to take over existing Zones of Peace and use them as bases to expel the MLF. The military then tried to forcibly relocate residents. Communities had to defy the government to establish and maintain their zones.

In Colombia, which has millions of internally displaced people as a result of more than fifty years of civil conflict, local communities set up one hundred Zones of Peace that practiced "active neutrality." Participants included Catholic clergy, indigenous groups, nongovernmental organizations, local officials, peasant organizations, and educators' groups. Associations of Zones of Peace met with guerrilla leaders to gain the release of abducted officials and set up safe passage for peasants to pass through roadblocks on their way to market. National organizations, such as the Network of Initiatives for Peace and against War (Redepaz), supported the local zones and helped them communicate with one another. Redepaz received a grant from the European Initiative for Democracy to set up the zones in the late 1990s.

Usually peace communities try to solve local disputes without violence. In this context, their activities consist of what Hancock and Mitchell call "almost invisible processes of people building peace in the midst of a civil war" on the local level, from the bottom up (25). Maintaining the zones under these circumstances is not easy. Peace communities start in areas that the state has abandoned, where armed insurgents have stepped in to fill the vacuum. Local residents resist their control at great risk. In one of many similar incidents, peace leaders in San Pablo, Colombia, had to flee and local supporting organizations had to discontinue their activities under attack by guerrilla forces in 2002–3.

To avoid such incidents, the peace communities sought outside and international support, to ensure that any attack or massacre in a Zone of Peace would entail a high political cost for the perpetrators. For example, the Fellowship of Reconciliation and Peace Brigades International sent peacekeepers to the village of San José de Apartadó, Colombia, to prevent paramilitaries from killing the inhabitants (Nolan and Hancock 2014: 3). However, in this settlement of 1,500 residents, more than 200 people, including the victims of twenty massacres, have been killed since 1997. Violence continues all around them. Their community website reported in October 2014 that an Italian peace organization had intervened on their behalf with the regional military commander. The website contains many pleas for help to the president of Colombia and other officials (San José de Apartadó 2014).

These homemade sanctuary communities are inhabitants' attempt to overcome the helplessness and hopelessness they suffer as a result of endemic violence (Hancock and Mitchell 2004: 39). Zones of Peace have been established during civil wars by the victims, during peace negotiations by the warring parties, or after wars by survivors seeking to recuperate and develop communities. They may provide relief and rescue, administer health care, protect sacred or historic sites or environmental resources, observe festivals and other events, or protect vulnerable groups, such as children.

The Zones of Peace are notable because they are grassroots efforts, usually unsupported or unacknowledged by the state, to establish and maintain havens without force of arms in the midst of civil conflict. Fragile though it may be, sanctuary in this context is a dynamic process that operates autonomously, beyond the polar antagonisms of war, in the small space where people can achieve the evanescent freedom to govern themselves by their own rules. Sanctuary may not last, but while it does, it satisfies a deep human longing. It defies the supremacy of arbitrary authority, coercion, and punishment. For as long as it lasts, it provides surcease to those who flee the imposition of brute force and a sense of accomplishment to those who shelter them. If the powers that be refuse to give sanctuary, then people make their own. If the persecuted cannot find refuge outside their home territory, they create it where they live.

A venerable and sacred institution, sanctuary is malleable and responsive to current conditions. Human beings in almost every time and place keep reinventing it as they go along. As Rabbi Gryn points out, asylum defines our level of moral and spiritual development, but sanctuary has a much more basic – and life-saving – significance for those who seek and give it. The legal institution of asylum may flourish or decline, but sanctuary – a spontaneous, voluntary, unregulated act of reciprocal altruism – is in our DNA and will survive in some form as long as we do.

Many incidents reported in this book show that as governments try to limit or undermine asylum, ordinary citizens provide or promote sanctuary, either secretly or openly. Each person must decide if he or she will defy the legal authorities for conscience's sake by offering refuge outside or against the law to persecuted strangers. Some sanctuarians, such as the activists of Humane Borders in Tucson, go right to the edge of legality but not over it. Most people do not feel compelled or able to go outside the law to provide sanctuary. Such actions are more likely to occur in extreme situations, such as the run-up to the American Civil War, Nazi-occupied Europe during World War II, or the Central American wars of the 1980s. Nevertheless, individuals and organizations may support sanctuarians in a variety of ways, from contributing funds to demonstrating against official policies and lobbying for changes in restrictive laws.

People in many countries have loudly or quietly expressed their opposition to measures limiting asylum. In some instances, grassroots sanctuary efforts have led to positive changes in government policies vis-à-vis asylum seekers, although they often take years to make any impact. Rich and powerful xenophobic forces get much more public attention and have considerable political clout and influence over government decision making. One can see numerous examples of the negative consequences of anti-immigrant sentiment and agitation on asylum policies in dozens of countries, including Australia, Britain, Canada, France, Germany, and the United States. Even so, persistent public support for sanctuary has helped asylum seekers and other migrants in those and other countries.

Time and time again, when governments have failed to abide by international law and their own laws, ordinary citizens have stepped in to enforce and advance human rights, even at great personal risk. Consider the example of Paul Rusesabagina, the Rwandan who saved about 1,200 people during the 1994 genocide by giving them sanctuary in the hotel he managed in Kigali. An unassuming man, Rusesabagina did what he had to do, including cheat, lie, and steal, to protect his own family and everyone else who sought his help in the midst of monstrous government-sponsored crimes and social chaos.

Thousands of other ordinary people have taken much less risky but modestly effective actions to give refuge to strangers or support those who did. If you donate money to pro-asylum groups, write letters to the editor on behalf of asylum seekers, teach English to refugees, hire an unemployed asylee, or volunteer to help torture survivors, you are a sanctuarian. Hundreds of organizations can use whatever help you choose to give. Through such actions, you, too, can know the pleasures of rescue. As a universal human right and an intrinsic part of our species' heritage, sanctuary belongs to everyone.

Appendix

Following is a partial list of organizations that help or advocate for asylum seekers, refugees, and immigrants.

International

European Council on Refugees and Exiles
Global Detention Project
International Catholic Migration Commission
International Detention Coalition
International Organization for Migration
International Rehabilitation Council for Torture Victims
United Nations High Commissioner for Refugees

Australia

Amnesty International
Asylum Seeker Resource Centre
Asylum Seekers Centre
Australian Catholic Migrant and Refugee Office
Australian Coalition to End Immigration Detention of Children
Australian Lutheran World Service
Australian National Committee on Refugee Women
Centre for Advocacy, Support and Education for Refugees
ChilOut
Coalition Assisting Refugees after Detention
Ecumenical Migration Centre
Immigrant Women's Speakout
Jesuit Refugee Service
Oxfam Australia
Red Cross of Australia
Refugee Action Collective
Refugee Advice and Casework Service

Refugee Council of Australia
Refugee Rights Action Network
Rise
Sanctuary Australia Foundation
Uniting Justice Australia

Canada

Amnesty International
Canadian Council for Refugees
Canadian Sanctuary Network
Jesuit Refugee Service
No One Is Illegal Toronto
Romero House
Southern Ontario Sanctuary Coalition

France

ANAFE (Association Nationale d'Assistance aux Frontières pour les Étrangers)
CIMADE (Comité Inter-mouvements auprès des Évacués)
Forum Réfugiés
France Terre d'Asile
GISTI (Groupe d'Information et de Soutien des Immigrés)

Germany

Amnesty International
Arbeiterwohlfahrt
Borderline-Europe
Bundesarbeitsgemeinschaft "Asyl in der Kirke"
Caritas
Diakonie
GECCA
German Red Cross
Pro Asyl
Raphaels-Werk

United Kingdom

Amnesty International
Asylum Support Appeals Project
Asylum Aid
AVID

Bail for Immigration Detainees
Black Women against Rape
British Refugee Council
Campaign to Close Campsfield
CARA
Citizens UK
Crossroads Women's Centre
Education Action International
Immigration Law Practitioners Association
Kalayaan
Medical Foundation for the Care of Victims of Torture
Medical Justice
Migrants' Rights Network
National Refugees Welcome Board
Positive Action in Housing
Quaker Asylum and Refugee Network
Refugee Action
Scottish Refugee Council
Women for Refugee Women

United States

American Civil Liberties Union
American Friends Service Committee
American Immigration Law Association
Amnesty International USA
Annunciation House, El Paso
Arab Community Center for Economic and Social Services (ACCESS)
Boston Center for Refugee Health and Human Rights
Capital Area Immigrant Rights Coalition
Catholic Legal Immigration Network (CLINIC)
Center for Victims of Torture, Saint Paul, MN
Church World Service
Detention Watch Network
Episcopal Migration Ministries
Ethiopian Community Development Council
Hebrew Immigrant Aid Society
Human Rights First
Human Rights Watch
Interfaith Refugee and Immigration Ministries
International Refugee Assistance Project
International Rescue Committee
Jesuit Refugee Service
Jewish Family Service

Karen American Communities Foundation
Kurdish Human Rights Watch
Lutheran Immigration and Refugee Service
Lutheran Social Services
National Immigrant Solidarity Network
New Sanctuary Movement of Philadelphia
Refugee Council USA
Scholar Rescue Fund
Southeast Asia Resource Action Center
Torture Abolition and Survivors Support Coalition
US Committee on Refugees and Immigrants
US Conference of Catholic Bishops/Migration and Refugee Services
Women's Refugee Commission

Notes

Introduction

1 The Human Relations Area Files, anthropological archives established by Yale University in 1949, are available at hraf.yale.edu.

2 See Markowitz 2010 for a review of the decades-long debate over Darwinian and neo-Darwinian explanations of human altruism and the "selfish gene."

3 According to the European Union's statistical agency, Eurostat, 942,400 people applied for asylum in the EU in 2015, up from 626,000 in 2014 (Eurostat 2015; BBC News 2016). The estimated population of the twenty-eight EU states was about 508 million as of January 1, 2015 (Eurostat 2015).

1. Asylum and Sanctuary Seekers' Stories

1 According to the United Nations High Commissioner for Refugees (2015), developing countries hosted 86 percent of refugees in 2013, up from 70 percent in 2003.

2 A refugee is a person who has fled across international boundaries, often as part of a group, and has officially obtained temporary or permanent sanctuary from a foreign government. An asylum seeker is someone who applies to a foreign government on his or her own initiative for refuge from persecution in the home country, usually on or after arrival in the receiving country. A successful asylum seeker, or asylee, is classified as a refugee and is eligible for various kinds of resettlement assistance. In the United States, asylees constitute a small proportion of refugees and relatively few people seek asylum, but in the United Kingdom and Europe, entering asylum seekers vastly outnumber entering refugees. Many receiving countries establish annual quotas of refugees, depending on varying (sometimes arbitrary) criteria. A person who flees persecution and seeks refuge inside his or her own country is designated as internally displaced. According to the United Nations High Commissioner

for Refugees (2015), in 2014 there were many more internally displaced persons (38.2 million) than refugees (19.5 million) in the world. Some 1.8 million people applied for asylum around the world in 2014. These totals were the highest in the history of the UNHCR.

3 For an anthropologist's perspective on the way the UK government's asylum system works, see Good (2007).

4 In 2012 (the most recent year for which I could find statistics), 29,484 applicants received asylum in the United States (Burt and Batalova 2014). During the year ending March 2014, 5,433 applicants received grants of asylum after their initial application in Britain. The British government did not indicate the number of asylum seekers' appeals granted during that period (United Kingdom Home Office 2014b).

5 Mary's story is based on the author's interview with an asylum seeker who requested anonymity, Providence, RI, August 2006.

6 This section is reprinted, with the author's permission, from "Detained: Women Asylum Seekers Locked Up in the UK" (Girma et al. 2014).

7 Michael Morpurgo is an award-winning British writer, the author of *War Horse*. Dame Joan Bakewell is a journalist and the president of Birkbeck College, University of London.

8 This account is based on Bernstein (2008).

9 Pierre's story is based on the author's interview with an asylee who requested anonymity, Takoma Park, MD, September 12, 2014.

10 Schengen and Dublin Convention rules prevent asylum seekers from making asylum claims in other EU countries if the first EU country they enter rejects or does not receive their application. These rules were set up to prevent "asylum shopping."

11 According to the Black Women's Rape Action Project of London (2006), 50 percent of women claiming asylum in Britain have been raped.

12 Matthew Gibney, professor of politics and forced migration at Oxford University, writes, "A kind of schizophrenia seems to pervade Western responses to asylum seekers and refugees; great importance is attached to the principle of asylum but enormous efforts are made to ensure that refugees . . . never reach the territory of the state where they could receive its protection" (2004: 2).

2. Sanctuary's Beginnings

1 Primatologists sometimes call these fleeing females "immigrants."

2 Ironically, Manus Island is now the site of asylum-seeker detention camps established by the Australian government under an agreement with Papua New Guinea. The local people are not happy about their presence. For more information about Australian asylum policies and practices, see chapter 8.

4. From Religious Sanctuary to Secular Asylum

Epigraph: Dallal Stevens found the English translation in Scott 1985: 125–26. The Latin original is from Grotius, *De jure belli ac pacis*, Book II, section xvi.

1 Original source is Hansard (House of Commons) Vol. 145, Cols. 755–79 (2 May 1905).

2 Emma Lazarus's famous sonnet about the Statue of Liberty, "The New Colossus" (1883), ends with the line, "I lift my lamp beside the golden door!" Lazarus, a descendant of eighteenth-century immigrants, transformed the meaning of the statue from a symbol of the American Revolution to "mother of exiles," who gives refuge to "huddled masses yearning to breathe free . . . wretched refuse . . . homeless, tempest-tost." The poem is engraved on a plaque mounted on the statue's base in 1903, at the height of mass immigration into the United States.

3 Emergency Quota Act of 1921: Act of May 10, 1921, Pub. L. No. 67-5, 42 Stat. 5.

5. Nineteenth-Century Sanctuary outside the Law

Epigraph: From an October 5, 1850, speech by Theodore Parker reproduced in *The Chronotype* of October 7, 1850, which was in a scrapbook compiled by Miss C. C. Thayer and housed in the archives of the Boston Public Library (quoted in Siebert 1968).

1 The primary UGRR states were Connecticut, Delaware, Illinois, Indiana, Iowa, Maryland, Massachusetts, Michigan, New Hampshire, New Jersey, New York, North Carolina, Ohio, Pennsylvania, Rhode Island, Vermont, and Wisconsin.

2 According to Larson (2004) Tubman rescued about seventy slaves rather than some three hundred.

3 Slavery was formally abolished in the (western) British Empire starting in 1833.

6. The Pleasures of Holocaust Rescue

Epigraph: translated by the author from Joutard, Poujol, and Cabanel 1987: 22.

1 Local historian Gérard Bollon collected the names of 3,458 refugees who were sheltered in Le Chambon and its environs.

7. The Twentieth-Century Heyday of Asylum

Epigraph: Elie Wiesel, "The Refugee," quoted in MacEoin 1985: 9.

1   Internal Security Act: Act of September 23, 1950, 64 Stat. 987, at 1010, and 1952 Immigration and Nationality Act, 66 Stat. 163, at 214, as cited by Bau.

2   In 1965 the McCarran-Walter Act was amended and national quotas were abolished. Priority was given to entry of close relatives of US citizens and those with special skills. See Pub. L. No. 89-236, 79 Stat. 911, at 918.

3   The original source is 121st meeting, November 3, 1948, 45, Draft International Declaration of Human Rights (E/800), p. 330 (UN Doc. A/X.3/SR. 121).

4   The history, by a Mr. Eaglestone, a Home Office civil servant, may be found at HO [Home Office] 213/1772.

5   Refugee Relief Act: Act of August 7, 1953, Pub. L. No. 82-203, 67 Stat. 400, as cited by Bau.

6   Quoted from Hansard (House of Commons) Vol. 864 Col. 518, written answers (22 November 1973).

7   The original source is Hansard (House of Commons) Vol. 153 Cols. 1257-66, oral answers (26 May 1989).

8   The original source is Hansard (House of Commons) Vol. 153 Cols. 1264-5 (26 May 1989).

9   Bau cites and analyzes *Nunez v. Boldin*, 537 F. Supp. 578 (S.D. Tex. 1982), and *Orantes-Hernandez v. Smith*, 541 F. Supp. 351 (C.D. Cal. 1982), among other US District Court decisions.

10 Elford was still conducting those vigils in 2014.

11 Cunningham wrote, "Church sanctuary was first declared publicly in the United States on October 16, 1967, by the Arlington Street Unitarian Church in Boston, Mass., when it claimed [*sic*] asylum for nearly 300 Vietnam War draft resisters" (1995: 84).

12 According to MacEoin (1985), support for the Sanctuary Movement came from numerous mainline churches and organizations, including the Presbyterian Church (USA), National Assembly of Religious Women, Mennonite Central Committee, National Coalition of American Nuns, United Methodist Board of Church and Society, Unitarian-Universalist Service Committee, United Church of Christ Office for Church and Society, Pax Christi, Board of National Ministries of American Baptist Church, Methodist Federation for Social Action, Lutheran Immigration and Refugee Service, and National Federal of Priests' Councils. From 1981 to 1986 Tucson church and community groups raised $725,000 to pay bonds and legal expenses for asylum seekers.

13 Obama administration officials echoed Reagan administration officials' words thirty years later, when they sought to deter mass entry of Central American asylum seekers in 2014–15.

8. Asylum Now in Canada, Australia, and the United Kingdom

1 In 2011, the Australian humanitarian quota was 13,750; in 2012 it was increased to 20,000; in 2014 it was lowered to 13,750 again (Parliament of Australia 2011; Doherty 2014).

2 The Howard government came under increasing pressure from many quarters to reform detention practices. In 2005, after a critical report by the Australian Human Rights Commission, Howard agreed to release all children from detention to the care of the Australian Red Cross. In 2007, two government-commissioned reports exposed the wrongful detention of more than 250 people. Subsequent reforms in case management and alternatives to detention were expanded by the new Rudd government (Grant Mitchell, personal communication, 2015; Triggs 2014).

3 The Australian government announced in 2014 that it would "voluntarily" relocate about a thousand detained asylum seekers from Nauru to Cambodia, one of the poorest countries in the world, whose people did not welcome the arrival of foreign refugees and which has a poor human rights record. By mid-2015, four asylum seekers had agreed to go to Cambodia.

4 According to Browne and Whyte (2015), 330 children were still in immigration detention as of February 12, 2015.

5 Seven percent of migrants to the United Kingdom are asylum seekers. Britain takes in less than 2 percent of the world's asylum seekers, and refugees constitute 0.3 percent of the UK population (United Nations High Commissioner for Refugees 2015).

6 Figures vary from year to year, with a sizable backlog of pending, lost, and abandoned cases. Pending asylum cases rose by 34 percent from 2013 to 2014, "reflecting a decrease in staffing levels instituted by the UK Border Agency" (United Kingdom Home Office 2015).

7 British immigration lawyer Steve Symonds explains, "Administrative removal is the removal of anyone from the UK under immigration powers. Hence, those who are in the UK without leave (permission) and need it (or have their leave taken away from them) may be removed. There is no bar on them returning to the UK. However, someone's immigration history may be relied upon to refuse a visa or refuse entry in the future; and from 2008, the UK introduced mandatory re-entry bans for a variety of immigration 'offenders' (i.e. those who had breached immigration rules as distinct from being convicted of a criminal offence, including a criminal immigration offence). In some instances, these last for 10 years" (personal communication, January 14, 2015). Symonds makes a distinction between removal and deportation, but I have difficulty understanding the difference.

8 See chapter 11 for the story of the Glasgow Girls' campaign against dawn raids.

9 According to Women for Refugee Women, "The UK is one of the few countries in Europe that has yet to limit the length of time a person can spend in immigration detention. The UK has opted out of the EU Returns Directive, which includes an absolute maximum of 18 months' detention, and ignored the UN Working Group on Arbitrary Detention's recommendation in 1998 to specify an absolute maximum duration" (Girma et al. 2014).

10 Mass-deportation charter flights, at a cost of £250,000 each, took place in 2012 and 2013. In some cases the flights had to return full to the United Kingdom, because judicial reviews, completed after they left Britain, saved the refused asylum seekers from deportation.

11 Steve Symonds points out that some asylum advocates have called for the British government to monitor the situation of returned asylum seekers, but others argue that such action could put them in danger (personal communication, February 4, 2015).

12 Nigeria is said to have the highest rate of female genital mutilation in the world (Okeke et al. 2012).

13 The 2013 parliamentary inquiry on asylum recommended that the government reinstitute English language classes for asylees (House of Commons, Home Affairs Committee 2013: 38).

14 Scrooge: "Are there no prisons? . . . And the union workhouses – are they still in operation?"
Visitor: ". . . Many can't go there, and many would rather die."
Scrooge: "Let them die and decrease the surplus population."
– From Charles Dickens, *A Christmas Carol* (1843)

9. Asylum Now in Europe and Beyond

1 Families that entered the Netherlands by land were not detained on arrival. The rationale for family detention at Schiphol Airport was "to protect the borders" (Goeman and van Os 2014).

2 "Despite Sweden's relatively small population of 9.5 million people, which is 1.9 percent of the European Union's total population, the country took in 19.5 percent of the 135,700 asylum seekers in 2013. Of the asylum seekers in Sweden, 46 percent were from Syria. In fact, of the 35,800 Syrians granted protection status in the EU 28, over 60 percent were recorded in Sweden. . . . After Syrians, most of Sweden's asylum seekers in 2013 were stateless at a total of 4,110. . . . In September [2013] Sweden granted permanent residence to all Syrian refugees, the first country in the EU to do so" (*The Local* 2014).

3 Sources of figures about Syrian refugees include UNHCR 2015, Hurvitz 2013, Sherwood 2014, Burman 2014, Migration Policy Centre 2014, and Swedish Migration Board 2014.

4 The Romani, or Roma, are believed to have migrated from India to

Europe and beyond, starting about a thousand years ago. Derisively
called gypsies, they do not use that word to describe themselves. They
have experienced persecution (including mass murder by the Nazis during World War II) and discrimination for centuries in many countries.
5 Israel ratified the 1951 Refugee Convention, the 1967 Protocol Relating
to the Status of Refugees, and the 1984 Convention against Torture. Like
other receiving countries, it has not signed or ratified the 1990 Convention on the Rights of Migrant Workers.

10. The Golden Door Ajar: US Asylum Policy

1 Percentages vary from year to year; they are approximate because the
US government does not provide complete information. For example, according to the government, in 2013 immigration courts received
36,674 asylum cases, granted 9,993, and denied 8,823; 1,439 were abandoned, and 6,400 were withdrawn. More than 11,000 cases were listed as
"Other," without explanation (United States Department of Justice 2014).
Also, the United States Department of Homeland Security (2013) reported
that 25,199 people were granted asylum in 2013 but did not indicate how
many cases were pending from previous years.
2 Illegal entry (without authorization) into the United States is now a federal misdemeanor, and illegal reentry is a felony. As a result, more people are now in federal prisons for immigration offenses than for violent
crimes (Chomsky 2014; Meissner et al. 2013). Chomsky explains confus-
ing immigration laws as follows: "It's illegal to cross the border without
inspection and/or without approval from U.S. immigration authorities. . . . Entering the country illegally is a crime, and a person who does
so can be subject to up to six months in prison. Entering the country
again after being deported is a more serious crime – a felony – punishable
by up to two years in prison. Simply *being* in the country without authorization, though, is not in itself a crime but rather a civil violation, rem-
edied by removal (either voluntary departure or deportation) rather than
a criminal penalty. Unlawful presence becomes a criminal offense only
'when an alien is found in the United States after having been formally
removed or after departing the United States while a removal order was
outstanding'" (Chomsky 2014: 98–99, quoting from a 2006 Congressional
Research Service report).
3 In September 2014, "the U.S. Justice Department and the group that
administers the AmeriCorps national service program awarded $1.8 mil-
lion in grants . . . to enroll about 100 lawyers and paralegals to provide
legal services to unaccompanied minors in immigration proceedings. But
groups including the American Civil Liberties Union are pursuing a lawsuit in July that accuses the federal government of not providing legal
representation to the minors. The groups have argued in legal papers

that the federal government's plan to underwrite the cost of representing some minors is too limited" (Dobuzinskis 2014).

4 Jaya Ramji-Nogales coined the term *refugee roulette* in a 2008 *Stanford Law Review* article, cited in Hamilton (2014).

5 Tam Tran's story is from Watanabe 2007 and her obituaries are from Stickgold 2010, Wong and Ramos 2011.

6 The ACLU and other legal advocacy groups filed suits challenging detention and expedited deportation procedures at the Artesia, Karnes, and Dilley family detention facilities in 2014.

7 In 2015, migrant advocacy groups from Alabama to Oregon were trying to persuade local police and city councils not to cooperate with PEP-Comm. In 2016 they were campaigning to end the program.

8 The nine VOLAGs are Church World Service, Episcopal Migration Ministries, Ethiopian Community Development Council, Hebrew Immigration Aid Society, International Rescue Committee, Lutheran Immigration and Refugee Services, US Committee on Refugees and Immigrants, US Conference of Catholic Bishops, and World Relief. Lutheran Immigration and Refugee Service has been responsible for reuniting unaccompanied minors with their families in the United States or finding temporary homes for them while their cases are considered.

11. Contemporary Sanctuary Movements

Epigraph: Quoted in Hayter 2004: 143.
1 Shakespeare, *The Merchant of Venice*, act 4, scene 1.
2 Over more than eighty years, the organization has gone through several incarnations under different names, including the Society for the Protection of Science and Learning and, since the 1980s, CARA.
3 The United Kingdom's Conservative-Liberal Democrat government (2010–15) imposed drastic austerity measures on all social welfare programs, including local government services and the National Health Service. The cuts left provision of many social services to charities, which were unable to replace the services that were lost. The Conservative government elected in 2015 continued cutting such programs.
4 In twenty-one of the thirty-six incidents that Lippert recorded, migrants gained legal status.

12. The News from Tucson

1 In the *American Baptist Churches v. Thornburgh* settlement of 1991, the Immigration and Naturalization Service agreed to reconsider thousands of Central American asylum claims it had rejected since 1980. In 1990 Congress passed a statute establishing Temporary Protected Status and

gave Salvadorans TPS for one year. The government renewed TPS for Salvadorans many times, most recently in 2014 until September 2016.

2   Sanctuary cities included Berkeley, Los Angeles, San Diego, San Francisco, and West Hollywood, CA; Burlington, VT; Cambridge, MA; Chicago, IL; Ithaca and Rochester, NY; Madison, WI; Olympia, WA; Duluth and Saint Paul, MN.

3   Sanctuary churches in late 2014 were in Tucson, Tempe, and Phoenix, AZ; Portland, OR; Chicago and Evanston, IL; Berkeley and Oakland, CA; Denver and Aurora, CO; Seattle and Auburn, WA; and Portland, ME.

4   "Winning" means receiving a stay of deportation so that the migrant can remain, undetained, in the United States while his or her case is in process.

5   Joe Arpaio, the longtime sheriff of Maricopa County, Arizona, has been accused of racially profiling Latinos and violating the civil rights of citizens, migrants, and detainees. In 2013 Maricopa County paid more than $7 million to settle lawsuits accusing Arpaio of abuse of power.

6   The number of migrants deported from the United States decreased from 412,000 in fiscal year 2014 to 235,000 in fiscal year 2015. Noel Andersen contends that this is because of increasing public pressure on the federal government (personal communication, October 7, 2015).

7   In February 2015 a federal judge issued a preliminary injunction in the RILR case, stopping the government from using detention without bond as a means to deter mass migration and allowing a class-action lawsuit by detainees to proceed.

8   By the time Artesia closed in December 2014, AILA attorneys had won asylum for fourteen detainees and bond for more than four hundred (Hylton 2015).

9   Most of the audiences I have spoken to express sympathy for asylum seekers and are shocked to learn about their detention and deportation. Nor are they generally aware that migrants with strong asylum claims, such as Central American children and families, may be denied the opportunity to apply for asylum, just as refugees from the same countries were thirty years ago, during the Sanctuary Movement. Some are too young to remember how history has repeated itself; others have forgotten those long-ago events.

Afterword

Epigraph: Seabrook 2009: 228.

References

Abass, Ademola, and Francesca Ippolito, eds. 2014. *Regional Approaches to the Protection of Asylum Seekers: An International Legal Perspective*. Farnham, Sussex: Ashgate.

Acer, Eleanor, and Jessica Chicco. 2009. "U.S. Detention of Asylum Seekers. Seeking Protection, Finding Prison." New York: Human Rights First.

Advocates for Human Rights and Detention Watch Network. 2014. "Report to the United Nations Working Group on Arbitrary Detention: Detention of Migrants in the United States."

Al Jazeera. 2015. "The Billion-Dollar Business of Refugee Smuggling." September 15. http://www.aljazeera.com/programmes/countingthecost/2015/09/billion-dollar-business-refugee-smuggling-150913113527788.html.

Alaya, Flavia, et al., eds. 2007. "Voices of the Disappeared: An Investigative Report of New Jersey Immigration Detention." Piscataway: New Jersey Civil Rights Defense Committee.

Allman, William. 1994. *The Stone Age Present*. New York: Simon and Shuster.

Allsopp, Jennifer, Nando Sigona, and Jenny Phillimore. 2014. "Poverty among Refugees and Asylum Seekers in the UK." Birmingham: University of Birmingham, Institute for Research into Superdiversity.

Amadiume, Ifi. 1987. *Male Daughters, Female Husbands: Gender and Sex in an African Society*. London: Zed Books.

American Bar Association, Commission on Immigration. 2014. "A Humanitarian Call to Action: Unaccompanied Alien Children at the Southwest Border."

———. 2015. "Family Immigration Detention: Why the Past Cannot Be Prologue."

American Civil Liberties Union. 2014a. "American Exile: Rapid Deportations That Bypass the Courtroom." New York: ACLU.

———. 2014b. "Warehoused and Forgotten: Immigrants Trapped in Our Shadow Private Prison System." New York: ACLU.

———. 2015. "Federal Court Blocks Government from Detaining Asylum Seekers as Tactic to Deter Others from Coming to U.S." Press release, February 20.

American Friends Service Committee. 1940–44. Archives, RG-67.007. Series I, Perpignan; Series II, Vichy France; Series VIII, Marseille; Series IX, Montauban. Washington, DC: Holocaust Museum Library.

———. 2013. "A New Path: Toward a Humane Immigration Policy." Philadelphia: AFSC.

American Immigration Lawyers Association. 2014a. "Stop the Obama Administration's Mass Detention and Rapid Deportation of Central American Mothers and Children." September 22. AILA InfoNet Document #14092255.

——. 2014b. "Artesia Family Detention Asylum Case Examples." December. AILA InfoNet Document #12102446.

Amit, Roni. 2013. "Security Rhetoric and Detention in South Africa." *Forced Migration Review* 44 (September): 32–33. www.fmreview.org/detention.

Amnesty International. 2010. "Stop Forced Evictions of Roma in Europe." EUR01/005/2010.

——. 2012a. "Israel: New Detention Law Violates Rights of Asylum Seekers." Press release, January 10.

——. 2012b. "SOS Europe: Human Rights and Migration Control." EUR01/013/2012.

——. 2014a. "We Ask for Justice: Europe's Failure to Protect Roma from Racist Violence." EUR01/007/2014.

——. 2014b. "Netherlands: Forced Returns of Somalis to South and Central Somalia, Including al-Shabaab Areas: A Blatant Violation of International Law." AFR 52/005/2014.

An-Na'im, Abdullahi Ahmed. 1990. *Toward an Islamic Reformation: Civil Liberties, Human Rights and International Law*. Syracuse, NY: Syracuse University Press.

Arbel, Afrat, and Alletta Brenner. 2013. "Bordering on Failure: Canada-US Border Policy and the Politics of Refugee Exclusion." Cambridge, MA: Harvard Immigration and Refugee Law Clinical Program, Harvard Law School.

Arnold, Samantha K. 2013. "Identity and the Sexual Minority Refugee: A Discussion of Conceptions and Preconceptions in the UK and Ireland." *Human Rights Brief* (Spring): 26–31.

Ashton, Rosemary. 1986. *Little Germany: Exile and Asylum in Victorian London*. Oxford: Oxford University Press.

Associated Press. 2007. "Dutch Government Approves Amnesty for 25,000 Rejected Asylum Seekers." *International Herald Tribune,* May 26. www.iht.com/bin/print.php?id=5876291.

Association of Visitors to Immigration Detainees [AVID]. 2013. Annual Report. London.

——. 2014. *Hidden Stories* (video). YouTube, December 13. www.youtube.com/watch?v=HgpfVnpxhic&app=desktop.

Australian Government. 2012. "Report of the Expert Panel on Asylum Seekers."

Back, Les, Bernadette Farrell, and Erin Vandermaas. 2005. "Report on the South London Citizens Enquiry into Service Provision by the Immigration and Nationality Directorate at Lunar House." London: South London Citizens.

Bade, Klaus J. 2003. *Migration in European History*. Oxford: Blackwell.

Bail for Immigration Detainees (BID). 2014. "Immigration Detention Frequently Asked Questions." www.biduk.org.

Barkow, Jerome, ed. 2006. *Missing the Revolution: Darwinism for Social Scientists*. New York: Oxford University Press.

Barry, Tom. 2009. "The Expanding Immigration Enforcement Apparatus." *Border Lines,* May 23. http://borderlinesblog.blogspot.com/2009/05/expanding-immigration-enforcement.html.

Bau, Ignatius. 1985. *This Ground Is Holy: Church Sanctuary and Central American Refugees*. New York: Paulist Press.

BBC. 2014. *Glasgow Girls* (video). YouTube, July 15. www.youtube.com/watch?v=Z4McEbBoh6k.

BBC News. 2013. "Australia to Send Asylum Seekers to PNG." July 19. www.bbc.com/news/world-asia-23358329.

——. 2016. "Migrant Crisis: Migration to Europe Explained in Graphics." January 28. www.bbc.com/news/world-europe-34131911.

BBC News Australia. 2014. "Australian Asylum: Why Is It Controversial?" December 5. www.bbc.com/ news/world-asia-28189608.

Beadle, Amanda Peterson. 2014. "New Family Detention Facility Opens in Dilley, Texas, despite Due Process Problems." Immigration Impact, December 18. http://immigrationimpact.com/2014/12/18 new-family-detention-facility-opens -dilley-texas-despite-due-process-problems/.

Bellamy, John. 1973. *Crime and Public Order in England in the Later Middle Ages.* London: Routledge and Kegan Paul.

Benari, Elad. 2012. "Knesset Approves Infiltration Law." *Arutz Sheva*, January 10. www.israelnationalnews.com.

Benenson, Larry. 2014. "A Trip to the Artesia Detention Facility." National Immigration Forum. www.immigrationforum.org/blog/display/a-trip-to-the-Artesia-detention-facility.

Berlo, Patrick von. 2014. "The Borderscapes of Australia's Offshore Asylum Policy: Examining the Impact of Operation Sovereign Borders on Pacific Borderscapes." Paper presented at the Borders of Crimmigration conference, Leiden, Netherlands, October 9.

Bernstein, Nina. 2008. "Ill and in Pain, Detainee Dies in U.S. Hands." *New York Times*, August 13.

——. 2010. "Officials Hid Truth of Immigration Deaths in Jail." *New York Times*, January 9.

Bernstein, Richard. 2010. "A Very Superior 'Chinaman.'" *New York Review of Books* 57, no. 16 (October 28).

Black Women's Rape Action Project. 2006. *Misjudging Rape: Breaching Gender Guidelines and International Law in Asylum Appeals.* London: Crossroad Books.

Blight, David W. 2004. *Passages to Freedom: The Underground Railroad in History and Memory.* Washington, DC: Smithsonian Books.

Boasberg, James E. 2015. U.S. District Court for the District of Columbia. *RILR et al, Plaintiffs, v. Jeh Charles Johnson, et al, Defendants.* Civil Action No. 15-11 (JEB). Case 1:15-cv-00011-JEB, Document 33, Filed February 20, 2015.

Boehm, Christopher. 1984. *Blood Revenge: The Anthropology of Feuding in Montenegro and Other Tribal Societies.* Lawrence: University of Kansas Press.

——. 2012. *Moral Origins: The Evolution of Virtue, Altruism and Shame.* New York: Basic Books.

Boer, René. 2013. "Architecture on the Move: Refugee Dwellings in Amsterdam." *Failed Architecture,* September 3. www.failedarchitecture.com/architecture-on-the-move -refugee-dwellings-in-amsterdam/.

Boesch, Christopher. 2010. "Patterns of Chimpanzees' Intergroup Violence." In *Human Morality and Sociality: Evolutionary and Comparative Perspectives,* ed. Henrik Høgh-Olesen. New York: Palgrave Macmillan.

Bolle, Pierre, ed. 1992. *Le plateau Vivarais-Lignon: Accueil et résistance 1939–1944.* Le Chambon-sur-Lignon: Société d'Histoire de la Montagne.

Bollon, Gérard. 2002. "La Montagne Protestante, terre d'accueil et de résistance pendant la seconde guerre mondiale (1939–1945)." *Cahiers du Mézenc* 14 (July): 25–32.

Booth, William, and Ruth Eglash. 2013. "Israel Says It Won't Forcibly Deport Illegal African Migrants, but It Wants Them to Leave." *Washington Post*, December 20.

Bordewich, Fergus M. 2005. *Bound for Canaan: The Underground Railroad and the War for the Soul of America*. New York: HarperCollins.

Borjas, George J., and Jeff Crisp, eds. 2005. *Poverty, International Migration and Asylum*. New York: Palgrave Macmillan.

Bourke, Latika, and AAP. 2014. "Sri Lanka Arrests 37 Asylum Seekers Sent Back by Australia." *Sydney Morning Herald*, November 29. www.smh.com.au/national/sri-lanka-arrests-37-asylum-seekers-sent-back-by-australia-20141129-11wj9f.html?rand=1417181350895.

Bowcott, Owen. 2014. "Asylum Seeker Subsistence Payment Defeat for Government in High Court." *Guardian*, April 9. www.theguardian.com/politics/2014/apr/09/asylum-seeker-subsistence-payments-defeat-government-theresa-may.

Brané, Michelle. 2007. "Locking Up Family Values: The Detention of Immigrant Families." Washington, DC: Women's Refugee Commission.

——, et al. 2014. "Locking Up Family Values, Again." Washington, DC: Lutheran Immigration and Refugee Service and Women's Refugee Commission.

Briggs, Billy. 2012. "Failed Asylum Seekers in Scotland Living below UN Global Poverty Threshold." *Guardian*, October 1. www.theguardian.com/uk/2012/oct/01/failed-asylum-seekers-scotland-poverty.

Brown, Anastasia, and Todd Scribner. 2014. "Unfulfilled Promises, Future Possibilities: The Refugee Resettlement System in the United States." *Journal on Migration and Human Security* 2, no. 2 (January): 101–20.

Browne, Rachel, and Sarah Whyte. 2015. "Children in Detention Report Not a Political Exercise: Human Rights Commission." *Sydney Morning Herald*, February 13. www.smh.com.au/federal-politics/political-news/children-in-detention-report-not-a-political-exercise-human-rights-commission-20150212-13cnnd.html.

Burman, Tony. 2014. "For Syrian Refugees, It's Shame Canada." *Toronto Star*, December 13.

Burnett, John. 2016. "US Churches Offer Safe Haven for a New Generation of Migrants." *All Things Considered*, February 9. www.npr.org/2016/02/09/466145280/u-s-churches-offer-safe-haven-for-a-new-generation-of-migrants.

Burnside, Julian. 2014. "By Bargaining with Children, Morrison's Refugee Strategy Has a Kidnapper's Logic." *Guardian*, December 7. www.theguardian.com/commentisfree/2014/dec/08/the-argument-is-over-morrisons-amendments-show-he-has-no-genuine-concern-for-asylum-seekers.

Burt, Lara, and Jeanne Batalova. 2014. "Refugees and Asylees in the United States." Washington, DC: Migration Policy Institute.

Butt, Audrey. 1952. *The Nilotes of the Anglo-Egyptian Sudan and Uganda*. London: International African Institute.

Cabot, Heath. 2014. *On the Doorstep of Europe: Asylum and Citizenship of Greece*. Philadelphia: University of Pennsylvania Press.

"Call for Integrity, Protection and Care for Asylum Seekers Undergoing Credible Fear Interviews in the U.S." 2014. Detention Watch Network listserv, May 7.

Caminero-Santangelo, Marta. 2013. "The Voice of the Voiceless: Religious Rhetoric, Undocumented Immigrants and the New Sanctuary Movement in the United States." In Lippert and Rehaag, eds., *Sanctuary Practices in International Perspective*.

Carman, Tara. 2014. "Most B.C. Asylum Seekers Housed in Jail." *Vancouver Sun*, June 19.

Casciani, Dominic. 2011. "UK Border Agency Attacked for 'Dumping' Missing Cases." BBC, November 4. www.bbc.co.uk/news/uk-politics-15581877.

Catholic Legal Immigration Network (CLINIC). 2014. "Children Traveling Alone: The Catholic Church's Response." June 20.

Center for Constitutional Rights. 2007. "American Baptist Churches v. Thornburgh." www.ccrjustice.org/ourcases/past-cases/american-baptist-churches-v.-thornburgh.

Center for the Study of Human Rights. 1992. *Twenty-four Human Rights Documents*. New York: Columbia University.

Chai, Jolie. 2013. "Threats to Liberty in Germany." *Forced Migration Review* 44 (September).

Chan, Wendy. 2014. "The Rise of Crimmigration Policies in Canada." Paper presented at the Borders of Crimmigration conference, Leiden, October 9.

Chapais, Bernard, and Carol M. Berman, eds. 2004. *Kinship and Behavior in Primates*. Oxford: Oxford University Press.

Chen, Angela. 2014. "Reformed Australian Immigration Policy Turns Refugees Away." *Human Rights Brief* 21, no. 2 (Spring): 53–54.

Chen, Michelle. 2014. "Does Homeland Security's Tough New Security Process Put Asylum Seekers at Risk?" *Nation*, June 3. www.thenation.com/article/does-homeland-securitys-tough-new-screening-process-put-asylum-seekers-risk.

Chishti, Muzaffar, Faye Hipsman, and Bethany Eberle. 2015. "As Implementation Nears, U.S. Deferred Action Programs Encounter Legal, Political Tests." *Migration Information Source*, February 11. http://migrationpolicy.org/article/implementation-nears-us-deferred-action-programs-encounter-legal-political-tests.

Chomsky, Aviva. 2014. *Undocumented: How Immigration Became Illegal*. Boston: Beacon Press.

Cissé, Madjiguene. 1997. "The Sans-Papiers: A Woman Draws the First Lessons," hartford-hwp.com, World History Archives, April 24. Also published as *The Sans-Papiers: A Woman Draws the First Lessons*. London: Crossroads Books.

Civic Leicester. 2014. *Glasgow Girls @Sanctuary Summit 2014* (video). YouTube. www.youtube.com/watch?v=vbMbOee7IvE.

Cochrane, Kira. 2014. "End the Despair of Detention for Female Asylum Seekers: 'I Saw What My Mother Went Through.'" *Guardian*, February 10. http://www.theguardian.com/uk-news/2014/feb/10/end-despair-detention-female-asylum-seekers-yarls-wood.

Connolly, Kate. 2015. "Dresden Crowds Tell a Chilling Tale of Europe's Fear of Migrants." *Guardian*, January 4. www.theguardian.com/world/2015/jan/04/dresden-germany-far-right-pegida.

Cook, Maria Lorena. 2007. "Advocacy on the Frontlines: Defending Migrant Rights in Southern Arizona." Paper delivered at Latin American Studies Association, Montreal, September.

Corbett, Jim. 1986. "Toward a Quaker View of Sanctuary: Preliminary Discussion Draft for Friends General Conference, June 28–July 5." Typescript, Friends House Library, London.

——. 1988. "Sanctuary, Basic Rights and Humanity's Fault Lines." *Weber Studies* 5, no. 1.

——. 1991. *Goatwalking.* New York: Viking.

Couch, Robbie. 2014. "US 'Steps Up,' Considers 9,000 Syrian Refugee Applications." *Huffington Post*, December 11. www.huffingtonpost.com/2014/12/11/syria-refugees-united-states_n_6308344.html.

Council of Europe. 2014. "Greece: Anti-torture Report Highlights 'Totally Unacceptable' Detention Conditions." www.humanrightseurope.org/2014/10/greece-report-highlights-totally-unacceptable-migrant-detention-conditions.

Courlander, Harold. 1987. *The Fourth World of the Hopis.* Albuquerque: University of New Mexico Press.

Cox, John Charles. 1911. *The Sanctuaries and Sanctuary Seekers of Mediaeval England.* London: George Allen.

Crittenden, Ann. 1988. *Sanctuary: A Story of American Conscience and Law in Collision.* New York: Weidenfeld and Nicolson.

Cunningham, Hilary. 1995. *God and Caesar at the Rio Grande: Sanctuary and the Politics of Religion.* Minneapolis: University of Minnesota Press.

——. 2013. "The Emergence of the Ontario Sanctuary Coalition: From Humanitarian and Compassionate Review to Civil Initiative." In Lippert and Rehaag, *Sanctuary Practices in International Perspective.*

Curio, Claudia. 2004. "'Invisible' Children: The Selection and Integration Strategies of Relief Organizations." *Shofar* 23, no. 1 (Fall): 41–56.

Dallas, Ted. 2014. "Maryland Officials Announce Key Developments in State's Plan to Assist Children Seeking Refuge." August 12. www.dhr.state.md.us/blog/?p=12548.

Daniels, Roger. 2004. *Guarding the Golden Door: American Immigration Policy and Immigrants since 1882.* New York: Hill and Wang.

Danticat, Edwidge. 2007. *Brother, I'm Dying.* New York: Knopf.

Darling, Jonathan, and Vicki Squire. 2013. "Everyday Enactments of Sanctuary: The UK City of Sanctuary Movement." In Lippert and Rehaag, *Sanctuary Practices in International Perspective.*

David, Ruth. 2003. "Help Given by Quakers to Refugees from Germany and Austria in the 1930s and 40s." Personal narrative, 13 pp. London: Friends House Library.

Davidson, Miriam. 1988. *Convictions of the Heart: Jim Corbett and the Sanctuary Movement.* Tucson: University of Arizona Press.

Davies, Lizzy. 2014. "Italy Remembers Cycling Champion Who Helped Save Jews from Nazis." *Guardian*, July 17. www.theguardian.com/world/2014/jul/17/italy-remembers-gino-bartali-cycling-hero-save-jews-nazis.

de Waal, Frans B. M. 1996. *Good Natured: The Origins of Right and Wrong in Humans and Other Animals.* Cambridge, MA: Harvard University Press.

——. 1998. *Chimpanzee Politics: Power and Sex among Apes.* Baltimore, MD: Johns Hopkins Press.

——. 2001. *Tree of Origin: What Primate Behavior Can Tell Us about Human Social Evolution.* Cambridge, MA: Harvard University Press.

——. 2006. *Primates and Philosophers: How Morality Evolved.* Edited and introduced by Stephen Macedo and Josiah Ober. Princeton, NJ: Princeton University Press.

———. 2009. *The Age of Empathy: Nature's Lessons for a Kinder Society.* New York: Harmony Books.

Deardoff, Merle H. 1951. *The Religion of Handsome Lake: Its Origin and Development.* Washington, DC: Smithsonian Institution.

Detention Watch Network. 2013. "Immigration Detention Backgrounder." www. detention watchnetwork.org.

Division Director. 2014. "Detainee Death Review of Tiombe Kimana CARLOS." Washington, DC: US Immigration and Customs Enforcement, Office of Professional Responsibility.

Dobuzinskis, Alex. 2014. "California Sets Up Fund for Legal Representation of Immigrant Children." *Reuters*, September 27. www.reuters.com/article/us-usa-immigration -california-idUSKCN0HN00B20140928.

Doherty, Ben. 2014. "Refugees' Plight in Australia: From Compassion to 'Vicious and Vindictive.'" *Guardian*, November 2. www.theguardian.com/australia-news/2014nov/03/ sp-refugees-plight-australia-compassion-vicious-and-vindictive.

Dominguez Villegas, Rodrigo. 2014. "Central American Migrants and 'La Bestia': The Route, Dangers and Government Responses." Washington, DC: Migration Policy Institute.

Douglass, Frederick. 1971. *Narrative of the Life of Frederick Douglass an American Slave, Written by Himself.* Cambridge, MA: Belknap Press.

Dow, Mark. 2004. *American Gulag: Inside U.S. Immigration Prisons.* Berkeley: University of California Press.

Doward, Jamie. 2014a. "Home Office 'Chaos' over Asylum Appeals." *Guardian*, October 18. www.theguardian.com/uk-news/2014/oct/18/asylum-appeals-home-office-chaos -theresa-may.

———. 2014b. "Church of England Urges End of 'Legal Limbo' for Asylum Seekers." *Guardian*, November 15. www.theguardian.com/uk-news/2014/nov/15/anglican-bishops-attack -asylum-seekers-detention.

Duffy, Corinne. 2014. "Key Statistics and Findings on Asylum Protection Requirements at the U.S.-Mexican Border." Washington, DC: Human Rights Watch.

Dunn, Jean. 2008. "Albanian Muslims Who Sheltered Jews Honored at Program." International Raoul Wallenberg Foundation, May 7. www.raoulwallenberg.net.

Editorial Board. 2014. "At an Immigration Detention Center Due Process Denied." *New York Times*, August 26. www.nytimes.com/2014/08/26/opinion/at-an-immigration -detention-center-due-process-denied.html?-r=0.

Epstein, Ruthie. 2014. "Mothers and Children Fleeing Violence Need a Fair Chance." Washington, DC: American Civil Liberties Union.

Epstein, Ruthie, and Eleanor Acer. 2011. "Jails and Jumpsuits: Transforming the U.S. Immigration Detention System – a Two-Year Review." New York: Human Rights First.

Erlanger, Steven. 2010. "Roma Expelled from Church." *New York Times*, November 5.

Eurostat. 2015. "Eurostat: Your Key to European Statistics." http://ec.europa.eu/eurostat.

Farmer, Alice. 2013. "The Impact of Immigration Detention on Children." *Forced Migration Review* 44 (September).

Farrell, Paul. 2014a. "Law Changes Could See Legitimate Refugees Sent Back, Senate Inquiry Told." *Guardian*, November 14. www.theguardian.com/australia-news/2014/

nov/14/law-changes-could-see-legitimate-refugees-sent-back-senate-inquiry-told.

———. 2014b. "Asylum Seekers Registered with UNHCR in Indonesia Blocked from Resettle-ment." *Guardian*, November 18. www.theguardian.com/australia-news/2014/nov/18/asylum-seekers-registered-with-unhcr-in-indonesia-blocked-from-resettlement.

———. 2016. "Churches Offer Sanctuary to Asylum Seekers Facing Deportation to Nauru." *Guardian*, February 3. www.theguardian.com/australia-news/2016/feb/04/churches-offer-sanctuary-to-asylum-seekers-facing-deportation-to-nauru.

Fein, Leonard. 2013. "Israel's Heartbreaking Policy to African Asylum Seekers." *Jewish Daily Forward*, May 4.

Feisen, Joe. 2012. "Canada to Raise Language Bar." *Guardian*, June 19. www.theguardian.com/education/2012/jun/19/canada-to-raise-language-bar.

Feltz, Renée. 2014. "Two Detention Centers for Migrant Women and Children Open on 5th Anniversary of End to Family Detention." *Democracy Now!* August 8. www.democracynow.org/blog/2014/8/8/two_detention_centers_for_migrant_women.

Ferguson, Kathryn, Norma A. Price, and Ted Parks. 2010. *Crossing with the Virgin: Stories from the Migrant Trail.* Tucson: University of Arizona Press.

Fischer, Nicolas. 2014. "Where Do I Go from Here? French Immigration Detention and Its Differential Impact on Immigrant Strategies." Paper presented at the Borders of Crim-migration conference, Leiden, October 10.

Fogelman, Eva. 1994. *Conscience and Courage: Rescuers of Jews during the Holocaust.* New York: Anchor Doubleday.

Ford, Robert. 2012. "Parochial and Cosmopolitan Britain: Examining the Social Divide in Reactions to Immigration." Washington, DC: German Marshall Fund of the United States.

Franko, Katja. 2014. "Policing with, against and through Humanity: European Borders and the Precariousness of Life." Paper presented at the Borders of Crimmigration confer-ence, Leiden, October 9.

Frelick, Bill, and Brian Jacek. 2013. "Immigration Reform Overlooks Asylum Seekers." *Los Angeles Times*, April 26. http://articles.latimes.com/2013/apr/25/opinion/la-oe-frelickjacek-asylum-immigration-2013042.

Friedman, Edie, and Reva Klein. 2008. *Reluctant Refuge: The Story of Asylum in Britain.* London: British Library.

Frontex. 2015. "Mission and Tasks." Accessed February 23, 2015. www.frontex.europa.eu/about-frontex/mission-and-tasks.

Gentile, Carmen. 2014. "In Pittsburgh, a Refuge for Endangered Writers." *Al Jazeera America*, September 10. http://america.aljazeera.com/articles/2014/8/10/in-pittsburgh-a-refugeforendangeredwriters.html.

Gentleman, Amelia. 2014. "Meet the Professional Refugees Lucky to Get the Minimum Wage in the UK." *Guardian*, March 8. www.theguardian.com/world/2014/mar/08/professional-refugees-lawyers-doctors-minimum-wage-uk.

Gershon, Karen, ed. 1966. *We Came as Children: A Collective Autobiography.* New York: Har-court, Brace and World.

Gibney, Matthew J. 2004. *The Ethics and Politics of Asylum: Liberal Democracy and the Response to Refugees.* Cambridge: Cambridge University Press.

Gibney, Matthew J., and Randall Hansen, eds. 2005. *Immigration and Asylum: From 1900 to the Present.* 3 vols. Santa Barbara: ABC-Clio.

Gilbert, Martin. 2003. *The Righteous: The Unsung Heroes of the Holocaust.* New York: Henry Holt.

Girma, Marchu, Sophie Radice, Natasha Tsangarides, and Natasha Walter. 2014. "Detained: Women Asylum Seekers Locked Up in the UK." London: Women for Refugee Women.

Global Detention Project. 2009. "Sweden Detention Profile." Geneva: Programme for the Study of Global Migration, the Graduate Institute. www.globaldetentionproject.org.

———. 2012. "Immigration Detention in Canada: A Global Detention Project Special Report." Geneva: Programme for the Study of Global Migration.

———. 2014. "Germany Detention Profile." www.globaldetentionproject.org/ countries/ europe/germany/introduction.html.

Goeman, Martine, and Carla van Os. 2014. "'Dad, Have We Done Something Wrong?' Children and Parents in Immigration Detention." Amsterdam: No Child in Detention Coalition.

Golash-Boza, Tanya. 2014. "Getting Caught in the Deportation Dragnet in the United States." Paper presented at the Borders of Crimmigration conference, Leiden, October 10.

Golden, Renny, and Michael McConnell. 1986. *Sanctuary: The New Underground Railroad.* New York: Orbis Books.

Good, Anthony. 2007. *Anthropology and Expertise in the Asylum Courts.* New York: Routledge-Cavendish.

Goodstein, Laurie. 2001. "Church Group Provides Oasis for Illegal Migrants to US." *New York Times,* June 10.

Gopfert, Rebekka. 2004. "Kindertransport: History and Memory." *Shofar* 23, no. 1 (Fall).

Gosztola, Kevin. 2012. "Why Did Ecuador Grant Asylum to Julian Assange?" *Nation,* August 16.

Grahl-Madsen, Atle. 1980. *Territorial Asylum.* New York: Oceana.

Grassler, Bernd. 2014. "German Parliament Discusses Asylum Law." *Deutsche Welle,* June 6. www.dw.com/en/german-parliament-discusses-asylum-law/a-17690245.

Greenslade, Roy. 2005. "Seeking Scapegoats: The Coverage of Asylum in the UK Press." Asylum and Migration Working Paper 5. London: Institute for Public Policy Research.

Greenwood, Phoebe. 2012. "Huge Detention Centre to Be Israel's Latest Weapon in Migration Battle." *Guardian,* April 17. www.theguardian.com/world/2012/apr/17/ detention-centre-israel-migration.

Grewal, Madhuri, and Silky Shah. 2014. "Expose and Close: Artesia Family Residential Center, New Mexico." Washington, DC: Detention Watch Network.

Gulf Coast Jewish Family and Community Services. 2014. "Country Conditions Report: El Salvador." www.gcjfcs.org/refugee.

Haines, David W. 2010. *Safe Haven? A History of Refugees in America.* Sterling, VA: Kumarian Press.

Hallie, Philip P. 1979. *Lest Innocent Blood Be Shed: The Story of the Village of Le Chambon and How Goodness Happened There.* New York: Harper and Row.

Hamilton, Keegan. 2014. "Asylum Insanity: Welcome to the Land of the Free." *Village Voice,* April 8.

Hancock, Landon, and Christopher Mitchell. 2004. *The Construction of Sanctuary: Local Zones of Peace amid Protracted Conflict.* Arlington, VA: George Mason University Institute for Conflict Analysis and Resolution.

Hangley, Bill. 2014. "Facing Deportation, Woman Finds Sanctuary in North Philly Church." *WHYY Newsworks*, December 24. www.newsworks.org/index.php/local/philadelphia/76686-facing-deportation-woman-finds-sanctuary-in-north-philly-church.

Harcourt, Alexander H., and Frans B. M. de Waal, eds. 1992. *Coalitions and Alliances in Humans and Other Animals.* Oxford: Oxford University Press.

Harris, Mark, dir. 2000. *Into the Arms of Strangers: Stories of the Kindertransport.* DVD.

Hatton, T. J. 2005. "European Asylum Policy." *National Institute Economic Review,* no. 194 (October): 108–19.

Hayter, Teresa. 2004. *Open Borders: The Case against Immigration Controls.* 2d ed. London: Pluto.

Healey, Justin, ed. 2013. *Asylum Seekers and Immigration Detention.* Issues in Society 353. Thirroul, NSW, Australia: Spinney Press.

Henry, Patrick. 2002. "Banishing the Coercion of Despair: Le Chambon sur Lignon and the Holocaust Today." *Shofar* 20, no. 2 (Winter). https://muse.jhu.edu/login?auth=0&type=summary&url=/journals/shofar/v020/20.2henry.html.

Heller, Becca. 2014. "America's Allies in Iraq, Forgotten and in Danger." *Washington Post,* June 20.

Hevisi, Dennis. 2007. "Johtje Vos, Who Saved Wartime Jews, Dies at 97." *New York Times,* November 4.

Hewett, Jennifer. 2012. "Asylum Policy a Great Leap Backward." *Australian Financial Review,* November 24. www.afr.com/p/opinion/asylum-policy-great-leap-backward-P07jGPLjUd9aezApt41qVI.

Heyman, Josiah. 1998. *Finding a Moral Heart for U.S. Immigration Policy: An Anthropological Perspective.* American Ethnological Society, Monographs in Human Policy Issues. Washington, DC: American Anthropological Association.

Ho, Christine G. T., and James Loucky. 2012. *Humane Migration: Establishing Legitimacy and Rights for Displaced People.* Sterling, VA: Kumarian Press.

Hobson, Chris, Jonathan Cox, and Nicholas Sagovsky. 2008. "Deserving Dignity: The Independent Asylum Commission's Third Report of Conclusions and Recommendations." London: Independent Asylum Commission.

Holley, Denise, ed. 2014. *No More Deaths* newsletter. Spring.

House of Commons, Home Affairs Committee. 2013. "Asylum: Seventh Report of Session 2013–14." Vol. 1, October.

Human Rights First. 2014. "How to Protect Refugees and Prevent Abuse at the Border: Blueprint for U.S. Government Policy."

Human Rights Watch. 2008. "Stuck in a Revolving Door: Iraqis and Other Asylum Seekers and Migrants at the Greece-Turkey Entrance to the European Union." New York: Human Rights Watch.

——. 2012. "Israel: Amend 'Anti-infiltration' Law." June 9. www.hrw.org/news/2012/06/10/israel-amend-anti-infiltration-law.

——. 2014. "United States: Parents of American Children Summarily Deported." November 20.

Hurvitz, Emily Singer. 2013. "The Plight of Syrian Refugees in Lebanon." *Human Rights Brief* 66 (Spring).

Hylton, Wil S. 2015. "The Shame of America's Family Detention Camps." *New York Times Magazine*, February 4. www.nytimes.com/2015/02/08/magazine/the-shame-of -americas-family-detention-camps.html?ref=magazine&_r=2.

Immigrant Legal Resource Center. 2014. "Organizer Alert: Life after 'PEP-Comm.'" www.ilrc.org/files/documents'ilrc-organizers-advisory-final.pdf.

Immigration and Refugee Board of Canada, Refugee Protection Division. 2013. "Refugee Status Determinations 1989 to December 2012."

Immigration Policy Center. 2011. "Understanding Prosecutorial Discretion in Immigration Law." Washington, DC: American Immigration Council. www.immigrationpolicy.org/ just-facts/understanding-prosecutorial-discretion-immigration-law.

Indymedia.org. 2013. "Ugandan Asylum Seeker and Movement for Justice Activist Killed by Reliance Thugs." March 14. www.indymedia.org.uk/en/2013/03/507609.html.

Information Centre about Asylum and Refugees. 2007. "Removals." London: ICAR.

Integrating Toryglen Community. 2007. "Integration and Orientation Programme: Information Pack."

Inter-American Commission on Human Rights. 2011. "Report on Immigration in the United States: Detention and Due Process." Washington, DC: Organization of American States. www.cidh.oas.org/countryrep/USImmigration/Chap.III.htm.

———. 2014. "Inter-American Commission on Human Rights Wraps Up Visit to the United States of America." October 2. www.cidh.org.

Inter-American Court of Human Rights. 2014. Advisory Opinion OC-21/14, "Rights and Guarantees of Children in the Context of Migration and/or in Need of International Protection." August 19.

Ira, Kumaran, and Antoine Lerougetel. 2008. "Undocumented Workers Occupy CGT Union Hall in Paris." World Socialist website, May 6. www.wsws.org.

Isbell, Lynne. 2004. "Is There No Place Like Home? Ecological Bases of Female Dispersal and Philopatry and Their Consequences for the Formation of Kin Groups." In *Kinship and Behavior in Primates*, edited by Bernard Chapais and Carol M. Berman. Oxford: Oxford University Press.

Jones, William R. 1994. "Sanctuary, Exile and Law: The Fugitive and Public Authority in Medieval England and Modern America." In *Essays on English Law and the American Experience*, edited by Elisabeth A. Cawthom and David E. Narrett. College Station: Texas A&M University Press.

Joutard, Philippe, Jacques Poujol, and Patrick Cabanel. 1987. *Cévennes, Terre de Refuge 1940–1944*. Montpellier: Presses du Languedoc/Club Cévenol.

Just, Wolf-Dieter. 2013. "The Rise and Features of Church Asylum in Germany: 'I Will Take Refuge in the Shadow of Thy Wings until the Storms Are Past.'" In Lippert and Rehaag, *Sanctuary Practices in International Perspective*.

Kalir, Barak. 2014. "The Deportation Mess: A Bureaucratic Muddling of State Fantasies." Border Criminologies blog, University of Oxford Faculty of Law, October 29. https:// www.law.ox.ac.uk/research-subject-groups/centre-criminology/centreborder -criminologies/blog/2014/10/deportation-mess.

Kaper-Dale, Seth. 2012. Press releases on eight Indonesians in sanctuary at Highland Park, NJ, Reformed Church, March 1, March 12, March 16.

Kassindja, Fauziya, and Layli Miller Bashir. 1998. *Do They Hear You When You Cry*. New York: Delacorte Press.

Kay, Matthew, and Jasper Kain. 2014. "African Migrants Speak Out about Life in Israel's Detention Centers." *Guardian*, December 19. www.theguardian.com/world/2014/dec/19/-sp-african-migrants-speak-out-about-life-in-israel-detention-centres-holot.

Keller, Kayla. 2014. "More than 160 Groups Condemn President Obama's Expansion of Family Detention." Detention Watch Network listserv, September 25.

Kelley, Ninette, and Michael Trebilcock. 2010. *The Making of the Mosaic: A History of Canadian Immigration Policy*. 2d ed. Toronto: University of Toronto Press.

Keneally, Thomas. 1982. *Schindler's List*. New York: Touchstone.

Kenney, David Ngaruri, and Philip G. Schrag. 2008. *Asylum Denied: A Refugee's Struggle for Safety in America*. Berkeley: University of California Press.

Kennon, Kenneth. 2001. *Prisoner of Conscience: A Memoir*. N.p.: Xlibris.

Kesselring, Krista. 1999. "Abjuration and Its Demise: The Changing Face of Royal Justice in the Tudor Period." *Canadian Journal of History* 34, no. 3 (December): 345–58.

Khonsari, Niloufar. 2014. "Update on USCIS Credible Fear Standards – Increased Deportations." Detention Watch Network listserv, April 22.

Koser, Khalid. 2007. *International Migration: A Very Short Introduction*. Oxford: Oxford University Press.

Kraus, Kevin. 2013. "Christian Indonesians in New Jersey Leave Church's Sanctuary." *ABC News*, February 18.

Kuper, Adam. 1994. *The Chosen Primate: Human Nature and Cultural Diversity*. Cambridge, MA: Harvard University Press.

Kushner, Tony. 2006. *Remembering Refugees: Then and Now*. Manchester: Manchester University Press.

Kushner, Tony, and Katharine Knox. 1999. *Refugees in an Age of Genocide: Global, National and Local Perspectives during the Twentieth Century*. London: Frank Cass.

Langer, Emily. 2012. "Albert O. Hirschman, 97, Influential Social Scientist, Author." *Washington Post*, December 10.

Larson, Kate Clifford. 2004. *Bound for the Promised Land*. New York: Ballantine.

Laughland, Oliver. 2014a. "Syrians on Manus Offered Repatriation despite Prospect of 'Certain Death.'" *Guardian*, March 14. www.theguardian.com/world/2014/mar/15/appalling-offer-syrian-asylum-seekers-offered-repatriation-manus-island.

——. 2014b. "The Life and Awful Death of a Tamil Asylum Seeker in Australia." *Guardian*, June 4. www.theguardian.com/world/2014/jun/05/the-life-and-awful-death-of-a-tamil-asylum-seeker-in-australia.

Laville, Sandra. 2014. "Nigerian Woman Fearing Daughters' FGM Wins Reprieve on Deportation." *Guardian*, April 25. www.theguardian.com/uk-news/2014/apr/25/nigerian-woman-saliu-mp-deportation-fgm.

Leddy, Mary Jo. 1997. *At the Border Called Hope, Where Refugees Are Neighbors*. Toronto: HarperCollins.

——. 2010. *Our Friendly Local Terrorist*. Toronto: Between the Lines.

Leerkes, Arjen, and Mieke Kox. 2014. "The Pains of Immigration Detention: A Study on the Specific Deterrent Effects of Custody with a View to Deportation." Paper presented at the Borders of Crimmigration conference, Leiden, October 10.

Levy, Taylor K. 2014. "In Search of Refuge: Mexican Refugees and Asylum Seekers to the United States from 1980 to the Present." Master's thesis, University of Texas/El Paso.

Lightsey, Dana. "Terrible Results of ICE Raid in Cheyenne, WY." Detention Watch Network listserv, February 16.

Lijnders, Laurie. 2013. "Deportation of South Sudanese from Israel." *Forced Migration Review* 44 (September): 66–67.

Lind, Dara. 2014. "Nine Ways Detaining Immigrant Families Is Turning into a 'Shitshow.'" *Vox Explainers*, August 6. www.vox.com/2014/8/6/5971003/artesia-immigrants -detention-due-process-families-lawyers-asylum-court-border.

Linthicum, Kate. 2014. "Immigration Officials Raise the Bar on Asylum Interview Process." *Los Angeles Times*, April 17. www.latimes.com/local/lanow/la-me-ln-asylum-credible-fear-20140417-story.html.

Lippert, Randy K. 2005. *Sanctuary, Sovereignty, Sacrifice: Canadian Sanctuary Incidents, Power, and Law*. Vancouver: University of British Columbia Press.

Lippert, Randy K., and Sean Rehaag, eds. 2013. *Sanctuary Practices in International Perspective: Migration, Citizenship and Social Movements*. New York: Routledge.

Local, The. 2014. "Sweden Takes 19 Percent of EU's Asylum Seekers." June 19. www.thelocal. se/20140619/sweden-takes-19-percent-of-eus-asylum-seekers.

Loewenstein, Antony. 2013. "Food Banks, English Classes, Politics: A Day with Two Refugee Organizations." *Guardian*, October 2. www.theguardian.com/commentisfree/2013/oct/ 02/ refugees-australia-groups-advocacy.

Loga, Jill, Miikka Pyykkönen, and Hanne Stenvaag. 2013. "Holy Territories and Hospitality: Nordic Exceptionality and National Differences of Sanctuary Incidents." In Lippert and Rehaag, *Sanctuary Practices in International Perspective*.

Long, Clara. 2014. "You Don't Have Rights Here: U.S. Border Screening and Returns of Central Americans to Risk of Serious Harm." Washington, DC: Human Rights Watch.

Lorentzen, Robin. 1991. *Women in the Sanctuary Movement*. Philadelphia: Temple University Press.

Lutheran Immigration and Refugee Service. 2014. "LIRS Condemns Administration's Plans to Expedite Deportations for Unaccompanied Children and Increase Detention of Families."

Lyall, James. 2014. "Welcome to Hell at the Border." *Huffington Post*, June 25. www .huffingtonpost.com/james-lyall/welcome-to-hell-the-borde_b_5527967.html.

MacEoin, Gary, ed. 1985. *Sanctuary: A Resource Guide for Understanding and Participating in the Central American Refugees' Struggle*. San Francisco: Harper and Row.

MacMichael, N. H. 1970. "Sanctuary at Westminster." Westminster Abbey Occasional Paper No. 27. London: Westminster Abbey.

Maese, Rick. 2014. "U.S.-Born Children Provide Key for Parents to Remain." *Washington Post*, November 28.

Mahanta, Siddhartha. 2014. "Haven Is for Real: How Dumbarton Methodist and Other D.C. Churches Helped Salvadoran Refugees Survive the 80s." *Washington City Paper*, September 19.

Maillebouis, Christian. 2005. *La Montagne Protestante: Pratiques chrétiennes socials dans la region du Mazet-St.-Voy 1920–1940*. Lyon: Editions Olivétan.

Malik, Shiv. 2012. "Tamils Deported to Sri Lanka from Britain Being Tortured, Victim Claims." *Guardian*, June 5. www.theguardian.com/uk/2012/jun/05/tamils-deported-sri-lanka-torture.

Maltby, Edward. 2008. "Parisian Migrant Workers Strike." *Workers' Liberty*, May 12, www.workersliberty.org.

Marino, Andy. 1999. *A Quiet American: The Secret War of Varian Fry*. New York: St. Martin's Press.

Markowitz, Miriam. 2010. "The Group." *Nation*, October 11.

Marshall, Catherine, Suma Pillai, and Louise Stack. 2013. "Community Detention in Australia." *Forced Migration Review* 44 (September): 55–57.

Martin, Susan, and Andrew I. Schoenholtz. 2006. "Promoting the Human Rights of Forced Migrants." In *Human Rights and Conflict: Exploring the Links between Rights, Law, and Peacebuilding*, edited by Julie Mertus and Jeffrey Helsing. Washington, DC: United States Institute of Peace Press.

Mason, Rowena. 2013. "UK Immigration Bill Could Create 'Climate of Ethnic Profiling' – UNHCR." *Guardian*, December 26. www.theguardian.com/uk-news/2013/dec/26/uk-immigration-bill-climate-ethnic-profiling-unhcr.

———. 2015. "Number of Syrian Refugees Brought to UK Passes 1,000." *Guardian*, December 16. www.theguardian.com/uk-news/2015/dec/16/number-syrian-refugees-uk-1000-david-cameron.

Masters, William Murray. 1953. "Rowanduz: A Kurdish Administrative and Mercantile Center." PhD diss., University of Michigan.

Mathewson, Tara Garcia, and Leonardo March. 2014. "Boston Interfaith Group Stands with Immigration Detainees." *Open Media Boston*, November 14. www.openmediaboston.org/ content/boston-interfaithgroup-stands-immigrant-detainees-3050.

Matza, Michael. 2013. "Sad Tale of Mental Illness and U.S. Detention." *Philadelphia Inquirer*, November 15. http://articles.philly.com/2013-11-15/news/44078208_1_immigration-detainees-detainee-deaths-u-s-immigration.

———. 2014. "Faith Groups to Fight Deportation." *Philadelphia Inquirer*, September 24.

———. 2015a. "Immigrant Wins Reprieve, Ends Sanctuary in Phila Church." *Philadelphia Inquirer*, January 17. www.philly.com/philly/news/20150116_Immigrant_wins_reprieve_ends_sanctuary_in_Phila_church.html.

———. 2015b. "Report Faults York County Prison on Immigrant Prisoner's 2013 Suicide." *Philadelphia Inquirer*, February 3. www.philly.com/philly/news/20150203_Report_faults_York_County_Prison_in_immigrant_prisoner_s_2013_suicide.html.

Mazzinghi, Thomas John de. 1887. *Sanctuaries*. Stafford: Halden.

McCarthy, Mary Meg. 2015. "Statement before House Subcommittee on Immigration and Border Security Hearing on 'Interior Immigration Enforcement Legislation.'" Chicago: National Immigration Justice Center.

McMartin, Pete. "Walk the Line: The Canadian Border Services Agency Crosses It." *Vancouver Sun*, March 6.

McVeigh, Karen. 2011. "Gay Asylum Claims Not Being Counted despite Pledge, Admit Ministers." *Guardian*, May 1. www.theguardian.com/uk/2011/may/01/gay-asylum-claims-not-being-counted.

——. 2012. "Iranian Fugitive: Identity Mix-Up with Shot Neda Wrecked My Life." *Observer*, October 14.

Mead, Margaret. 1956. *New Lives for Old: Cultural Transformation – Manus 1928–1953*. New York: Morrow.

Medhora, Shalailah, and Ben Doherty. 2015. "Tony Abbott Calls Report on Children in Detention a 'Transparent Stitch-Up.'" *Guardian*, February 11. www.theguardian.com/ australia-news/2015/feb/12/tony-abbott-rejects-report-children-detention-blatantly-political.

Medical Justice. 2012. *Annual Report FY 2012*. London.

——. 2014. *Annual Report FY 2014*. London.

Meissner, Doris, Donald M. Kerwin, Muzaffar Chisti, and Clair Bergeron. 2013. "Immigration Enforcement in the United States: The Rise of a Formidable Machinery." Washington, DC: Migration Policy Institute.

Merjian, Armen H. 2009. "A Guinean Refugee's Odyssey: In Re Jarno, the Biggest Asylum Case in U.S. History and What It Tells Us about Our Broken System." *Georgetown Immigration Law Journal* 23 (Summer): 649–90.

Michels, David H., and David Blaikie. 2013. "'I Took Up the Case of the Stranger': Arguments from Faith, History and Law." In Lippert and Rehaag, *Sanctuary Practices in International Perspective*.

Migration Policy Centre. 2014. "Syrian Refugees: A Snapshot of the Crisis – in the Middle East and Europe." European University Institute. www.syrianrefugees.eu.

Miller, Nick. 2014. "Australia's Detention of Refugees Is Forbidden by International Law: UN Committee against Torture." *Sydney Morning Herald*, November 29. www.smh. com.au/national/australias-detention-of-refugees-is-forbidden-by-international-law-un-committee-against-torture-20141128-11wjas.html.

Miller, Scott, and Sarah Ogilvie. 2006. *Refuge Denied: The* St. Louis *Passengers and the Holocaust*. Madison: University of Wisconsin Press.

Millner, Naomi. 2013. "Sanctuary sans Frontières: Social Movements and Solidarity in Postwar Northern France." In Lippert and Rehaag, *Sanctuary Practices in International Perspective*.

Moorehead, Caroline. 2005. *Human Cargo*. New York: Holt.

Morton, John. 2011. "Exercising Prosecutorial Discretion Consistent with the Civil Immigration Enforcement Priorities of the Agency for the Apprehension, Detention and Removal of Aliens." Memorandum, U.S. Department of Homeland Security, June 17.

Moss, Stephen. 2014. "'British Schindler' Nicholas Winton: I Wasn't Heroic. I Was Never in Danger." *Guardian*, November 9. www.theguardian.com/world/2014/nov/09/ british-schindler-nicholas-winton-interview.

Mountz, Alison. 2010. *Seeking Asylum: Human Smuggling and Bureaucracy at the Border*. Minneapolis: University of Minnesota Press.

Muižnieks, Nils. 2014. "Report by Commissioner for Human Rights of the Council of Europe Following His Visit to the Netherlands from 20 to 22 May 2014." Strasbourg: Council of Europe.

Musson, Anthony, ed. 2005. *Boundaries of the Law: Geography, Gender and Jurisdiction in Medieval and Early Modern Europe*. Aldershot, UK: Ashgate.

Nail, Thomas. 2012. "Violence at the Borders: Nomadic Solidarity and Non-status Migrant Resistance." *Radical Philosophy Review* 15, no. 1: 241–57.

——. 2013. "Migrant Cosmopolitanism." www.e-ir.info/2013/04/11/migrant-cosmopolitanism.

National Alliance of Latin American and Caribbean Communities. 2014. "Backgrounder: NALAAC Delegations to Central America Summer 2014: Myths and Realities of Child Migration and Migration Policy."

New York Times. 2014. "Israel: Court Condemns Policy of Detaining Migrants." September 23.

No More Deaths. 2010. "'Littering' Conviction of Border Volunteer Overturned by Appeals Court." September 2. www.nomoredeaths.org.

Noferi, Mark. 2015. "A Humane Approach Can Work: The Effectiveness of Alternatives to Detention for Asylum Seekers." Washington, DC: American Immigration Council.

Nolan, Ruairi, and Landon E. Hancock. 2014. "Local Zones of Peace: Communities Withdrawing from Conflict." *Insight on Conflict,* January 24. www.insightonconflict. org/2013/01/zones-of-peace-landon-e-hancock/.

North, James. 2014. "How the US's Foreign Policy Created an Immigrant Refugee Crisis on Its Own Southern Border." *Nation*, July 9. www.thenation.com/article/180578/ how-us-foreign-policy-created-immigrant-refugee-crisis-its-own-southern-border.

Notess, Laura. 2014. "Conditions for Hondurans in the American Asylum Process." Washington, DC: Jesuit Conference of the United States.

Obermeyer, Gerald J. 1969. *Structure and Authority in a Bedouin Tribe: The 'Aishabit of the Western Desert of Egypt.* Ann Arbor: University Microfilms.

Oda, Hiroshi. 2013. "Ethnography of Relationships among Church Sanctuary Actors in Germany." In Lippert and Rehaag, *Sanctuary Practices in International Perspective.*

Okeke, T. C., U. S. B. Anyaehie, and C. C. K. Ezenyeaku. 2012. "An Overview of Female Genital Mutilation in Nigeria." *Annals of Medical and Health Sciences Research* 2, no. 1 (January–June): 70–73.

Oldfield, Sybil. 2004. "'It Is Usually She': The Role of British Women in the Rescue and Care of the Kindertransport Kinder." *Shofar* 23, no. 1 (Fall): 57–70.

Olivo, Antonio. 2014. "So Close to Mexico, Fear – and Hope – Run High." *Washington Post*, November 28.

Ortiz Uribe, Monica. 2014. "Fewer Deportations Happening from New Mexico Detention Center." *Fronteras*, November 5. www.fronterasdesk.org/content/9835/ fewer-deportations-happening-new-mexico-detention-center.

Otter, Elna L., and Dorothy F. Pine. 2004. *The Sanctuary Experience: Voices of the Community.* San Diego, CA: Aventine Press.

Owen, Jonathan. 2015. "Detention: The Black Hole at the Heart of British Justice." *Independent*, January 6. www.independent.co.uk/news/uk/crime/detention-the-black-hole-at-the-heart-of-british-justice-9961576.html.

Parliament of Australia. 2011. "Refugee Resettlement to Australia: What Are the Facts?" December 2.

Patel, Sunita, and Tom Jawetz. 2007. "Conditions of Confinement in Immigration Detention Facilities." Washington, DC: American Civil Liberties Union National Prison Project.

Patsias, Caroline, and Nastassia Williams. 2013. "Religious Sanctuary in France and Canada." In Lippert and Rehaag, *Sanctuary Practices in International Perspective.*

Payne, Lisa. 2014. "Review of Government Action on United Nations' Recommendations for Strengthening Children's Rights in the UK, 2014." London: Children's Rights Alliance for England.

Pedley, John. 2005. *Sanctuaries and the Sacred in the Ancient Greek World*. Cambridge: Cambridge University Press.

Perla, Hector, Jr., and Susan Bibler Coutin. 2013. "Legacies and Origins of the 1980s U.S.-Central American Sanctuary Movement." In Lippert and Rehaag, *Sanctuary Practices in International Perspective*.

Pew Research Center for the People and the Press. 2014. "Immigration Action Gets Mixed Response, but Legal Pathway Still Popular." December 11. www.people-press.org/2014/12/11/immigration-action-gets-mixed-response-but-legal-pathway-still-popular/.

Phelps, Jerome. 2013. "Alternatives to Detention in the UK: From Enforcement to Engagement." *Forced Migration Review* 44 (September).

Philo, Greg, Emma Briant, and Pauline Donald. 2013. *Bad News for Refugees*. London: Pluto Press.

Pirouet, LouisHurvitz, Emily Singer. 2013. "The Plight of Syrian Refugees in Lebanon." *Human Rights Brief* 66 (Spring). e, 2001. *Whatever Happened to Asylum in Britain? A Tale of Two Walls*. New York: Berghahn Books.

Planas, Roque. 2014. "Children Deported to Honduras Are Getting Killed: Report." *Huffington Post*, August 20. www.huffingtonpost.com/2014/08/20/minors-honduras-killed_n_5694986.html.

———. 2015. "Family Detention Center in Texas Is 'Utterly Unnecessary,' Says Immigration Attorney." *Huffington Post*, January 14. www.huffingtonpost.com/2015/01/14/dilley-texas-detention-center_n_6473274.html.

Povoledo, Elisabetta. 2013. "Italy's Migrant Detention Centers Are Cruel, Rights Groups Say." *New York Times*, June 5. www.nytimes.com/2013/06/05/world/europe/italys-migrant-detention-centers-are-cruel-rights-groups-say.html?_r=0.

Preston, Julia. 2011. "Immigration Crackdown Also Snares Americans." *New York Times*, December 14. www.nytimes.com/2011/12/14/us/measures-to-capture-illegal-aliens-nab-citizens.html.

———. 2013. "Huge Amounts Spent on Immigration, Study Finds." *New York Times*, January 7. www.nytimes.com/2013/01/08/us/huge-amounts-spent-on-immigration-study-finds.html.

———. 2014. "Detention Center Presented as Deterrent to Border Crossings." *New York Times*, December 15. www.nytimes.com/2014/12/16/us/homeland-security-chief-opens-largest-immigration-detention-center-in-us.html?_r=0.

Price, Jonathan. 2007. "History of Asylum in London." Researching Asylum in London. www.researchasylum.org.uk/?lid=282.

Puthooparambil, Soorej Jose, Beth Ahlberg, and Magdelena Bjerheid. 2013. "Do Higher Standards of Detention Promote Well-Being?" *Forced Migration Review* 44 (September): 39.

Quaker Asylum and Refugee Network. 2014. Letter to Parliamentary Inquiry, October 1. www.qarn.org.uk. 2014-Oct-1-Submission-to-APPG-inquiry.pdf.

Rabben, Linda. 1997. "Conditions of Asylum Seekers in INS Detention Centers and Contract Prison Facilities." Immigration Policy Report No. 34. Washington, DC: American Immigration Law Foundation.

———. 2011. *Give Refuge to the Stranger: The Past, Present, and Future of Sanctuary*. Walnut Creek, CA: Left Coast Press.

———. 2013. "Credential Recognition in the United States for Foreign Professionals." Washington, DC: Migration Policy Institute.

———. 2014. "Bound by Law to Aid Refugees." *Philadelphia Inquirer*, July 25.

Raskin, Debra L. 2014. Letter to Barack Obama. "New York City Bar Association's Opposition to Expansion of Detention for Immigrant Mothers and Children." November 21. www2.nycbar.org/pdf/report/uploads/1_20072779-LetteronDenialofCounselandFair HearingsforDetainedImmigrantMothersChildren.pdf .

Raskin, Debra L., and Lenni B. Benson. 2014. Letter to Barack Obama. "Denial of Access to Counsel and Fair Hearings for Immigrant Mothers and Children Detained in Artesia, New Mexico," August 20. Author's collection.

Reider, Dimi. 2012. "Testimonies: Israelis Tear-Gassed Pleading Asylum Seekers, Dragged Them to Egypt." +972, September. http://972mag.com/testimonies-israelis-tear-gassed-pleading-asylum-seekers-dragged-them-to-egypt/55732/.

Religionlink. 2008. "The New Sanctuary Movement: Protecting and Welcoming." www.religionlink.com/tip_081208.php.

Reuters. 2015. "Greece Vows to Shut Down Holding Sites for Migrants." *Washington Post*, February 15.

Rhodes, Diane Lee, and Linda Wedel Greene. 2001. "A Cultural History of Three Traditional Hawaiian Sites on the West Coast of Hawaii Island." Denver: US Department of Interior, National Park Service. Accessed November 7, 2014. www.cr.nps.gov/history/online_ books/Kora/history1i.htm.

Ridgley, Jennifer. 2013. "The City as a Sanctuary in the United States." In Lippert and Rehaag, *Sanctuary Practices in International Perspective*.

Riggs, Charles H., Jr. 1963. *Criminal Asylum in Anglo-Saxon Law*. University of Florida Monographs, Social Sciences, no. 18. Gainesville: University of Florida Press.

Rights Working Group. 2012. "The NSEERS Effect: A Decade of Racial Profiling, Fear and Secrecy." College Park: Pennsylvania State Law School.

Rittner, Carol, and Sondia Myers, eds. 1986. *The Courage to Care: Rescuers of Jews during the Holocaust*. New York: New York University Press.

Rose, Ananda. 2014. "Seeking Refuge: Life and Death at the Border." *Commonweal*, December 18. www.commonwealmagazine.org/users/ananda-rose.

Ross, Oakland. 2014. "In Canada's Immigration Law, Anyone Can Be a Terrorist." *Toronto Star*, April 27.

Rosser, Gervase. 1989. *Medieval Westminster, 1200–1540*. Oxford: Clarendon Press.

———. 1996. "Sanctuary and Social Negotiation in Medieval England." In *The Cloister and the World: Essays in Medieval History in Honour of Barbara Harvey*, edited by John Blair and Brian Golding, 57–79. Oxford: Clarendon Press.

Rossi, Victoria. 2015. "Seeking Asylum in Karnes City." *Texas Observer*, February 2. www.texasobserver.org/seeking-asylum-karnes-city.

Rourke, Alison. 2012. "Australia to Deport Boat Asylum Seekers to Pacific Islands." *Guardian*, August 13. www.theguardian.com/world/2012/aug/13/australia-asylum -seekers-pacific-islands.

Rubenstein, Edwin S. 2012. "The High Cost of Cheap Detentions." *Social Contract* 22, no. 3 (Spring): 80–85.

Rubio-Marin, Ruth. 2014. *Human Rights and Immigration*. Oxford: Oxford University Press.

Rushdie, Salman. 2013. *Joseph Anton: A Memoir*. New York: Random House.

Safi, Michael. 2014. "Asylum Seeker Children on Christmas Island Transferred to Detention in Darwin." *Guardian*, December 21. www.theguardian.com/australia-news/2014/dec/21/asylum-seeker-children-christmas-island-transferred-detention-darwin.

Salman, Saba. 2011. "More Action Needed on Illegal Immigration, Says Report." *Guardian*, April 20. www.theguardian.com/society/2011/apr/20/more-action-illegal-immigration-ippr-report.

San Antonio Express-News Editorial Board. 2014. "Alternatives to Detention." *San Antonio Express-News*, October 16. www.mysanantonio.com/opinion/editorials/article/Alternatives-to-detention-5827949.php.

San José de Apartadó. 2014. "Extreme Efforts to Mask Horrors." *Comunidad de Paz San José de Apartadó*, October 14. www.cdpsanjose.org.

Sartain, Dorthea M. 2002. "Sanctuary in the Reign of Henry VII, with Particular Reference to Beverley and Durham." PhD diss., Cambridge University.

Saslow, Eli. 2014. "'Band-Aid' for 800 Children: Nora Sandigo Is Legal Guardian to Hundreds of Young American Citizens Born to Illegal Immigrants Who Are Subject to Deportation." *Washington Post*, July 6.

Sauvage, Pierre. 1989. *Weapons of the Spirit*. DVD.

Schoenholtz, Andrew I., Philip G. Schrag, and Jaya Ramji-Nogales. 2014. *Lives in the Balance: Asylum Adjudication by the Department of Homeland Security*. New York: New York University Press.

Schönbauer, R. 2015. "Deported Children Face Deadly New Dangers on Return to Honduras." UN High Commissioner for Refugees. www.unhcr.org/54ca32d89.html.

Scott, J. Brown. 1985. *The Classics of International Law*. London: Routledge.

Seabrook, Jeremy. 2009. *The Refuge and the Fortress: Britain and the Flight from Tyranny*. London: Palgrave Macmillan.

Sherwood, Harriet. 2014. "UK Has Only Let In 24 Syrian Refugees under Relocation Scheme for Conflict Victims." *Guardian*, June 20. www.theguardian.com/world/2014/jun/20/uk-24-syrians-vulnerable-persons-relocation-scheme.

Shisheva, Mariya, Gary Christie, and Gareth Mulvey. 2013. "Improving the Lives of Refugees in Scotland after the Referendum: An Appraisal of the Options." Glasgow: Scottish Refugee Council.

Shoeb, Marwa, Harvey M. Weinstein, and Jodi Halpern. 2007. "Living in Religious Time and Space: Iraqi Refugees in Dearborn, Michigan." *Journal of Refugee Studies* 20, no. 3 (September): 441–60.

Siebert, Wilbur H. 1968 [1898]. *The Underground Railroad from Slavery to Freedom*. New York: Arno Press/New York Times.

Siebold, Martin. 1937. "Sanctuary." In *Encyclopaedia of the Social Sciences*, edited by Edwin Seligman, 534–37. New York: Macmillan.

Sieff, Kevin. 2013. "Alleged Terrorism Ties Foil Some Afghan Interpreters' U.S. Visa Hopes." *Washington Post*, February 2.

Silkenat, James R. 2014. "Statement on Behalf of the American Bar Association, Committee on the Judiciary, U.S. House of Representatives." June 25. www.americanbar.org.2014 june25_unaccompaniedalienminors_t.authcheckdam-1.pdf.

Simmie, Scott. 2014. "Dodging Death on the Mediterranean." *Toronto Star*, November 7.

www.thestar.com/news/world/2014/11/07/dodging_death_on_the_mediterranean.html.

Slavin, Barbara. 2014. "US to Accept Thousands of Syrian Refugees for Resettlement." *AL-Monitor*, December 22.

Smith, Adam, et al. 2014. Congressional letter to Secretary of Homeland Security Jeh Johnson, August 1. www.immigrantjustice.org/stop-detaining-families/2014_08_Ltr_Sec-Johnson_FamilyDetention-1.pdf.

Soltani, Neda. 2012. *My Stolen Face: The Story of a Dramatic Mistake*. Munich: Ariadne-Buch.

Sovcik, Annie. 2013. "Tortured and Detained: Survivor Stories of U.S. Immigration Detention." Minneapolis: Center for Victims of Torture.

Stastny, Charles. 1987. "Sanctuary and the State." *Contemporary Crises* 11, no. 3 (September): 279–301.

Stevens, Dallal. 2004. *UK Asylum Law and Policy: Historical and Contemporary Perspectives*. London: Sweet and Maxwell.

Stickgold, Emma. 2010. "Tam Tran, Brown Student: Fought for Immigrant Rights." *Boston Globe*, May 17.

Stinchcomb, Dennis, and Eric Hershberg. 2014. "Unaccompanied Migrant Children from Central America." CLALS Working Paper Series, no. 7. Washington, DC: American University Center for Latin American and Latino Studies.

Stowe, Harriet Beecher. 1952 [1852]. *Uncle Tom's Cabin*. New York: Dodd, Mead.

Struggles in Italy. 2014. "Immigration Policies in Italy." Accessed December 15, 2014. www.strugglesinitaly.wordpress.com/equality/en-immigration-policies-in-italy.

Stumpf, Juliet. 2014. Keynote address. Presented at the Borders of Crimmigration conference, Leiden, October 9.

Sullivan, Michael. 2014. "Refugee Deal between Australia and Cambodia Sparks Outrage." *National Public Radio*, October 8. www.npr.org/2014/10/08/354507395/refugee-deal-between-australia-and-cambodia-sparks-outrage.

Swedish Migration Board. 2014. Statistics. November 3. www.migrationsverket.se.

Switala, William J. 2004. *Underground Railroad in Delaware, Maryland and West Virginia*. Mechanicsburg, PA: Stackpole Books.

Syal, Rajeev, and Alan Travis. 2014. "Britain's Immigration System in Chaos, MP's Report Reveals." *Guardian*, October 28. www.theguardian.com/uk-news/2014/oct/29/britain-immigration-system-in-chaos-report-reveals.

Sydney Morning Herald. 2007. "Dutch Amnesty for 30,000 Asylum Seekers." May 26.

Symonds, Steve. 2007. "Experiences of the UK Immigration Service: Report Launch and Information Day, Refugee and Migrants' Forum." London: Immigration Law Practitioners Association.

Tan, Michael. 2011. "No Bond, No Bars." American Civil Liberties Union, September 1. www.aclu.org/blog/no-bond-no-bars.

Taylor, Diane. 2012. "£2m Paid Out over Child Asylum Seekers Illegally Detained as Adults." *Guardian*, February 17. www.theguardian.com/uk/2012/feb/17/home-office-payout-child-asylum-seekers.

Taylor, Diane, and Mark Townsend. 2014. "Gay Asylum Seekers Face 'Humiliation.'" *Observer*, February 8. www.theguardian.com/uk-news/2014/feb/08/gay-asylum-seekers-humiliation-home-office.

Taylor, Jerome. 2012. "Government Accused of Wasting Taxpayer Money on 'Half-Empty'

Chartered Deportation Flights to Sri Lanka." *Independent*, October 22.

Taylor, Lenore. 2013. "Rudd Announces Deal to Send All Asylum Boat Arrivals to Papua New Guinea." *Guardian*, July 19. www.theguardian.com/world/2013/jul/19/ kevin-rudd-asylum-boats-png.

Taylor, Matthew, and Guy Grandjean. "At Least 15 Migrants Died in 'Shameful' Calais Conditions in 2014." *Guardian*, December 23. www.theguardian.com/uk-news/2014/ dec/23/15-migrants-trying-enter-uk-die-shameful-calais-conditions.

Tazreiter, Claudia. 2004. *Asylum Seekers and the State: The Politics of Protection in a Security -Conscious World*. Aldershot, UK: Ashgate.

——. 2015a. "Lifeboat Politics in the Pacific: Affect and the Ripples and Shimmers of a Migrant Saturated Future." *Emotion, Space and Society* 16 (August): 99–107.

——. 2015b. "'Stop the Boats!' Externalising the Borders of Australia and Imaginary Pathologies of Contagion." *Immigration, Asylum and Nationality Law* 29, no. 2 (January): 141–57.

This Is Local London. 2009. "New Waiting Area at Croydon's Lunar House Finally Completed." December 22. www.thisislocallondon.co.uk/whereilive/ southlondon/ croydon/4816303/New_waiting_area_at_Croydon_s_Lunar_House_finally_completed/.

Thomas, Adrian. 2012. "Asylum Seekers Continue to Be Stigmatised by the British Press." *Guardian*, October 31. www.theguardian.com/media/2012/oct/31/asylum-seekers -stigmatised-british-press.

Thornley, Isobel. 1924. "The Destruction of Sanctuary." In *Tudor Studies*, edited by R. W. Seton-Watson. London: Longmans, Green.

Tomsho, Robert. 1987. *The American Sanctuary Movement*. Austin: University of Texas Press.

Topping, Alexandra. 2014. "Pressure on Richard Branson to Block Deportation of Nigerian FGM Mother." *Guardian*, May 29. www.theguardian.com/society/2014/may/29/ branson-deportation-nigerian-mother-fgm-virgin-atlantic.

Transactional Records Access Clearinghouse (TRAC). 2015. "Immigration Court Backlog Tool." http://trac.syr.edu/phptools/immigration/court_backlog.

Trauner, Helene. 2005. "Dimensions of West African Immigration to France: Malian Immigrant Women in Paris." *Stichproben: Wiener Zeitschrift für kritische Afrikastudien* 8: 221–35.

Travis, Alan. 2010. "Home Office Bids to Restrict Jobs for Asylum Seekers." *Guardian*, July 29. www.theguardian.com/uk/2010/jul/29/restrictions-sought-asylum-seekers-jobs.

——. 2012. "Border Agency Condemned over Asylum and Immigration Backlog." *Guardian*, November 22. www.theguardian.com/uk/2012/nov/22/border-agency-asylum-claims -backlog.

——. 2013. "Inspector Finds UKBA Backlog Dating Back 10 Years." *Guardian*, January 24. www.theguardian.com/uk/2013/jan/23/inspector-uk-border-agency-backlog.

——. 2014. "Net Migration to UK Soars by 39% to 243,000." *Guardian*, August 28. www.theguardian.com/uk-news/2014/aug/28.

Treviso, Perla. 2014. "Status of Kids, Families in '14 Immigration Spike Isn't Clear." *Arizona Daily Star*, November 23.

Triggs, Gillian. 2014. *The Forgotten Children: National Inquiry into Children in Immigration Detention*. Sydney: Australian Human Rights Commission.

Trigilio, Trisha, Ranjana Natarajan, and Kelly Haragan. 2014. Letter to the Department of Homeland Security and the Environmental Protection Agency, October 30. Civil Rights Clinic, University of Texas School of Law, Austin.

Trocmé, André. N.d. "Autobiographie." Typescript, Trocmé Collection, Peace Collection, Swarthmore College, Pennsylvania.

———. 1940. "This Is My Will and Testament." Typescript, Trocmé Collection, Peace Collection, Swarthmore College, Pennsylvania.

———. 2004. *Jesus and the Nonviolent Revolution*. Farmington, PA: Bruderhof Foundation.

Tsangarides, Natasha. 2012. "The Second Torture: The Immigration Detention of Torture Survivors." London: Medical Justice.

Tsurkov, Elizabeth. 2012. "Knesset Passes Bill on Prolonged Detention of Refugees without Trial." +972. www.972mag.com/knesset-passes-controversial-bill-on-prolonged-detention-of-asylum-seekers/32487/.

Tuitt, Patricia. 1996. *False Images: The Law's Construction of the Refugee*. London: Pluto Press.

Tumulty, Karen. 2014. "At Home Legally – for Now." *Washington Post*, November 28.

United Kingdom Home Office. 2014a. Statistical News Release: Immigration Statistics, October–December 2013. February 27.

———. 2014b. Immigration Statistics, January to March 2014. May 22.

———. 2014c. "Immigration Bill Becomes Law." May 14. www.gov.uk/government/news/immigration-bill-becomes-law.

———. 2015. Immigration Statistics, October to December 2014. February 26. www.gov.uk/government/publications/immigration-statistics-october-to-december-2014/immigration-statistics-october-to-december.

United Kingdom National Asylum Support Service. 2014. "Asylum Support." December 8. www.gov.uk/asylum-support-what-you'll-get.

United Nations High Commissioner for Refugees. 2012. "Guidelines on the Applicable Criteria and Standards relating to the Detention of Asylum Seekers and Alternatives to Detention." www.unhcr.org.

———. 2013. "UN's High Commissioner for Refugees Urges Europe to Do More for Syrian Asylum Seekers." www.unhcr.org.

———. 2014a. Sweden. January. www.unhcr.org.

———. 2014b. "2015 UNHCR Country Operations Profile – Syrian Arab Republic." www.unhcr.org/pages/49e486a76.html.

———. 2015. "World at War. UNHCR Global Trends: Forced Displacement in 2014." www.unhcr.org/556725e69.htm.

United States Commission on Civil Rights. 2015. "With Liberty and Justice for All: The State of Civil Rights at Immigration Detention Facilities; Statutory Enforcement Report."

United States Commission on International Religious Freedom. 2013. "Special Report: Assessing the U.S. Government's Detention of Asylum Seekers; Further Action Needed to Fully Implement Reforms."

United States Department of Homeland Security. 2002. "Endgame: Office of Detention and Removal Strategic Plan, 2003–2012." Washington, DC: Bureau of Immigration and Customs Enforcement.

———. 2013. "Annual Flow Report 2013." Washington, DC: Office of Immigration Statistics.

———. 2014. "Detainee Deaths, 2003 to Present." Washington, DC: Bureau of Immigration and Customs Enforcement. www.ice.gov/doclib/foia/reports/detaineedeaths2003 -present.pdf.

United States Department of Justice. 2014. *FY 2009–FY 2013 Asylum Statistics by Nationality*. Washington, DC: Executive Office of Immigration Review. www.justice.gov/eoir/efoia/ FY2009-FY2013AsylumStatisticsbyNationality.pdf.

Walzer, Michael. 1983. *Spheres of Justice: A Defense of Pluralism and Equality*. New York: Basic Books.

Warikoo, Niraj. 2011. "Immigration Raid outside Detroit Church Sparks Outrage." *Detroit Free Press*, September 22. www.freep.com/article/20110922/NEWS05/109220492/ Immigration-raid-outside-Detroit-church-sparks-outrage.

Washington College of Law. 2013. "Italy's Return of Asylum Seekers to Greece Raises Human Rights Concerns." *Human Rights Brief* (Spring): 63–64.

Washington Post. 2007. "Takoma Park Stays Immigrant 'Sanctuary.'" *Washington Post*, October 31.

Watanabe, Teresa. 2007. "Vietnamese Refugee Family in Limbo." *Los Angeles Times*, October 9.

Webber, Frances. 2012. *Borderline Justice: The Fight for Refugee and Migrant Rights*. London: Pluto Press.

Welch, Michael. 2002. *Detained: Immigration Laws and the Expanding INS Jail Complex*. Philadelphia: Temple University Press.

Welch, Michael, and Liza Schuster. 2005. "Detention of Asylum Seekers in the United States, United Kingdom, France, Germany and Italy: A Critical View of the Globalizing Culture of Control." *Criminal Justice* 5, no. 4: 331–55.

Werkman, Geesje. 2013. "Report of a Meeting between PCN (Protestant Church in the Netherlands) and Asylum Seekers and Rejected Asylum Seekers Whose Right on Shelter, Food and Clothing Is Denied by the Dutch Government." Typescript, March 27.

Westermarck, Edward. 1909. "Asylum." In *Encyclopaedia of Religion and Ethics*, edited by J. Hastings. Edinburgh: T & T Clark.

Westhead, Rick. 2012. "Failed Refuge Claimants Find Sanctuary in Toronto Churches." *Toronto Star*, October 14. www.thestar.com/news/world/2012/10/14/ failed_refugee_ claimants_ find_ sanctuary_in_toronto_churches.html.

Wiesel, Elie. 1985. "The Refugee." In MacEoin, *Sanctuary*.

Williams, Zoe. 2013. "For Failed Asylum Seeker, Life on Section 4 Is a Nightmare Worse Than Kafka." *Guardian*, January 30. www.theguardian.com/commentisfree/2013/ jan/30/asylum-theresa-may-private-fiefdom.

Willsher, Kim. 2014. "Broken Camp, Broken Lives, as Vigilante Attack Makes Itself Felt on Roma." *Guardian*, June 22. www.theguardian.com/world/2014/jun/22/broken-lives -vigilante-justice-roma.

Winder, Robert. 2004. *Bloody Foreigners: The Story of Immigration to Britain*. London: Little Brown.

Withers, Tracy. 2012. "Gillard says Australian Asylum Policy Change in National Interest." *Bloomberg Business*, August 19. www.bloomberg.com/news/articles/2012-08-19/gillard -says-australia-asylum-policy-change-in-national-interest.

Witte, Griff. 2014. "In Heart of Europe, Migrants Offer a One-Stop Tour of Worldwide Misery." *Washington Post*, November 26.

Wong, Kent, and Matias Ramos. 2011. "Undocumented and Unafraid: Tam Tran and Cinthya Felix." *Boom: A Journal of California* (Spring).

Wozniacka, Gusia. 2014. "Francisco Aguirre, Undocumented Activist, Takes Sanctuary at Portland Church." *Huffington Post*, September 23. www.huffingtonpost.com/2014/09/23/francisco-aguirre-sanctuary-church_n_5867778.html.

Wyman, David S. 1984. *The Abandonment of the Jews: America and the Holocaust, 1941–1945.* New York: Pantheon Books.

Yukich, Grace. 2013. "'I Didn't Know If This Was Sanctuary': Strategic Adaptation in the U.S. Sanctuary Movement." In Lippert and Rehaag, *Sanctuary Practices in International Perspective.*

Index

non-refoulement, 96, 122, 125, 186. *See also* refoulement

non-Western societies, sanctuary in, 34–36

Noonan, John, 36

North American Free Trade Agreement (NAFTA), 246

Norway, sanctuary in, 227

Obama, Barack, 190, 199, 210, 215, 216, 250

Oberlin College, 74

Oda, Hiroshi, 223

Office of Refugee Resettlement, 216, 217

offshore detention centers, Australian. *See* Pacific Solution

Omzo Foundation, 226

Ontario Sanctuary Coalition, 238

On the Laws and Customs of England (Bracton), 46, 47

Operation Liberty Shield, 209

orbit, refugees in, 176

Organization for Economic Co-operation and Development, 180

OSE (Organisation de Secours aux Enfants), 117

"other," social construction of, 5

Oxford Resolutions, 63

Pacific Solution, 154–56, 242

Parker, William, 78

Parliamentary Committee for Refugees, 103

Pashtunwali, Code of, 43

Patriot Act, 210

Peace of Westphalia, 57

Pedley, John, 33

Pegida movement, 224–25

Pentecostal church, 227

People magazine, 141

Perez, Cinthya Felix, 208

Perutz, Max, 99

Pevsner, Sir Nikolaus, 99

Philip, Mireille, 118

Philippines, refugees and asylum seekers from, 223; Zones of Peace in, 275–76

philopatric, 30

Pick, Hella, 102,

"Pierre" (asylum seeker), 20–21, 24, 25, 286n9

Pinal County (AZ) Jail, 203

Pinochet, Augusto, 129

pleasures of rescue, 2, 120, 279

political weapon, asylum as, 127, 131

Popper, Karl, 99

post-medieval Europe, sanctuary and asylum in: French Revolution and Napoleonic Wars, 57–58; nineteenth century, 59–63; Renaissance and Reformation, 55–57

Powell, Enoch, 127

Presbyterians, 82, 132, 133, 135, 136, 138, 142, 144, 254, 256, 288n12

Prevention of Infiltration Law of 1954 (Israel), 193

primates, nonhuman: altruism in, 4, 285n2; exogamy among, 29; migration among, 29; reciprocal altruism in, 28

Primitive Marriage (McLennan), 30

prisons, detention centers as. *See* correctional detention model

private prison corporations, 200–201, 204

pro bono legal representation: for Central American detainees, 260; for Fauziya Kassindja, 1, 2; for "Mary," 12; for Neda Soltani, 22–23; for "Pierre," 20, 24, 25; for Rosa Robles Loreto, 255; for "Stephen," 21; in UK, 229

Professional Alliance for the Health of Asylum Seekers and Their Children, 242

prosecutorial discretion, 251, 253, 254

Protestant Church of the Netherlands, 185, 225

Protocol Relating to the Status of Refugees, 124, 127, 138, 195, 206, 291n5

public opinion. *See* anti-immigrant political pressures